Paddling Tennessee

A Guide to 38 of the State's Greatest Paddling Adventures

Johnny Molloy

FALCONGUIDES

GUILFORD, CONNECTICUT
HELENA, MONTANA

AN IMPRINT OF GLOBE PEQUOT PRESS

To buy books in quantity for corporate use
or incentives, call **(800) 962–0973**
or e-mail **premiums@GlobePequot.com**.

FALCONGUIDES®

Copyright © 2011 by Morris Book Publishing, LLC

ALL RIGHTS RESERVED. No part of this book may be reproduced or transmitted in any form by any meangs, electronic or mechanical, including photocopying and recording, or by any information storage and retrieval system, except as may be expressly permitted in writing from the publisher. Requests for permission should be addressed to Globe Pequot Press, Attn: Rights and Permissions Department, P.O. Box 480, Guilford, CT 06437.

FalconGuides is an imprint of Globe Pequot Press.

Falcon, FalconGuides, and Outfit Your Mind are registered trademarks of Morris Book Publishing, LLC.

TOPO! Explorer software and SuperQuad source maps courtesy of National Geographic Maps. For information about TOPO! Explorer, TOPO!, and Nat Geo Maps products, go to www.topo.com or www.natgeomaps.com.

Project editor: David Legere
Layout artist: Kevin Mak
Maps by Design Maps Inc. © Morris Book Publishing, LLC.

Library of Congress Cataloging-in-Publication Data is available on file.

ISBN 978-0-7627-4639-2

Printed in the United States of America

10 9 8 7 6 5 4 3 2

The author and Globe Pequot Press assume no liability for accidents happening to, or injuries sustained by, readers who engage in the activities described in this book.

To Patrick Molloy

Contents

◀ *Paddler drops his kayak into the Harpeth River.*

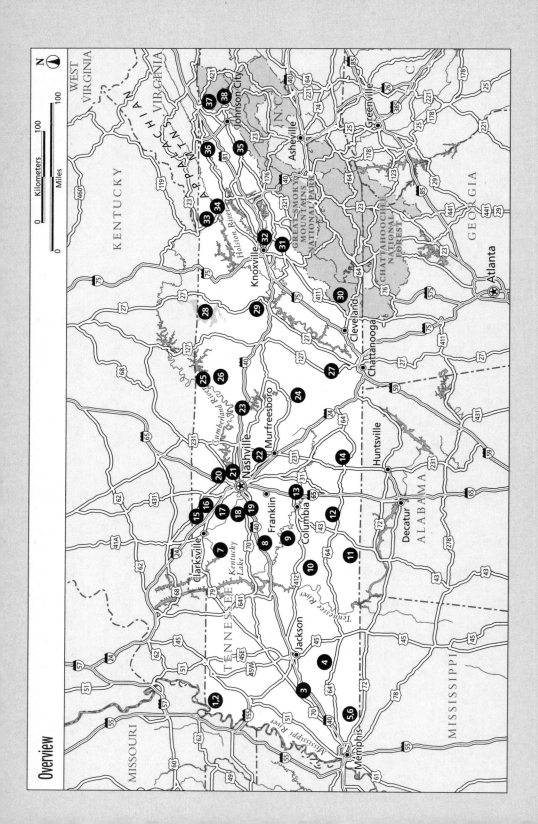

East Tennessee

Map Legend

Transportation

40	Freeway/Interstate Highway
231	U.S. Highway
57	State Highway
	Other Road
	Railroad

Trails

------	Paddling Route
--------	Land Trail
→	Direction of Travel

Water Features

	Body of Water
	Major River
	Minor River or Creek
	Intermittent River or Creek
	Rapids
	Waterfalls
	Marsh
	Spring

Land Management

	National Forest, National Park
	State/County Preserve, Wilderness, Recreation Area

Symbols

	Boat Launch
	Bridge
■	Building/Point of Interest
▲	Campground
∩	Cave
✪	Capital
◉	City
	Church
	Dam
1	Mileage Marker
	Observation Tower
	Powerline
	Put-in/Takeout
◎	Town
	Scenic View/Overlook
▲	State Park
○	Village

Acknowledgments

Thanks to Pam Morgan for paddling many rivers from Memphis to Mountain City. Thanks also to Bill Armstrong; Steve Grayson; Wes Shepherd; my brothers Steele, Pat, and Mike; Mark and Frank Carroll; Cisco Meyer; John Cox; Tim Balthrop; and all the people who helped me with shuttles and rides.

Thanks to Merrell for the great hiking shoes and river sandals and to DeLorme for the Earthmate PN-40 GPS and their excellent Topo USA mapping program. Thanks to Wenonah for providing me a great canoe to paddle on many rivers—the Spirit II. The 17-footer handled wonderfully, and its light weight made for easy loading and unloading.

Introduction

My camping, hiking, and paddling obsession began in the Smoky Mountains more than two decades ago. A native Tennessean, I have lived in all parts of the state, growing up in Memphis, living in Nashville and Knoxville, and finally settling in Johnson City. For many years I have explored the great outdoors of the Volunteer State, roaming the mountains from top to bottom, trekking throughout Middle Tennessee, and camping the lowlands of the west. I also began paddling many of the state's rivers and lakes, from the Nolichucky to the Buffalo and waterways beyond, flowing off the Appalachians, the Cumberland Plateau, and throughout the Highland Rim and Central Basin. Sea kayaking trips led me west to Reelfoot Lake and the Hatchie River. I have since made repeated trips to these Tennessee treasures, paddling along dark water trails of swamp rivers that contrast mightily with the crashing, whitewater streams, enjoying the natural aquatic abundance of my home state.

Time passed, and I began writing outdoor guidebooks for a living. The opportunity arose to write this guidebook and I jumped on it excitedly. I began systematically exploring the waterways of the Tennessee landscape for great paddling destinations. I sought to include paddling destinations that would not only be rewarding but would also be exemplary paddles of the varied landscapes offered. In the east, the Hiwassee River forms the crown jewel of Blue Ridge paddling destinations. But these mountains offer other paddling places, such as the crystalline Watauga River or the brawling Nolichucky. And what good is a Tennessee paddling guidebook without including Tennessee's contribution to great rivers of the world—the Duck? The Duck River flows through the botanically rich heart of Tennessee and has a little bit of everything, flowing from the Cumberland Plateau through the Central Basin and into the Western Highland Rim before emptying into the Tennessee River. The stunning Buffalo offers sheer bluffs rising from clear green waters across from which lie inviting gravel bars. The Hatchie makes a serpentine course through the back of beyond. And there simply is no other Reelfoot Lake. Created by an earthquake two centuries ago, this stillwater wildlife refuge is something you must experience for yourself—with the help of this guidebook of course. Then, when you cobble the paddling destinations together, it presents a mosaic of Volunteer State beauty and biodiversity that's hard to beat!

As you may guess, the hardest part of writing this book may have been picking out the paddling destinations. With each of these waterways I sought out a combination of scenery, paddling experiences, ease of access—including shuttling when necessary—and a reasonable length for day-tripping. Now it is your turn—get out there and paddle Tennessee!

◀ *Bluff view of Big Swan Creek.*

1

Weather

Each of the four distinct seasons lays its hands on Tennessee. Elevation factors into weather patterns in East Tennessee. Summer can get hot, but is generally cooler in the east than in other parts of the state. The mountains receive the most precipitation, though it arrives with slow-moving frontal systems in winter, including snow, and with thunderstorms in summer. Fall offers warm days followed by cool, crisp evenings. Spring varies with elevation, too, and climbs its way up the mountains. Mountain paddlers must be prepared for cool to cold conditions on the water in winter and early spring, the time when the highland waters will be running at their fullest—and their coldest. However, most streams included in this guidebook can be paddled well into the summer, most year-round.

Middle Tennessee offers warm to hot summers and mostly moderate winters. Early spring is the most variable, with periodic warm-ups, broken by cold fronts bringing rain, then chilly temperatures. Later, temperatures stay warm, and become hot by July. Typically, mornings start clear, then clouds build and hit-or-miss thunderstorms occur by afternoon. The first cool fronts hit around mid-September. Fall sees warm clear days and cool nights with the least amount of rain. Precipitation picks up in November, and temperatures generally stay cool to cold, broken by occasional mild spells. Most Middle Tennessee streams can be paddled year-round, though as with the mountains they'll be running their boldest during winter and early spring. Summertime paddlers should consider beginning their trips in the morning to avoid the heat of the day and afternoon thunderstorms.

West Tennessee offers the warmest climate, yet has four distinct seasons. During the long summer highs regularly reach the 90s, and a thunderstorm will come most any afternoon. Warm nights stay up in the 70s. Fall brings cooler nights and warm days with less precipitation than summer. Winter is variable. Highs push 50 degrees. Expect lows in the 30s, with temperatures in the 20s during cold snaps. There are usually several mild days during each winter month. Precipitation comes in strong continental fronts, with persistent rains followed by sunny, cold days. Snow is uncommon, though not unheard of. The longer days of spring begin the warm-up process, even becoming hot, but temperatures can vary wildly. West Tennessee has a marginally longer paddling season, but you must also be prepared for the variety of conditions on the water there. Mild winter days can offer decent paddling in this region, as the insects will be absent and the sun will be at its weakest.

Flora and Fauna

The landscape of Tennessee offers everything from mountain bears furtively roaming beneath trees more common in New England than down South to dense swamp forests bordering remote waterways to high bluffs overlooking rocky streams. A wide variety of wildlife calls these dissimilar landscapes home.

Deer is the land animal you are most likely to see as you paddle Tennessee's waterways. They can be found throughout the state, and number over one million. A quiet paddler may also witness turkeys, raccoons, or even a coyote. Don't be surprised if you observe beaver, muskrat, or a playful otter in the water.

Overhead, many raptors will be plying the waterways for food, including eagles, falcons, and owls. Of special interest is the osprey. Watch for this bird flying overhead with a freshly caught fish in its talons! Depending upon where you are, other birds you may spot range from kingfishers to woodpeckers. Under the water Tennessee once had over 130 species of mussels. Some are thought to be extinct, and forty-two are on the federal endangered species list. The Clinch and Powell Rivers, both detailed in this guidebook, are the richest mussel streams of today. Finned species range from coldwater fish such as trout to warmwater largemouth bass and endangered species of fish, from sturgeons to darters to sunfish.

The flora offers just as much variety. Along the riverways of the east, towering white pines and imperiled hemlock reign over rhododendron and mountain laurel that bloom in late spring and early summer. Still other shorelines will harbor river birch, sycamore, and willow. Massive cypress trees are a common sight along slower, warmer waterways in West Tennessee. Wildflowers will grace shorelines throughout the state well into fall.

Tennessee River Regions

Tennessee is drained by three primary river systems—the Mississippi, Tennessee, and Cumberland Rivers. These drainages cut across this wide and narrow state, dividing it into its three regions—East, West, and Middle Tennessee (the reason for the three stars on our state flag). Starting in the west, the Mississippi drains the lowlands of West Tennessee in the Mississippi Plain. Unfortunately, most of Old Man River's Tennessee tributaries have been channelized, but still the wild Hatchie and upper Wolf make for quality paddling destinations. Reelfoot Lake, Tennessee's only natural lake, is an earthquake-created former channel of the Mississippi. The Tennessee River drainage is the master watercourse of the Volunteer State. Its headwaters enter from the northeast, gathering to become the Tennessee River proper near Knoxville, to cut southeast through the Cumberland Plateau and temporarily leave the state, only to flow back north into Kentucky, forming the division between West and Middle Tennessee. Including waters outside the state, the Tennessee River basin encompasses over 40,000 square miles. This river is noted for its watery diversity, supporting over 240 fish species alone. Important tributaries for paddlers include the Duck, Buffalo, Elk, Sequatchie, Hiwassee, Little, Emory, Clinch, Holston, French Broad, and Nolichucky.

The Cumberland River drains the north and north-central part of the state along its boundary with Kentucky. The streams of the Cumberland, from the Big South Fork to the Collins River to the Caney Fork and the forks of the Stones River, also reflect the changes in topography that follow the elevational transition from the

Cumberland Plateau to the state's Central Basin, home to Nashville and environs. The Eastern Highland Rim and Western Highland Rim surround the Central Basin, adding more physiographic variety through which the state's rivers flow. Paddling tributaries include the Caney Fork, East Fork Stones, Red River, Roaring River, Harpeth River, and Sycamore Creek.

Your Rights on the River

Luckily for Tennessee paddlers, navigable waters are considered public highways under state law. Generally speaking, streams that are floatable by a canoe are considered navigable waterways. Better yet, streams do not have to be floatable year-round to be considered floatable; they need only be floatable seasonally and regularly, meaning not just during a flood.

Over the years, cases brought before the state have declared the following: In Tennessee, navigability is determined by a waterway being "capable of being navigated." If a vessel can be employed in the ordinary purposes of commerce, and the stream or waterway is "sufficient capacity in depth, width and volume" for commerce, then it is navigable. To the flood question, it has been determined that a stream is not navigable if only capable of being floated during a flood, but a stream is navigable if it is "routinely swollen" during rains. Following this, if the stream is determined to be navigable, then the use of the water belongs to the public.

A navigable stream cannot be privately owned. Public uses of navigable streams include not only commerce but also navigation, hunting, and fishing. Interestingly, the public also owns the land under the water. Owners of land bordering a navigable stream own the land to the ordinary low water mark only and not to the center of the stream. Finally, since a navigable stream is considered a public highway, adjacent landowners cannot obstruct navigation.

In reality, on the water, what does this mean for the Tennessee paddler? The vast majority of landowners do not mind passage through waters along their property. While paddling be considerate—don't litter, bother livestock, climb on a dock, or traipse through someone's backyard. If encountered or confronted, be friendly and approachable. However, if you are stopped, or you are asked to get off riverside property, then I suggest you paddle on. Adhere to the landowner's request and live to paddle another day. Be apprised that you could be considered trespassing when you portage, camp, or even stop for a lunch break on streamside lands if not on public property. At that point, it is not a great time for debate on Tennessee waterway law.

How to Use This Guide

This guidebook offers trips covering every corner of Tennessee. The paddles are divided into the three primary regions of the state—West Tennessee, Middle Tennessee, and East Tennessee. Each paddle included in the book is chosen as a day trip, though overnight camping can be done where noted. The following is a sample of what you will find in the information box at the beginning of each paddling destination:

1 Yellow Creek

This swiftwater gravel-bottomed creek makes for a fun spring paddle.

County: Houston, Montgomery
Start: Williamson Branch Road near Ellis Mills, N36° 17.786', W87° 33.264'
End: McFall Road near Lake Barkley, N36° 22.841', W87° 32.777'
Length: 9.9 miles
Float time: 4 hours
Difficulty rating: Moderate
Rapids: Class I-I+
River type: Big creek
Current: Moderate to swift
River gradient: 5.1 feet per mile
River gauge: Yellow Creek at Ellis Mills, minimum runnable level 120 cfs

Season: Winter, spring, early summer, and after heavy rains
Land status: Private
Fees or permits: None
Nearest city/town: Cumberland City
Maps: USGS: Ellis Mills, Needmore; *DeLorme: Tennessee Atlas and Gazetteer,* Page 51 B6
Boats used: Canoes, kayaks
Organizations: Cumberland River Compact, P.O. Box 41721, Nashville 37204; (615) 837-1151; www.cumberlandrivercompact.org
Contacts/outfitters: Tennessee Clean Water Network, 123A S. Gay St., Knoxville 37902; (865) 522-7007; www.tcwn.org

From the information box we can see that the paddle is in Houston and Montgomery Counties. It begins at Williamson Branch Road near Ellis Mills. The GPS coordinates for the put-in are given using NAD 27 datum (the base mapping collected by the United States Geological Service), which you can plug into your GPS for direction finding. The paddle ends at McFall Road near Lake Barkley. It is 9.9 miles in length, which I acquired from using a GPS during my research. The paddle should last around four hours, but this is just an average. The time you will spend on the water depends upon whether you fish, picnic, swim, paddle, or simply relax. Use the float time as a gauge to help you determine how long you need/want to spend on your particular trip. The paddle is rated as moderate. Here, the difficulty arises from shallows created by a shifting streambed and also tree strainers. The river has no rapids per se, but the swift water rates as Class I+. This river difficulty rating system goes from Class I to Class VI. Class I has easy waves requiring little maneuvering and few obstructions. Class II rapids may have more obstructions and require more maneu-vering, and the rapids may be flowing faster. Most paddles in this guidebook are Class I–II. Class III rapids can be difficult with numerous waves and no clear defined passage and require precise maneuvering. Classes IV to VI increase in difficulty with Class VI being unrunnable, except by the best of experts.

The river type classification reflects its geographical placement within the state and what type of river it is, in this case a large creek. The current is moderate to swift, depending upon the width of the water where you are paddling. The river gradient reflects the rate at which the river descends during the paddle.

The river gauge listed will be near the destination and will help you determine the paddleability of the river. Some rivers, such as this one, have minimum flow rates listed so you will get on the river only when it has enough water—or stay off when the water is too high. Others that don't have a minimum runnable level can be pad-dled year-round. Concerning water gauges, the key variable is the height of the river at a fixed point. Gauge houses, situated on most rivers, consist of a well at the river's edge with a float attached to a recording clock. The gauge reads in hundredths of feet. Rating tables are constructed for each gauge to get a cubic feet per second (cfs) reading for each level. Other gauges are measured in height, given in feet. This gauge information can be obtained quickly, often along with a gauge reading of recent rainfall at the same location! USGS Real-time Water Levels for the United States can be found on the web at http://waterdata.usgs.gov/nwis/rt. This in-depth website has hundreds of gauges for the entire country updated continually, and graphs showing recent flow trends, along with historic trends for any given day of the year, available at the touch of a mouse. Consult these gauges before you start your trip!

The best paddling seasons are given, followed by land status. The lands bordering Yellow Creek are private. Many paddling destinations included in this guidebook border public lands. See above for information about your rights on the river. For this sample paddle, no fees or permits are required. Cumberland City is the nearest municipality. This listing will help you get oriented to the paddle destination area while looking at a map or looking up map information on the Internet. Though quality maps and driving directions are included with each paddle, the Maps section lists pertinent maps you can use for more detailed information, including United States Geographical Survey (USGS) 7.5' quadrangle maps. These "quad maps," as they are known, cover every parcel of land in this country. They are divided into very detailed rectangular maps. Each quad has a name, usually based on a physical feature located within the quad. In this case the paddle traverses a quad map named "Ellis Mills." Quad maps can be obtained online at www.usgs.gov. The map section also lists the page for this paddle in the *Tennessee Atlas and Gazetteer* produced by DeLorme. The gazetteer is an invaluable aid in making your way through the Volunteer State.

Boats Used simply informs you of what other river users will be floating. The Organizations section lists groups that charge themselves with taking care of the par-ticular waterway included in the paddle. If you are interested in learning more about the river's health and other water quality issues, as well as simply getting involved in preserving Tennessee's waterways, consult these groups. Their contact information is listed. The Contacts/Outfitters listing will give you information if an outfitter operates on the segment of river given. This can help with shuttles.

In addition to the information in the sample above, each paddle has several additional sections. Put-in/takeout information gives you directions from the nearest interstate or largest community first to the takeout, where you can leave a shuttle vehicle, then from the takeout to the put-in. By the way, look before you leap! Some of the put-ins and takeouts use dirt or sand roads just before reaching the waterways. After periods of extreme weather, such as heavy rains or long dry periods, the roads can become troublesome. If you are at all unsure about the road ahead of you stop, get out, and examine it on foot before you drive into a deep mudhole or get stuck in the sand.

A paddle summary follows the put-in/takeout directions. This does what it sounds like it should do—it gives an overview of the paddle trip, giving you an idea of what to expect that will help you determine whether or not you want to experience this waterway. A river summary follows. This gives an overview of the entire river, not just the section paddled. This way you can determine whether you want to paddle other sections of the river being detailed. It also gives you a better understanding of the entire watershed, rather than just a section of river in space and time. Next comes The Paddling, which is the meat and potatoes narrative, giving you detailed information about your river trip, including flora, fauna, and interesting not-to-be-missed natural features. It also details important information needed to execute the paddle, including forthcoming rapids, portages, bridges and stops along the way, and the mileages at which you will come across them.

Finally, each paddle has a sidebar. This is interesting information about the waterway that doesn't necessarily pertain to the specific paddle but gives you some human or natural tidbit that may pique your interest to explore beyond the simple mechanics of the paddle.

Fixing to Paddle

Which Boat Do I Use?

This book covers waterways from crashing mountain rivers to massive waterways a mile across to still and silent swamp streams to narrow creeks barely wide enough for a boat. So with such variety, what boat do you use? There are multiple possibilities.

Canoes and kayaks offer different venues for plying the waters of Tennessee. When looking for a canoe, consider the type of water through which you will be paddling. Will it be through still bodies of water or moving rivers? Will you be on big lakes, or mild whitewater, or sluggish streams? Canoes come in a wide array of oil-based materials, and are molded for weight, performance, and durability. Don't waste your time or money with an aluminum canoe. They are extremely noisy, and are more likely to get hung on underwater obstacles rather than slide over them. Consider material and design. Canoe materials can range from wood to fiberglass to composites such as Polylink 3, Royalex, Kevlar, and even graphite. I prefer more durable canoes, and thus seek out the tougher composites, such as Royalex.

Canoe design comprises the following factors: length, width, depth, keel and bottom curve, as well as flare and tumblehome.

- **Length.** Canoes should be at least 16 feet, for carrying loads and better tracking. Be apprised that shorter canoes are available, and are often used in ponds, small lakes, and smaller streams for shorter trips.

- **Width.** Wider canoes are more stable and can carry more loads but are slower. Go for somewhere in the middle.

- **Depth.** Deeper canoes can carry more weight and shed water, but they can get heavy. Again, go for the middle ground.

- **Keel.** A keel helps for tracking in lakes, but decreases maneuverability in moving water.

- **Bottom curve.** The more curved the canoe bottom, the less stable the boat. Seek a shallowly arched boat, as it is more efficient than a flat bottom boat, but not as tippy as a deeply curved boat.

- **Flare.** Flare, the outward curve of the sides of the boat, sheds water from the craft. How much flare you want depends upon how much whitewater you expect to encounter.

- **Tumblehome.** Tumblehome is the inward slope of the upper body of the canoe. A more curved tumblehome allows paddlers to get their paddle into the water easier. Rocker, the curve of the keel line from bow to stern, is important. More rocker increases maneuverability at the expense of stability. Again, go for the middle ground.

And then there are situation-specific canoes, such as whitewater or portaging canoes. Whitewater boats will have heavy rocker and deeper flare, but will be a zigzagging tub on flatwater. Portaging canoes are built with extremely light materials and will have a padded portage yoke for toting the boat on your shoulders. I recommend multipurpose touring/tripping tandem canoes, those with adequate maneuverability, so you will be able to adjust and react while shooting rapids. You want a boat that can navigate moderate whitewater, can handle loads, and can track decently through flatwater. If you are solo paddling a tandem canoe, weight the front with gear to make it run true. But if you have a solo boat, you can't change it to a two-person boat.

Consider the Old Town Penobscot 17, long a favorite of mine. It is a great all-around boat that I have used on varied trips, from day paddles on rivers to multi-night adventures, over years and years. Ultralightweight canoes, such as those built by Wenonah, are designed to be carried from lake to lake via portages, but have their place throughout Tennessee's waterways. I highly recommend the 17-foot Wenonah Spirit II. At forty-two pounds, this ultralight Kevlar boat can perform well in the water and not break your back between your vehicle and the water. I used it often while writing this book. Other times you may be going down rivers with significant stretches of whitewater, where you will want a boat that can take bone-jarring hits from rocks in East Tennessee. Finally, choose muted colors that blend with the land and water.

The first consideration in choosing a kayak is deciding between a sit-on-top model and a sit-in model, also known as a touring kayak. Sit-on-tops are what their name implies—paddlers sit on top of the boat—whereas a touring kayak requires you to put your body into the boat, leaving your upper half above an enclosed cockpit. Ask yourself, what type of waters are you going to paddle? Are you going to paddle near shore, on calm flat waters, or are you going to paddle bigger waters, such as Kentucky Lake near Land Between the Lakes National Recreation Area? If paddling bigger water you will need a cockpit. Sit-on-top kayaks are generally more comfortable, and allow for more freedom of movement. They also take on water more readily and are used almost exclusively in warmer water destinations. Sit-in touring kayaks are inherently more stable, since the user sits on the bottom of the boat, rather than on top of the boat. Sit-on-top kayaks make up for this stability shortcoming by being wider, which makes them slower. Base your decision primarily on what types of waters you will be paddling and whether you will be going overnight in your kayak. Sit-on-top kayaks are a poor choice when it comes to overnight camping. However, sit-on-tops do have their place. Smaller waters, such as ponds and gentle, smaller streams, are good for sit-on-top kayaks.

Sit-in kayaks are the traditional kayaks, based on models used by Arctic aboriginals. Some factors to consider when choosing a touring sit-in kayak are length, volume, and steering. These longer touring kayaks are built to cover water and track better. Look for a boat anywhere from 14 to 18 feet in length if overnighting. Sit-on-top kayaks will range generally from 8 to 15 feet. Narrow touring kayaks have less "initial stability"—they feel tippier when you get into them—although their narrowness prevents waves from flipping the boat over. Waves will tip wider sit-on-top kayaks, which have better initial stability.

Kayak materials vary from the traditional skin-and-wood of the Inuits to plastic and fiberglass composites like Kevlar and the waterproof cover of folding kayaks. For touring kayaks I recommend a tough composite model, simply because they can withstand running up on sandbars, scratching over oyster bars, or being accidentally dropped at the boat launch. I look for durability in a boat and don't want something that needs babying.

For touring boats, consider storage capacity. Gear is usually stored in water-proof compartments with hatches. Look for watertight hatches that close safely and securely. The larger the boat, the more room you will have. This is a matter of personal preference. Today, not only are there single kayaks, but also double kayaks, and even triple kayaks. Most touring kayaks come with a foot pedal–based steering system using a rudder. Overall, kayakers need to be fussier when choosing their boats than do canoeists, as kayaks are more situation specific. Surf the Internet and read reviews thoroughly to get an idea of what you want, then go to a store that sells kayaks and try them out. Look for "demo days" at outdoor stores. Borrow a friend's kayak. A well-informed, careful choice will result in many positive kayaking experiences. What about whitewater kayaks? These are used for many of Tennessee's wild whitewater streams, most of which are not included in the guidebook. This volume is designed for a larger audience of recreational paddlers.

Which Paddle Do I Use?

Wood is still holding on strong as a material for paddles, though plastics dominate the market, especially lower-end paddles, such as those used by outfitters, and also ultralight high-end paddles. Some cheap varieties combine a plastic blade with an aluminum handle. Bent shaft paddles are popular as well, though I don't recommend them myself. They are efficient as far as trying to get from point A to point B, but while floating you are often drifting and turning, making constant small adjustments, turning the boat around and doing all sorts of maneuvers other than straightforward paddling in a line. Bent shaft paddles are poor when it comes to precision steering moves. How about a square vs. rounded blade? I prefer a rounded blade for precision strokes, whereas a power paddler, maybe the bow paddler, will desire a square blade. Paddles can vary in length as well, generally from 48 to 60 inches. I recommend a shorter paddle for the stern paddler, because that is the person who makes the small adjustments in boat direction. A shorter paddle is easier to maneuver when making all these small adjustments, not only in the water but also when shifting the paddle from one side of the boat to the next.

Kayak paddles are double-bladed, that is they have a blade on both sides, resulting in more efficient stroking. Kayakers seem more willing to part with a lot of money to use an ultralight paddle. Almost all kayak paddles are two-piece, snapping in the middle.

This makes them easier to haul around, but more importantly it allows paddlers to offset the blades for more efficient stroking. Four-piece blades are not unusual though. Kayak blades are generally 6 inches by 18 inches, with paddles averaging between 7 and 8 feet in length. Weight wise, expensive paddles can go as low as twenty-four ounces or less, while average paddles are thirty to forty ounces. Like anything, you get what you pay for. A paddle leash is a wise investment to prevent losing your paddle.

Whether in a canoe or a sea kayak, an extra paddle is a smart idea. It's easy to stow an extra paddle in the canoe, but a kayak can be more troublesome. A four-piece paddle is easier for a kayaker to stow.

Paddling Accessories

Life Vest

I admit to never wearing my life vest unless I feel threatened by the waters in which I ply. But I do always have a life vest with me. In the bad old days, I would use anything that would meet Coast Guard standards just to get by. But now I carry a quality life vest, not only for safety but also for comfort. The better kinds, especially those designed for sea kayaking, allow for freedom of arm movement. Speaking of sea kayaking, that is when I most often wear my life vest.

Chair Backs

These hook on to the canoe seat to provide support for your back. I recommend the plastic models that cover most of your back, especially giving lower lumbar support. The more elaborate metal and canvas chair backs get in the way of paddling. However, having no chair back on multi-day trips can lead to "canoer's back."

Dry Bags

Waterproof dry bags are one of those inventions that give modern paddlers an advantage of leaps and bounds over those of yesteryear. These dry bags, primarily made of rubber and/or plastic, have various means of closing themselves down that result in a watertight seal, keeping your gear dry as you travel waterways, whether they are oceanic or riverine. Today's dry bags, which can range from tiny personal-sized, clear bags in which you might throw things such as sunscreen, keys, bug dope, and a hat, to massive rubber "black holes" with built-in shoulder straps and waist belts designed not only to keep your stuff dry but also to be carried on portages. They come in various sizes and shapes, designed to fit in the tiny corners of a kayak or an open canoe. Long and thin bags can hold a tent, while wide bags will fit most anything. Kayakers should consider deck bags, which are attached to the top of the kayak just in front of the paddler for storing day-use items.

Plastic Boxes

Plastic storage boxes, found at any mega-retailer, come in a variety of sizes and shapes. They are cheap, easily sit in the bottom of the canoe, and can double as a table. Store items in here such as bread that you don't want smashed. However, they are not nearly as waterproof as a rubber dry bag. Consider using these if you are on flatwater.

Paddlers' Checklist

- ☐ Canoe/kayak
- ☐ Paddles
- ☐ Spare paddle
- ☐ Personal flotation device
- ☐ Dry bags for gear storage
- ☐ Whistle
- ☐ Tow line

- ☐ Bilge pump for kayak
- ☐ Spray skirt for kayak
- ☐ Paddle float/lanyard for kayak
- ☐ Maps
- ☐ Throw lines
- ☐ Boat sponge

Depending on your personal interests, you may also want to consider some other items: fishing gear, sunglasses, trash bag, GPS, weather radio, camera, watch, sunscreen, lip balm, extra batteries, binoculars, and wildlife identification books.

Traveling with Your Boat

Boats, whether they are canoes or kayaks, need to be carried atop your vehicle en route to the water. How you load your boat not only depends upon whether it is a canoe or kayak, it also depends upon what type of vehicle it is and also whether or not you have an aftermarket roof rack. No matter how you carry your boat, tie it down securely, for the sake of not only your boat but also your fellow drivers, who will be endangered if your boat comes loose. I have seen a canoe fly off the car in front of me, and have seen what a boat will do to a car after sliding off the side of said car while still tied on! After cinching your boat down, drive a short distance, then pull over and recheck your tie job. I recommend using the flat straps with buckles, which are sold at any outdoor retailer and also big box stores.

A quality aftermarket roof rack installed atop your vehicle makes for a much safer way to transport boats. Invest in one of these if paddling frequently. Roof racks can be customized to different types and numbers of boats as well. And don't skimp on tie-down straps either; this is what holds the boat to the rack.

Parking

In writing this book, and other Tennessee guidebooks, among over forty outdoor guidebooks, I have parked all over the country, often for days and weeks at a time. Use your intuition when leaving your vehicle somewhere. It is always best to arrange with someone to look after your car, and a small fee is worth the peace of mind. National, state, and county parks with on-site rangers are a good choice for leaving your vehicle overnight. Also, check with fish camps and liveries, as many of these provide shuttle service and a safe place to park. Private businesses sometimes allow overnighters to park in their lots. Be sure to ask permission and offer to pay. When parking for day trips, it is better to leave the vehicle near the road rather than back in the woods out of sight.

Shuttles

River trips require a shuttle. Setting up these shuttles is a pain, but the payoff is getting to explore continually new waters in an ever-changing outdoor panorama. The closer you are to home, the more likely you are to be self-shuttling. Always remember to go to the takeout point first, leaving a car there, with the put-in point car following. Leave no valuables in your car. Take your keys with you and store them securely while you are floating!

Outfitters can save you the hassle of shuttling and allow you to leave your car in a safe, secure setting. Of course, you will pay for this service. This especially helps on river trips that are far away from home. Don't be afraid to ask about prices, distances, and reservations. Also ask about camping and potential crowds, especially during weekends. If outfitters are available, they are listed with each paddle.

Paddling Safety

A safe paddler is a smart paddler. Be prepared before you get on the water and you will minimize the possibility of accidents. And if they do happen, you will be better prepared to deal with them.

Lightning

Lightning can strike a paddler. Play it smart. When you sense a storm coming, have a plan as to what you will do when it hits. Most plans will involve getting off the water as quickly as possible. Seek shelter in a low area or in a grove of trees, not against a single tree, and then wait it out.

Poisonous Plants

Yep, poisonous plants are growing out there. You know the adages, such as leaves of three leave it be. If you are highly allergic to poisonous plants, check ahead for the area in which you will be paddling, then take the appropriate action, such as having Benadryl-based creams.

Bugs

Sometimes when paddling we consider the possibility of death by blood loss from mosquitoes, but actually your chances of dying from a bug bite in the wild are less than your chances of dying on the car ride to the river. Watch out for black widow spiders, and ticks with Lyme disease (though you can't tell the ones with Lyme disease until you get it). For those who are allergic, bee stings are a real danger.

Snakes

Paddlers will see snakes along rivers, especially on sunny streamside rocks. This is a preferred area for copperheads. I have seen other snakes swimming while floating by in a boat. Give them a wide berth and they'll do the same for you.

Sun

When paddling Tennessee, the sun can be your enemy and your friend. You welcome its light and warmth. Then it tries to burn your skin, penetrate your eyes, and kick up gusty winds. Finally you lament its departure every night as darkness falls. Sun can be a real threat no matter where you are. While boating, you will be on the water, and thus open to the prowess of old Sol. Be prepared for sun. Have sunscreen, a hat, bandanna, long pants, and a long-sleeved shirt. Clothes are your best defense. Put on the sunscreen before you get in the sun. Consider covering your hands. I have personally seen several cases of sun poisoning on paddler's hands.

Heat

While paddling, take shade breaks and swim to cool off in the heat of summer.

Cold

In our eagerness to hit the river, especially after a string of nice March days, we take off for the nearest stream, disregarding the fact that twenty-one days of March are classified as winter, and the waterways can be really cold then. The possibility of hypothermia is very real if you take a tumble into the water. Try to stay dry if at all possible—it is easier to stay dry and warm, or even dry and not so warm, than to get wet and cold, then warm up.

Medical Kit

Today, medical kits have come a long way. Now you can find activity-specific medical kits that also come in different sizes for each activity, including paddling. Medical kits designed for water sports come in waterproof pouches. I recommend Adventure Medical Kits. They not only have a good variety of kits but also divide their kits into group-size units as well, so whether you are a solo paddler or on a multiple-boat multiple-day river trip, you will have not only the right kit but the right size one.

Camping

Overnight camping can add to the Tennessee paddling experience. Where camping is a possibility, I have noted it in the paddling narratives. Other places may have strict private property situations or other elements that prohibit camping. However, you may want to consider camping either before or after your paddle. Check out the plethora of Tennessee state parks, national parks, national forests, and other public lands.

Final Note

Just remember, paddling Tennessee is about having a good time, whether you are sea kayaking on Reelfoot Lake, winding along a remote Cumberland Plateau stream, or stroking a translucent mountain waterway. Now, get out there and make some memories!

West Tennessee

1 Bayou du Chien at Reelfoot Lake

This paddle skirts the eastern edge of Reelfoot Lake, the iconic body of water that stands as one of Tennessee's most notable physical features. Paddle down a slender cypress-lined waterway before opening onto the big lake. From there, pick up a canal, reaching more open water before ending your paddle near a wildlife observation tower. Be apprised this paddle can be done as a one-way or an out-and-back.

County: Obion
Start: Walnut Log Boat Ramp, N36° 28' 1.4", W89° 19' 7.0"
End: Wildlife Drive Boat Ramp, N36° 26' 35.1", W89° 21' 7.3"
Length: 3.5 miles one way, 7 miles there and back
Float time: 2 hours one way, 4 hours there and back
Difficulty rating: Moderate, could have wind problems in open water sections
Rapids: None
River type: Narrow swamp channel, lake
Current: Little to none
River gradient: 0.0 feet per mile

River gauge: None
Season: Year-round
Land status: Public
Fees or permits: No fees or permits required
Nearest city/town: Tiptonville
Maps: USGS: Samburg; *DeLorme: Tennessee Atlas & Gazetteer,* Page 47 A6
Boats used: Canoes, kayaks, johnboats
Organizations: Reelfoot Lake National Wildlife Refuge, 4343 Hwy. 157, Union City 38261, (731) 538-2481, www.fws.gov/Reelfoot/
Contacts/outfitters: Reelfoot Lake State Park, 2595 State Rte. 21E, Tiptonville 38079, (731) 253-9652

Put-in/Takeout Information

To takeout: From exit 13 on I-155 near Dyersburg, take TN 78 north for 23 miles to Tiptonville and a four-way stop. Turn right here on TN 22 east/TN 21 south. Come along Reelfoot Lake, passing the Reelfoot Lake State Park Visitor Center to reach a road split at 5.6 miles. Veer left with TN 22 east. Stay with TN 22 east for 8.3 more miles to turn left on TN 157 north. Follow TN 157, passing Reelfoot National Wildlife Refuge Visitor Center at 1 mile. Continue for a total of 2.1 miles to the turn left on Walnut Log Road (there will be a sign here for the wildlife refuge's Grassy Island Auto Tour). Follow Walnut Log Road for 0.8 mile as it reaches a boat ramp on your right. This is the put-in. Continue past the put-in on Walnut Log Road, as it turns into Wildlife Drive, proceeding for 2.5 miles to dead-end at another boat ramp.

To put-in from takeout: Backtrack on Wildlife Drive 2.5 miles to the Walnut Log boat ramp.

Paddle Summary

You will be using paddle power while exploring this slice of Reelfoot Lake, Tennessee's only natural large lake. Travel Bayou du Chien, a linear, still waterway bordered with magnificent tall cypress. After cruising the bayou open onto one of the three large basins of Reelfoot Lake, enjoying some big water scenery before taking a canal southward to a second basin. Make your way to an observation platform where you can look over the lake and the waterfowl, wildlife, and maybe even bald eagles, for which this earthquake-created body of water is known.

Since there is little to no current you can either paddle back, doubling your mileage from 3.5 to 7 miles, or use the ramps located on both ends of the paddle. Wildlife Drive makes for a scenic bike shuttle. I have done this using a foot shuttle, adding in the hiking trail located along Wildlife Drive. Be apprised that winds can be a factor in the open water. Water levels of Reelfoot Lake are managed using a spillway at the lake's south end. However, paddlers will have ample water year-round. Spring and fall are the best times to visit here. Be apprised this section of the refuge is closed from November 15 through January 30.

River Overview

Reelfoot Lake, located in the most northwesterly corner of Tennessee, was formed after a series of major earthquakes during the winter of 1811 and 1812. It is said that during the biggest of a thousand-plus shocks, the land opened wide and the Mississippi River flowed into the newly created maw, filling over a twenty-four-hour period, taking so much water from the Mississippi that boats down in Vicksburg, hundreds of miles distant, reported the Mississippi flowing backwards! The quakes, in the heart of the active New Madrid Fault, altered the landscape over a 40,000-square-mile area. The lake covers approximately 25,000 acres, but much of this is hardwood swamp and wetland. Around 15,000 acres are open water. A registered National Natural Landmark, the large contiguous protected area makes for an important habitat for rare plants, birds, and animals. The lake's closest point to the Mississippi River is but 3 miles, making Reelfoot an important migration stopover and wintering area for winged critters on the Mississippi Flyway. This unique area of the state is managed by the Fish and Wildlife Service as well as Tennessee State Parks and Tennessee Wildlife Resources Agency. Therefore it is a wildlife-rich area, from fish below the water to beavers, deer, woodpeckers, and waterfowl. Concentrations of waterfowl can number in the tens of thousands during winter. This is also when eagles can be seen in the hundreds.

The Paddling

There are two boat ramps located at Walnut Log. The first you come to is very evident. The second is a little down the way, and you probably won't see it until begin-

Golden fall cypresses line Bayou du Chien.

ning your paddle. As you look out from the main boat ramp, three channels open. To your right is the northbound waterway of Bayou du Chien. Ahead, westerly, is the man-made Walnut Log Ditch connecting the community of Walnut Log to Upper Blue Basin, one of the three open bodies of water that make up Reelfoot Lake. This paddle heads left, southwesterly, down Bayou du Chien. Immediately pass the second, smaller boat ramp, partly shrouded by forest. The mostly straight waterway stretches about 50 feet wide. Regal bald cypress trees rise high above the water, yet there is not a complete canopy over the bayou. Lily pads, water grasses, and sawgrass mixed with cypress knees border the waterway. Occasional sycamore trees occupy higher and drier ground. There will only be current if the lake is very high and the lake spillway is open. The normally clear water will have a green or brown tint, depending on the season. Duck moss will find its place on the surface. Occasional wood duck nesting boxes are scattered along the waterway At this point, Wildlife Drive is to your left through the trees.

At 0.3 mile, Bayou du Chien narrows to 30 feet and curves to the right. Continue generally southwest, paralleling Upper Blue Basin. At 1.5 miles, a channel leads right to Upper Blue Basin. At 2.2 miles, a slender channel leads left and shortcuts the paddle. However, it may be silted in or log-choked. Bayou du Chien widens and turns

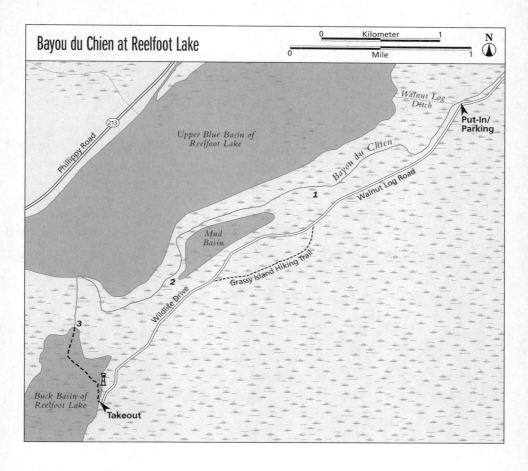

Bayou du Chien at Reelfoot Lake

north, opening onto Upper Blue Basin at 2.6 miles. You can see westerly across the lake to the community of Gray's Camp, as well as scattered cypress amid open water.

Once in Upper Blue Basin, keep the shoreline to your left, heading westerly. Views open to the north of Upper Blue Basin. Reach a straight southbound canal at 2.7 miles. Turn left here, heading south on the 60-foot-wide channel. Buck Basin opens at 3.0 miles. Begin looking left, southeasterly, for the elevated observation platform. You may have to work around lily pads, so be prepared to keep south in the open water before curving east. The squared-off shape of the platform contrasts with the fluid shapes of nature at Reelfoot Lake. Reach the platform at 3.4 miles. You can access this platform from Wildlife Drive, but consider tying your boat up to go ahead and climb the platform. In winter you may be looking down on waterfowl by the thousands. Leave the platform to join a southerly channel bordered by scattered cypress. The Wildlife Drive ramp will come into view. This is the takeout and is reached at 3.5 miles. If the winds are low, you can easily paddle back. Or walk Wildlife Drive, using the Grassy Island Hiking Trail on your trek back.

THE EAGLES OF REELFOOT

Reelfoot Lake is known for wildlife viewing, and bald eagles stand at the head of the class. The bald eagle evokes wildness and freedom and has been our national symbol since 1782. Bald eagles have called Reelfoot home since the lake came into existence in the early 1800s. Why wouldn't a bald eagle love a place like Reelfoot? The lake is a nationally known fishery, and a bald eagle's diet is about 90 percent fish, along with small mammals. It also preys on injured waterfowl, and with Reelfoot's high winter waterfowl populations, wounded ducks aren't unusual.

Interestingly, female bald eagles are larger, averaging two pounds heavier by weight. The biggest American bald eagles are in Alaska and weigh up to sixteen pounds, then generally get smaller the farther south you go. Bald eagles have a wingspan that extends from 6 to 7.5 feet. However, their wingspan is not their giveaway—these birds are identified by their white-feathered heads and tails. While maturing, bald eagles are completely brown. Their heads generally whiten around four to six years. At this time, their beaks also change from black to yellow. In the wild, their life spans extend nearly four decades.

No nesting pairs of bald eagles were observed in the Volunteer State from the early 1950s until 1983. The pesticide DDT was blamed. Nowadays, with numerous artificial lakes in the state creating favorable habitats for eagles, their populations are up, not only on lakes but also rivers you may paddle.

2 Reelfoot Lake Loop

This paddle trail explores numerous watery environments in a relatively short distance at Reelfoot National Wildlife Refuge. Follow an old canal to open water, before backtracking a bit to meander through a brushy wet prairie to enter a slender wooded channel, where cypress rises high. The final leg passes a little civilization before returning to the boat ramp of origin, making a shuttle unnecessary.

County: Obion
Start: Walnut Log Boat Ramp, N36° 28' 1.4", W89° 19' 7.0"
End: Walnut Log Boat Ramp, N36° 28' 1.4", W89° 19' 7.0"
Length: 2.7 miles
Float time: 1.5 hours
Difficulty rating: Easy
Rapids: None
River type: Narrow swamp channels, lake
Current: Little to none
River gradient: 0.0 feet per mile
River gauge: None

Season: Year-round
Land status: Public
Fees or permits: No fees or permits required
Nearest city/town: Tiptonville
Maps: USGS: Samburg; *DeLorme: Tennessee Atlas & Gazetteer,* Page 47 A6
Boats used: Canoes, kayaks, johnboats
Organizations: Reelfoot Lake National Wildlife Refuge, 4343 Hwy. 157, Union City 38261, (731) 538-2481, www.fws.gov/Reelfoot/
Contacts/outfitters: Reelfoot Lake State Park, 2595 State Rte. 21E, Tiptonville 38079, (731) 253-9652

Put-in/Takeout Information

To takeout: From exit 13 on I-155 near Dyersburg, take TN 78 north for 23 miles to Tiptonville and a four-way stop. Turn right here on TN 22 east/TN 21 south. Come along Reelfoot Lake, passing the Reelfoot Lake State Park Visitor Center to reach a road split at 5.6 miles. Veer left with TN 22 east. Stay with TN 22 east for 8.3 more miles to turn left on TN 157 north. Follow TN 157, passing Reelfoot National Wildlife Refuge Visitor Center at 1 mile. Continue for a total of 2.1 miles to the turn left on Walnut Log Road (there will be a sign here for the wildlife refuge's Grassy Island Auto Tour). Follow Walnut Log Road for 0.8 mile as it reaches a boat ramp on your right. This is the put-in and takeout.

To put-in from takeout: The takeout is the same as the put-in.

Paddle Summary

Many paddlers are reluctant to explore small channels in wooded swamps. And I can't blame them. However, this canoe trail has been marked and thus decreases the potential for getting lost. Another advantage is the paddle starting and ending in the same location, eliminating the need for a shuttle. Begin your trek in the community of Walnut Log, a small collection of houses on the eastern edge of Reelfoot Lake. Follow a canal through swamp woods, then meet Upper Blue Basin, one of three open water areas on Reelfoot Lake. Backtrack a bit to pick up a slender channel bordered by brush, a sort of wetland prairie through which you paddle. Sawgrass lines the channel in many spots here. Drift into a couple of open water sections before joining an even smaller channel that is navigable only by self-propelled craft. It leads you to Bayou du Chien. Trace the bayou past Walnut Log, then return to the boat ramp where you started.

This paddle can be done on a windy day, since it travels very little open water. Your only troubles may be beaver dams that sometimes partially block the smallest channel. Even at that you will only have to drag your boat over the dam, and at normal water levels that shouldn't be a problem. Be apprised that the Grassy Island refuge waters, where this paddle takes place, are closed from November 15 to January 30. Spring and fall are the best times to make this paddle. Spring offers high water and the emergence of life on Reelfoot Lake. Autumn paddlers will have less chance of wind and bronze-colored cypress trees reflecting in the lake.

River Overview

Reelfoot Lake, located in the most northwesterly corner of Tennessee, was formed after a series of major earthquakes during the winter of 1811 and 1812. It is said that during the biggest of a thousand-plus shocks, the land opened wide and the Mississippi River flowed into the newly created maw, filling over a twenty-four-hour period, taking so much water from the Mississippi that boats down in Vicksburg, hundreds of miles distant, reported the Mississippi flowing upstream! The quakes, in the heart of the active New Madrid Fault, altered the landscape over a 40,000-square-mile area. Reelfoot Lake covers approximately 25,000 acres, but much of this is hardwood swamp and wetland. Around 15,000 acres are open water. A registered National Natural Landmark, the large contiguous protected area makes for an important habitat for rare plants, birds, and animals. The lake's closest point to the Mississippi River is but 3 miles, making Reelfoot a significant migration stopover and wintering area for winged critters on the Mississippi Flyway. This unique area of the state is managed by the Fish and Wildlife Service as well as Tennessee State Parks and Tennessee Wildlife Resources Agency. Therefore it is wildlife rich, from fish below the water to beavers, deer, woodpeckers, and waterfowl. Concentrations of waterfowl can number in the tens of thousands during winter. This is also when eagles can be seen in the hundreds.

The Paddling

Looking out from the Walnut Log boat ramp, you will see three distinct channels. To your right is the north channel of Bayou du Chien, your return route. To your left is the south channel of Bayou du Chien. And dead ahead is a dug canal called Walnut Log Ditch. Take Walnut Log Ditch, heading westerly. You can see the open water of Upper Blue Basin in the far distance. The canal stretches about 35 feet wide, bordered

At this point, Walnut Log Ditch joins the open waters of Upper Blue Basin.

with silver maple, cattails, water lilies, cypress, willow, and sycamore. After about 0.25 mile, a northbound channel, smaller than Walnut Log Ditch, opens on the right. You will take this channel to complete your loop, but for now keep westerly, heading toward the open waters of Upper Blue Basin.

Reach the big water at 0.4 mile, gaining a glimpse of Upper Blue Basin, one of the three named open water areas of Reelfoot Lake. Views extend to the north and south. There's even some scattered cypress in the open water here. This lake has many faces, including the open waters of the basins where waterfowl gather, as well as wooded wetlands, small bays, narrow channels, and open wet prairies. This mosaic of waterscapes is what makes Reelfoot Lake visually rich for humans and an attractive environment for wildlife.

Backtrack to the northbound channel. This channel is but 20 feet wide, though wet vegetated areas stretch beyond the paddleable waters. Short trees mix with brush, but the sky is open overhead. The already intimate channel narrows, adding to the sense of remoteness. Punch your paddle down and you will likely touch bottom. The spongy, peatlike bottom reveals the long-term fate of this lake, which will eventually silt in over centuries. At 0.8 mile, a short channel leads left to Upper Blue Basin. Here, the channel curves right and becomes lined with sawgrass with little tree cover.

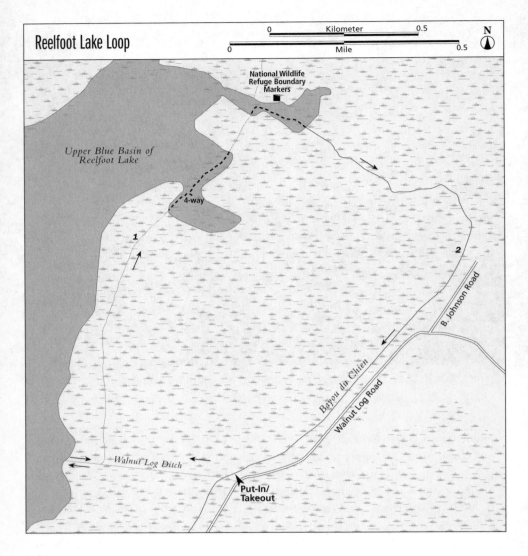

Kilometer

Mile

N

Upper Blue Basin of
Reelfoot Lake

National Wildlife
Refuge Boundary
Markers

4-way

1

2

B. Johnson Road

Bayou du Chien

Walnut Log Road

Walnut Log Ditch

Put-In/
Takeout

Reach a four-way junction of waterways at 1.2 miles. The water leading right dead-ends in a bay. The water leading left opens to Upper Blue Basin. Continue northeast on the 10-foot-wide channel bordered by low brush. At 1.4 miles, reach another area of multiple channels in open water. At this junction you will see national wildlife refuge boundary markers. Turn right, easterly, keeping the national wildlife boundary markers on your left. The channel narrows and widens into small bays. Elaborate duck blinds will be seen here. Trees rise near Bayou du Chien. Leave the open swamp behind. The wandering watercourse meets Bayou du Chien at 1.9 miles. Houses border the east bank of the bayou. Turn right, heading southwesterly down Bayou du Chien. This channel is about 60 feet wide and is wooded on the east bank.

Paddle roughly parallel to Walnut Log Road and return to the boat ramp where you started at 2.7 miles, ending your paddle.

OUR NATIONAL WILDLIFE REFUGE SYSTEM

The American system of national wildlife refuges goes hand in hand with its system of national parks. With our first national parks established in the late 1800s, it was only a step further to care for unique plant and animal habitats that demonstrate the biodiversity that makes not only Tennessee but the entire country great for paddling, hiking, and exploring. Furthermore, keeping the web of life as densely interwoven as possible enhances our country for future generations and keeps our natural heritage intact.

The mission of the national wildlife refuges is to "manage a national network of lands and waters for the conservation, management, and where appropriate, restoration of fish, wildlife and plant resources and their habitat." It all started on Pelican Island down Florida way, in 1903. At that time, throughout the Sunshine State, habitat for shorebirds was being eliminated as population, illegal hunting, and feather-gathering pressures built. Recognizing this, President Theodore Roosevelt declared Pelican Island a national wildlife refuge and set aside the land purely for the protection of brown pelicans and other birds that called Pelican Island home. From this small island oasis for America's native critters, the national wildlife refuge system has expanded to over ninety-five million acres spread over nearly 540 refuges. These refuges not only preserve wildlife but also offer recreation for hunters, anglers, birders, and photographers. Hundreds of species of fish, reptiles, mammals, and birds call these refuges home. Many of them are on the endangered species list, and several refuges have been established primarily to preserve these endangered species.

Reelfoot National Wildlife Refuge is one of four refuges in the area, known as the West Tennessee Refuge Complex. Chickasaw National Wildlife Refuge covers over 25,000 acres and protects the largest bottomland hardwood forest in the state. Like Reelfoot, it is important for waterfowl wintering, with bird populations exceeding 200,000. The Lower Hatchie National Wildlife Refuge protects the last 17 miles of the Hatchie, the only Mississippi River tributary in West Tennessee that hasn't been artificially straightened. It is one of the wildest and least accessible spots in the state. Lake Isom National Wildlife Refuge is almost a southerly extension of Reelfoot Lake and is much like Reelfoot, except smaller. Together, these refuges protect some of the wildest areas in West Tennessee and are important additions to the countrywide wildlife refuge system.

3 Hatchie River near Brownsville

This unchanneled swamp river is further protected as part of the Hatchie National Wildlife Refuge. It's a long trip, but a hasty current helps the scenic paddle.

County: Haywood
Start: TN 76 at Hatchie National Wildlife Refuge, N35° 31.228', W89° 15.138'
End: TN 70 southwest of Brownsville, N35° 31.210', W89° 20.588'
Length: 12.9 miles
Float time: 6.5 hours
Difficulty rating: Moderate
Rapids: None
River type: Swamp river
Current: Moderate to sometimes swift
River gradient: 1.0 feet per mile
River gauge: USGS Hatchie River near Bolivar, TN, minimum runnable level 160 cfs

Season: Year-round
Land status: Private
Fees or permits: No fees or permits required
Nearest city/town: Brownsville
Maps: USGS: Brownsville; *DeLorme: Tennessee Atlas & Gazetteer,* Page 31 D6
Boats used: Johnboats, canoes, kayaks
Organizations: Lower Mississippi River Conservation Committee, 2524 South Frontage Rd., Suite C, Vicksburg, MS 39180, (601) 629-6602, www.lmrcc.org
Contacts/outfitters: Hatchie National Wildlife Refuge, 6772 Hwy. 76 South, Stanton 38069, (731) 772-0501, www.fws.gov/hatchie/

Put-in/Takeout Information

To takeout: From exit 56 on I-40 near Brownsville, take TN 76 north toward Brownsville just a very short distance then look left for Windrow Road. (Windrow Road is so close to I-40, a sign states that it is not an on-ramp to 40. Also look for the sign stating the way to a Tennessee Department of Transportation facility.) Follow Windrow Road for 1.1 miles to a stop sign. Here, Windrow Road turns right. Keep straight, now on Sugar Creek Road. Follow Sugar Creek Road 1.4 miles to reach Shaw Chapel Road at a three-way intersection. Turn left on Shaw Chapel Road and follow it for 4.3 miles to US 70/US 79. Turn left and take US 70 west/US 79 south to bridge the Hatchie River at 0.8 mile. Just after the bridge, turn right on Fin-Feather Bend Road and reach the TWRA boat ramp.

To put-in from takeout: Backtrack to exit 56 on I-40. This time take TN 76 south from the interstate for 1.2 miles to bridge the Hatchie River. The Hatchie River National Wildlife Refuge boat ramp is on the southwest side of the bridge.

Paddle Summary

The distance of this swamp river paddle—12.9 miles—can seem scary for day-trippers, but the current is surprisingly swift and will help you move along, especially if you're a willing paddler. That being said, if going on a fall leaf viewing trip—when the water is its lowest and current weakest—allow yourself ample time. The Hatchie River takes

Sandbars are exposed on a bend during a fall paddle on the Hatchie.

a decidedly westerly turn as it wanders through Haywood County within the Hatchie Wildlife Refuge. Though the refuge designation is good, it isn't necessary, as most of the river travels through remote terrain with little human habitation. Interestingly the river also banks against numerous bluffs, which rise on the northern flank of Hatchie Bottom. The bluffs and bottoms provide an interesting contrast and add to the biodiversity of an already botanically rich paddle. Expect to see wildlife on the trip whether it be bird, reptile, or beast. The Hatchie Bottom harbors a rich array of species, and having part of the lands managed as a national wildlife refuge only helps the situation. Dwellings are nearly nonexistent, but you will find a few scattered hunt/fish camps along the banks beyond the refuge boundaries.

The first part of the paddle repeatedly runs into bluffs before the river turns its back on the hills at around 4 miles. The waterway then wanders through pure bottoms and connects to other channels on a torturously winding track that travels all the cardinal directions. However, the main route is easily evident at normal flows as the strongest current travels the widest, most open paddling path. However, do expect to work your way around fallen trees and other woodsy debris. If you are concerned about your position, bring a GPS. Also, a recent overhead satellite image will be

Hatchie River near Brownsville

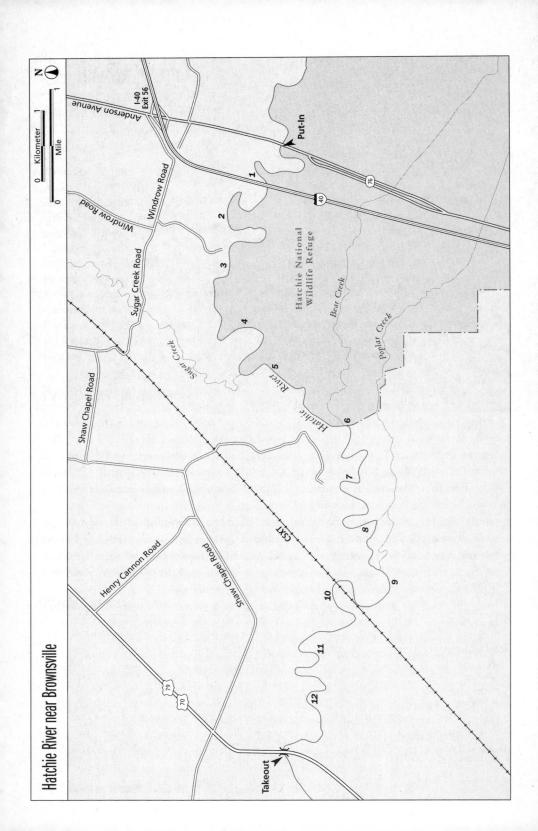

helpful. At this point the river is about halfway to the confluence with the Mississippi River and is a larger, brawnier waterway than upstream near the Mississippi state border. You'll be surprised at the speed of the current as it pulses over a sandy floor.

River Overview

The Hatchie River begins in north Mississippi, flowing as a small stream just a short distance into the Volunteer State before meeting the much larger Tuscumbia River, which by all rights should retain the name instead of the Hatchie. Name aside, the Hatchie then works its way north and west through Hardeman County, picking up tributaries and creating wide bottoms. Unlike the Hatchie itself, some of these tributaries were channelized. For this is the Hatchie's claim to fame—it is the only river in West Tennessee that remains unchanneled its entire length of over 170 miles. This intact extensive bottomland makes for a wildlife corridor matched only by the Mississippi River itself. The Hatchie works its way northwest past the town of Bolivar, then enters Haywood County, where it is protected as the Hatchie National Wildlife Refuge. The river continues its serpentine meanderings, now heading more westerly as it forms the dividing line between Tipton County and Lauderdale County, where it also passes in the shadow of Fort Pillow State Historic Area. Finally, the waterway drifts into the Lower Hatchie National Wildlife Refuge before meeting the Mississippi River. Paddlers can enjoy every wild mile of the river, and those looking for a first-rate backcountry swamp river camping experience, can paddle from the TN 57 bridge in Pocahontas all the way to the mighty Mississippi.

The Paddling

The concrete boat ramp can be muddy if the river has come up recently. You will probably not escape getting your feet dirty entering the boat. The Hatchie stretches about 120 feet from bank to bank and has a brown tint that will often belie its clarity. It won't be mistaken for a Smoky Mountains stream, but you should be able to see your paddle in the water and throw lures if you are an angler—barring recent rain.

Vertical mud banks rise 5 to 10 feet above the water. The shore rises from the water at an angle inside bends. This is where you'll find sandbars. Interestingly, some sandbars are partially vegetated and are becoming wooded due to the river changing course or not rising to extreme heights and depositing sand, as it can during historically very high but infrequent floods. Cypress and tupelo define the swamp river. Other water-loving trees such as sycamore, willow, and river birch will be found along the shores. Brush can be impenetrably thick in summer. Oaks and hickories occupy the driest sites. Fallen trees are frequent on the river but rarely block passage. Live trees overhanging the waterway also effectively narrow the paddling corridor. Local river rats keep the Hatchie clear for boat passage. Look for trees at the edge of vertical banks with exposed roots waiting for the next high water event to come and wash them into the river.

The hum of I-40 is inescapable during the paddle's beginning. Come alongside your first high white clay bluff at 0.9 mile. Shortly pass under the twin I-40 bridges. The stains on the bridge abutments show how high the Hatchie gets on a regular basis. Watch the south bank for blue and white signs indicating the national wildlife refuge, though in essence no difference can be told between the refuge bank and the unprotected bank. At 1.7 miles, swing alongside more incredible bluffs. Multicolored layers of red and pale soil are easily visible. Pass a few dwellings on river right here, taking advantage of the elevated ground.

The Hatchie winds its way away from the bluffs only to bank up against a wooded hill at 2.8 miles. Return to the bluff yet again at 3.2 miles as the Hatchie continues bouncing against hills that delineate Hatchie Bottom. At 3.7 miles, pass an old river shack as the Hatchie makes a sharp turn to the south. Alluring wooded flats lie above the vertical wood banks, where hickories and oaks will be laden with mast in the fall. At 4.3 miles look for a large sandbar suitable for stopping on the inside of a bend where the Hatchie curves to the northwest. Sugar Creek comes in on river right at 4.7 miles. Another cabin is located here, and the landowner has placed rock riprap along the shoreline.

Bear Creek comes in on river left at 6 miles. This marks the end of the refuge. Large sandbars are prevalent on bends but will be grassy in summer. Branches of Poplar Creek enter river left at 8.3 and 8.6 miles. The Hatchie widens. CSXT Railroad comes into view at 9.1 miles, and the Hatchie slips under its bridge at 9.8 miles. Sandbars are fewer below the confluence with Poplar Creek. At 12 miles, an unnamed stream comes in on river right. Pass some developed properties on river left just before going under the US 70/US 79 bridge. The takeout is on river left just after the bridge. Beware, as this boat ramp can be muddy also.

MAKE YOUR HATCHIE BASE CAMP AT CHICKASAW STATE PARK

I've used Chickasaw State Park as a paddling base when plying the Hatchie River. It offers fine state park facilities amid a larger rustic state forest. The state park and the surrounding Chickasaw State Forest comprise over 14,000 acres. Part of the acreage has been developed for intense recreational use and offers three state park campgrounds near Lake Placid. Horse, hiking, and motor trails spill out from the state park into the adjacent state forest, offering plenty of avenues to roam. Separate camps are designed for tent campers, trailer/RV campers, and equestrian campers. Hot showers are available, as is a camp store.

Tent campers can walk from their site to the Lakeshore Nature Trail. It loops Lake Placid. Or you could cross the footbridge over to the designated swim beach. The clear, cool lake is inviting during the summertime. Paddleboats and rowboats are available for rent. Unfortunately, no private canoes or kayaks are allowed. Many folks choose to wet a line from the bank or a boat, vying for bass and bluegill.

If you want to stay on land, hike the Forked Pine Nature Trail, which leaves from near the picnic shelters. If horseback riding is your thing, an on-site equestrian stable leads trail rides. Beyond the park recreation area, the state forest has over 50 miles of gravel roads and trails for horses, hikers, mountain bikers, and autos. A forest map is available at the park office. All they ask is that you stay on the established paths and roads.

Chickasaw also has a more developed side, with tennis, basketball, and volleyball courts; horseshoe pits; an archery range; and playgrounds. Parents will be glad to know that during summer a park recreation director keeps kids busy with arts, crafts, games, movies, and evening programs. The recreation opportunities here at Chickasaw run the gamut, so you shouldn't suffer from boredom, especially when you throw in a paddle on the Hatchie. For more information visit www.tnstateparks.org.

4 Hatchie River near Bolivar

This gorgeous and remote swamp river wanders through a wide bottomland offering wildlife viewing and a distinct paddling experience. The shuttle is easy too.

County: Hardeman
Start: US 64 east of Bolivar, N35° 16.519', W88° 58.255'
End: TN 18 northeast of Bolivar, N35° 14.344', W88° 55.178'
Length: 8.3 miles
Float time: 4.5 hours
Difficulty rating: Moderate
Rapids: None
River type: Swamp river
Current: Moderate to swift
River gradient: 1.1 feet per mile
River gauge: USGS Hatchie River near Bolivar, TN, minimum runnable level 160 cfs
Season: Year-round

Land status: Private
Fees or permits: No fees or permits required
Nearest city/town: Bolivar
Maps: USGS: Hebron, Bolivar East; *DeLorme: Tennessee Atlas & Gazetteer,* Page 16 B2
Boats used: Johnboats, canoes, kayaks
Organizations: Lower Mississippi River Conservation Committee, 2524 South Frontage Rd., Suite C, Vicksburg, MS 39180, (601) 629-6602, www.lmrcc.org
Contacts/outfitters: Nature Conservancy—Tennessee, 2021 21st Ave. South, Suite C-400, Nashville 37212, (615) 383-9909, www.nature.org

Put-in/Takeout Information

To takeout: From the town square in Bolivar, take TN 18 north for 1.5 miles, bridging the Hatchie River. Keep straight on TN 18 for a total of 1.9 miles to the boat ramp on the left. You will see a building at the left turn. This will be just after the second bridge over the Hatchie and its adjacent channels.

To put-in from takeout: Backtrack to the town square in Bolivar on TN 18 south, then join US 64 east and travel for 3.8 miles to the boat ramp on your right just before bridging the Hatchie River.

Paddle Summary

When you look at a topographic map of the Hatchie River, the mazelike channels shown can be intimidating—it looks like you'll never find the proper route. However, in reality Hatchie River is much easier to follow, as most of the channels are slack to slow at normal water levels while the primary channel flows distinctly stronger. Also, many of the spur channels will be log choked or otherwise impassible. That being said, this is a good river to have a GPS with you, especially when the water is up. The brownish-clear water flows surprisingly swift, except for the first mile or so, then the bends begin. From here on out the watercourse twists and curves, forming sandbars in places, despite having mud banks. The shoreline vegetation is incredibly thick, prohibiting landing in many spots. Sandbars will be your best option, and at high water these will be underwater. The river run remains mostly wild save for a few hunt camps set on higher ground.

The Hatchie continues working its way northwesterly through the greater Hatchie Bottom, flowing fast over sandy shallows and slower where deep. Eventually the sounds of TN 18 echo through the forest and you pass under it. But your paddle isn't over as the river makes a wide curve back to the public landing located off TN 18.

River Overview

The Hatchie River begins in north Mississippi, flowing as a small stream just a short distance into the Volunteer State before meeting the much larger Tuscumbia River, which by all rights should retain the name instead of the Hatchie. Name aside the Hatchie then works its way north and west through Hardeman County, picking up tributaries and creating wide bottoms. Unlike the Hatchie itself, some of these tributaries were channelized. For this is the Hatchie's claim to fame—it is the only river in West Tennessee that remains unchanneled its entire length of over 170 miles. This intact extensive bottomland makes for a wildlife corridor matched only by the Mississippi River itself. The Hatchie works its way northwest past the town of Bolivar, then enters Haywood County, where it is protected as the Hatchie National Wildlife Refuge. The river continues its serpentine meanderings, now heading more westerly as it forms the dividing line between Tipton County and Lauderdale County, where it also passes in the shadow of Fort Pillow State Historic Area. Finally, the river enters the Lower Hatchie National Wildlife Refuge before meeting the Mississippi River. Paddlers can enjoy every wild mile of the river, and those

Bridge view of the Hatchie River.

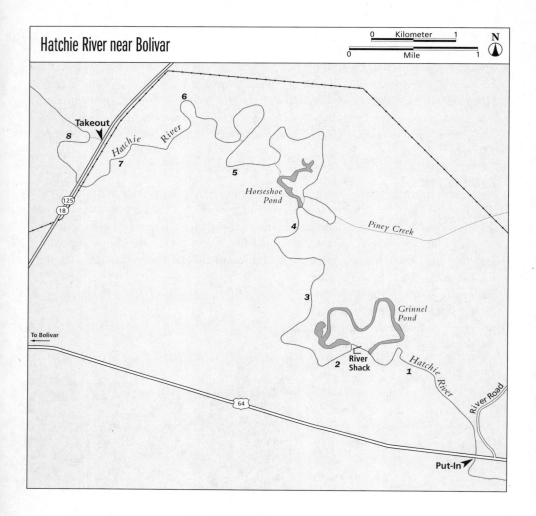

Hatchie River near Bolivar

0   Kilometer   1

0   Mile   1

N

Takeout

8

Hatchie River

7

6

125
18

5

Horseshoe Pond

4

Piney Creek

3

Grinnel Pond

To Bolivar

2

River Shack

1

Hatchie River

River Road

64

Put-In

looking for a first-rate backcountry swamp river camping experience can paddle from the TN 57 bridge in Pocahontas all the way to the mighty Mississippi.

The Paddling

Leave the concrete boat ramp and immediately flow under the US 64 bridge. A few houses are located on river right just below the bridge. Cypress and tupelo trees occupy the lowermost shoreline, along with brushy willows, river birch, and sycamore. Water oaks, hickory, and laurel oaks occupy the higher ground. The river is tinted brown but will run clear, especially in late summer and fall, which is the recommended time to paddle the river, as the overflow channels aren't running and this cuts down on navigational confusion. Winter and early spring offer the highest flows and a chance to explore adjacent sloughs.

Expect substantial deadfall in the river. You may have to work around them, but passages are generally kept cut open. The mud banks range about 6 to 8 feet high and can be nearly vertical at times but will be more sloped on the insides of bends, where sandbars rise from the water. The Hatchie extends 100 feet across, yet it is often narrower, especially when it divides into channels. Punch your paddle into the river bottom when going over swift segments and you will be surprised, as it is nearly all sand. Listen for deer in the bordering bottoms. Beaver and muskrat will splash away. Turtles will dive into water upon your approach. Woodpeckers howl in the distance. Waterfowl gathers along the shoreline. Wild turkeys roost in the trees and wander the forest floor. The Hatchie Bottom is simply alive with nature's beasts in their primitive glory.

The current begins to speed after mile one. The serpentine convolutions snake through the bottom. Large partially vegetated sandbars begin appearing. Silent channels and sloughs are flanked with cypress and tupelo. Sharp channels are sometimes cut by overflow routes. No matter what, stay with the main flow and you should be fine at normal water levels. Rivers such as this can and do change course, so bring your GPS. Also look for man-made saw marks in fall in trees, which also help identify the main channel. Since bona fide rapids are nonexistent, your steering challenges will be working around fallen trees. Most trees will have fallen from high water and natural erosion, but other trees will have been taken down by beavers. River debris will pile up on the upstream sides of these fallen trees.

At 1.8 miles, the main river curves left and passes a river shack on river left while a large channel leaves right into the Grinnel Pond. At 3.4 miles, the Hatchie curves sharply left, west, as a notable channel comes in on the right. The river narrows to as little as 50 feet on sharp bends. At 4.3 miles the river meets another notable channel and makes another sharp bend to the west. It then passes the Horseshoe Pond at 4.5 miles, but you probably won't even notice it. At 5.3 miles, the river cuts through an old meander and heads sharply west yet again. The river is constantly being pushed northwesterly by hills that rise to its east and form one boundary of the greater Hatchie Bottom. Note the occasional grassy shoreline. These are sand- or mudbars that haven't been inundated recently or aren't being shaped because the river channel has rerouted itself and is now revegetating.

At 5.9 miles, the river curves left and backs against a steep hill on river right. TN 18 becomes audible in the distance, yet you still have miles to go due to the river meanderings. Pass under the TN 18 bridge at 7.5 miles. A broken down metal bridge lies just downstream as you begin one last extensive curve. At 8.2 miles, a channel leads right and the boat ramp is a short distance up this side channel. You will be able to see a bridge on TN 18 from the main Hatchie when you look up this channel.

EXPLORING NEARBY BIG HILL POND STATE PARK

Located southeast of Bolivar within easy driving distance, consider coupling a trip to Big Hill Pond State Park with your paddle—the best-kept secret in West Tennessee. The park was created in part because of its wetlands, which lie in the floodplain of the Tuscumbia River, the major tributary of the Hatchie. But Big Hill Pond is mostly steep hills broken with rock outcrops hovering over sharp wooded ravines. A 30-mile trail system is special enough to have been designated a National Recreation Trail. And when darkness comes, you will find a quality campground.

The thirty-site camp is set on a ridge above Dismal Branch. This rolling backdrop offers vertical variation. Tall pines, hickories, and oaks shade sites leveled by landscaping timbers. Campsite privacy, while excellent, isn't much of an issue, as this undiscovered getaway is rarely crowded. A fully equipped bathhouse lies in the center of the loop. Spring and fall are the most popular seasons, but even then Big Hill Pond very rarely fills.

The name Big Hill Pond comes from a pond dug in 1853 after fill was needed for completing the railroad running near the park. A newer impoundment, Travis McNatt Lake, is just a short piece from the campground. Spring fed and 165 acres in size, the lake is popular for its supply of bass, bream, and catfish. Even if you don't catch anything, the "no gas motors" lake is a pleasure to paddle, especially in spring when the azaleas are blooming, or when autumn's paintbrush reflects off the water.

The trail system explores the high and the low of Big Hill Pond State Park. The highest of the high is an observation tower where there are 360-degree views of the surrounding countryside and far south into Mississippi. The lowest of the low is the 0.8-mile boardwalk traversing Dismal Swamp, a bottomland forest that attracts waterfowl and other wildlife. In between are wooded hills and surprisingly steep valleys. For more information visit www .tnstateparks.org.

5 Wolf River–Ghost River Section

This marked paddling trail begins a swift bottomland swamp river, then enters canoe-width channels and the "Ghost River," which meanders through a cypress–tupelo swamp. It then opens into a lakelike open swamp before speeding to its end.

County: Fayette
Start: LaGrange, N35° 1.584', W89° 14.502'
End: Bateman Road near Moscow, N35° 1.394', W89° 21.11'
Length: 8.4 miles
Float time: 6 hours
Difficulty rating: Moderate to difficult due to tight channels and navigation through wooded swamp
Rapids: None
River type: Swamp river
Current: Moderate to swift
River gradient: 1.9 feet per mile
River gauge: USGS Wolf River at LaGrange, TN, minimum runnable level 60 cfs

Season: Year-round
Land status: Mostly public—Ghost River State Natural Area, private also
Fees or permits: No fees or permits required
Nearest city/town: LaGrange
Maps: USGS: Grand Junction, Moscow SE; *DeLorme: Tennessee Atlas & Gazetteer,* Page 15 D6
Boats used: Canoes, kayaks, a few johnboats
Organizations: Wolf River Conservancy, P. O. Box 11031, Memphis 38111-0031, (901) 452-6500, www.wolfriver.org
Contacts/outfitters: Ghost River Rentals, 952 Quail Chase, Collierville 38017, (901) 485-1220, www.ghostriverrentals.com

Put-in/Takeout Information

To takeout: From the intersection of TN 76 and TN 57 in Moscow, take TN 57 east for 2.4 miles to Bateman Road. Turn right on Bateman Road and follow it 1.7 miles to the boat ramp on river left just before bridging the Wolf River.

To put-in from takeout: Backtrack to TN 57 and drive east to LaGrange. Reach a four-way intersection and turn right on Main Street. Head southbound as Main Street becomes Yager Drive, driving for 0.8 mile from TN 57 to reach the boat ramp on the right before bridging the Wolf River.

Paddle Summary

This is one incredible paddle. For starters, most of the river corridor you will be paddling is protected as the Ghost River State Natural Area, where the unchannelized swamp river flows westerly through bottomland hardwoods, offering numerous faces as it works its way from LaGrange toward Moscow. At times it is a narrow and swift swamp river curving through dense woodlands and the next minute it separates, braiding into multiple channels that would ordinarily make it quite difficult to follow. However, the correct route is signed, easing the burden of navigation and thus allowing you to enjoy the superlative scenery that abounds along this waterway. Next, the

Wolf enters a bona fide cypress-tupelo swamp with little to no current, thus receiving the name Ghost River. Here you will be paddling shaded watery woodland evoking primeval nature that once covered much of West Tennessee's waterways. Then the paddle opens into a wide lakelike expanse where open water, lily pads, and swamp hardwoods together form a wetland mosaic. The Wolf eventually gathers steam and speeds for one final push to reach Bateman Bridge. Be apprised this is as challenging as swamp paddling can get—you will be working around fallen trees, navigating swift channels no wider than your boat, searching for signs while squeezing between cypress and tupelo, paddling open still water then making fast turns over sandy shallows. Even the most experienced paddlers will be playing "bumper boats" along the way. Allow every bit of six hours for your paddle, and don't start this trip if daylight is lacking. Also, there are few places to pull over and get out, so be prepared to spend a lot of time in your boat. Hazards aside, a Tennessee paddler will not have their passport validated until adding this river to their résumé!

River Overview

The Wolf River begins in Mississippi's Holly Springs National Forest, just a few miles south of the Tennessee state line. Here the Wolf wanders westerly, leaving the national forest, aiming for the Volunteer State, then says goodbye to Mississippi near the hamlet of Michigan City. The river then enters Fayette County, creating part of the 40,000 some odd acres of bottomland that lie along the river between this point and its confluence with the Mississippi River. The Wolf makes a northward jog, nearing the town of LaGrange. Here it turns west and flows within the protected corridor of the Ghost River State Natural Area, where it wanders westerly in many incarnations while bordered by hills to its north. The Wolf then speeds its way toward Moscow to pick up the North Fork Wolf River, significantly increasing its flow from waters that drain eastern Fayette County and extreme western Hardeman County. The bottomland strip continues west, passing near Rossville. It becomes hemmed by habitation upon entering Shelby County and the greater Memphis area. The river still meanders until it meets Grays Creek, where this tributary and the Wolf are both channelized, done in the 1960s. The Wolf continues to remain channelized the duration of its length. Some wildness remains due to adjacent bottoms, especially where it passes through the protected Shelby Farms Park. The Wolf continues to be fed by municipal streams and becomes muddier and a victim of urban litter before meeting the Mississippi River just north of downtown Memphis. Paddlers can enjoy the river from LaGrange all the way to Memphis, even though the channelized area is less appealing. Public accesses are springing up along the river as the corridor is being recognized as a vital natural resource for West Tennesseans.

◀ *The marked paddle route passes under a tree.*

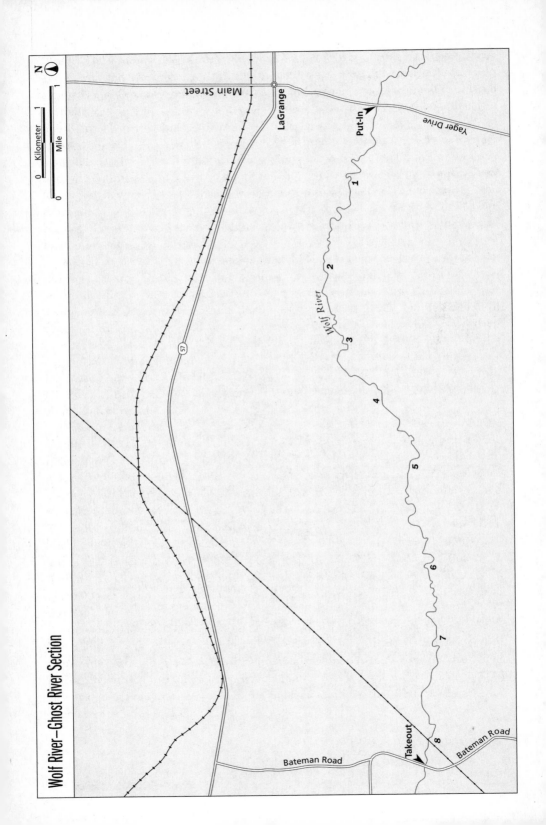

Wolf River–Ghost River Section

The Paddling

Leave boat ramp to immediately see your first canoe trail markers. The Wolf is about 30 feet wide and bordered by tupelo, cypress, and willow. Mud banks rise 4 to 6 feet above the water, allowing laurel oak, beech, river birch, and ironwood. Maple ash, cane, and brush round out the riverside vegetation. Fallen tree snags rise above the water surface, as do distinctly odd cypress knees. Cut limbs on these snags clear slender passages for the paddler. The river often braids around islands, so be prepared to choose the correct channel. You will be aided by the canoe trail markers as well as the limbs sawn by previous river travelers. Expect to duck under live trunks and limbs overhanging the river as you paddle.

The Wolf where shallow will have a sandy bottom, otherwise the floor and banks will be mud. Depths vary wildly depending upon whether you are in moving water or not. The river has a greenish-brown tint, but will be surprisingly clear unless muddied by recent rains. Tan sandbars form inside bends. Underwater grasses sway in the current while lily pads occupy still waters. Cypress trees stand sentinel in silent sloughs.

At 1.3 miles, pass a private section of land bordered in rock riprap. Pass Marker #1 at 1.5 miles. At 2.3 miles, the banks are quite low and wooded overflow swamps border the river. At higher water levels the whole area will be inundated, but the main channel is evident. The sense of remoteness overwhelms. At 3 miles, pass marker #2. Numerical markers have been placed along the canoe trail to keep you apprised of your position. At 3.5 miles, pass marker #3. The sandbar just upstream is known as "the lunch spot," as it offers a high, dry stopping point. The current is traveling into standing cypress and tupelo trees. The twists and turns continue; the Wolf continues to braid then come together, and the channels correspondingly widen and narrow.

At 5.0 miles, reach a very important junction. Here you will find marker #4. The main channel goes forward while the marked canoe trail enters the Ghost River section of the Wolf. A sign states, GHOST RIVER CANOE TRAIL ENTRANCE HERE. Enter a slender channel barely wide enough for your boat bordered with stunted pumpkin ash. Prepare to turn like you've never turned a boat before while making your way through bona fide swamp forest. Stay with the trail markers, take your time, and enjoy the float. This is the only route through the swamp forest. Reach Marker #5 at 5.6 miles and end the Ghost River section. The waterway widens, but make sure and stay with the trail markers continuing in a swamp forest.

The current slackens as you enter a stillwater section known as Spirit Lake, a region where lily pads, open water, and swamp woods along with a main channel all bleed into one another. Also note the wood duck nesting boxes. Reach marker #6 at 7.4 miles. Here, the Wolf begins to move again as the channel narrows. Solid land banks and a few sandbars reappear. Swift waters resume while you twist among trees then emerge into open yet fast waters, passing under a power line at 8.1 miles. From here keep your eyes ahead, looking for the concrete boat ramp at Bateman Bridge, completing the paddle at 8.4 miles.

PROTECTING THE WOLF RIVER CORRIDOR

As greater Memphis has moved easterly, the wild upper Wolf River has increased in importance as a natural resource. Not only is the Wolf River important as an ecosystem giving refuge to plant and animal species, but it is also a feeder of the Memphis aquifer, so keeping it clean is in the interests of all who live in the Bluff City. Throughout the history of Memphis the Wolf River was used as a dumping ground for trash and human waste. As Memphis grew the Wolf was channelized for land use and drainage purposes. However, much of the Wolf east of Memphis remained in its natural state, protected by wide and wild bottoms. Eventually concerned citizens formed the Wolf River Conservancy in 1985 and have been working to protect the greater Wolf River watershed.

The conservancy worked with numerous groups including the state of Tennessee, which has since established the 720-acre Lucius Burch State Natural Area within 4,500-acre Shelby Farms and the 2,200-acre Ghost River State Natural Area through which this paddle travels. The Ghost River area was established in 1999 and includes a loop trail and boardwalk that complements the paddling experience.

The greater Wolf River Wildlife Management Area adds another 7,000 acres. This along with other lands add to over 17,000 protected acres of the 42,000-acre hundred-year floodplain of the Wolf River in Tennessee. Another goal of the conservancy is to establish a 30-mile greenway along the Wolf River stretching from downtown Memphis to Collierville, adding another 2,000-plus acres. They are also working with the Army Corps of Engineers to restore the channelized river portion and protect upstream erosion known as head cutting. Interestingly, the protection of the wild upper reaches has increased awareness of the Wolf River in Memphis. Stay tuned as the Wolf River continues to be recognized as a special area and natural resource for all in the Mid-South. For more information visit www.wolfriver.org.

6 Wolf River–Moscow Section

This swamp paddle is shorter than the more well-known Ghost River section of the Wolf. It does offer additional technical segments, which pass through wooded swamps. The lesser mileage makes it a better choice for those with less time.

County: Fayette

Start: Bateman Road near Moscow, N35° 1.394', W89° 21.11'

End: TN 57 in Moscow, N35° 3.362', W89° 24.231'

Length: 6.1 miles

Float time: 3.5 hours

Difficulty rating: Moderate to difficult due to some tight channels and navigation through wooded swamp

Rapids: None

River type: Swamp river

Current: Moderate to swift

River gradient: 1.9 feet per mile

River gauge: USGS Wolf River at LaGrange, TN,

minimum runnable level 70 cfs

Season: Year-round

Land status: Private

Fees or permits: No fees or permits required

Nearest city/town: LaGrange

Maps: USGS: Grand Junction, Moscow SE; *DeLorme: Tennessee Atlas & Gazetteer,* Page 15 D5

Boats used: Canoes, kayaks, a few johnboats

Organizations: Wolf River Conservancy, P. O. Box 11031, Memphis 38111-0031, (901) 452-6500, www.wolfriver.org

Contacts/outfitters: Ghost River Rentals, 952 Quail Chase, Collierville 38017, (901) 485-1220, www.ghostriverrentals.com

Put-in/Takeout Information

To takeout: From the intersection of TN 194 and TN 57 in Rossville, take TN 57 east to the bridge over the Wolf River in Moscow. Just after the bridge look left for a road leading into a small shopping center. The takeout is the end of a narrow dug ditch reached from the southwest corner of the shopping center parking area. Make sure to physically check the takeout spot. The bridge over the Wolf is 0.7 mile *west* of the intersection of TN 76 and TN 57 in Moscow.

To put-in from takeout: Backtrack to TN 57 and drive east to the intersection of TN 76 and TN 57 in Moscow. From there, take TN 57 east for 2.4 miles to Bateman Road. Turn right on Bateman Road and follow it 1.7 miles to the boat ramp on river left just before bridging the Wolf River.

Paddle Summary

This is one of two excellent paddles on the upper Wolf River. The other, the Ghost River paddle, is more renowned, but this paddle has plenty to offer—namely a wandering swamp river coursing through a wide wooded bottom where wildlife thrives. The trip is a feast for your eyes but will test your paddling skills as you navigate sharp bends and slice between tupelo and cypress trees. Begin your trip at the Bateman

Paddler posing by the sun-dappled Wolf River at the Bateman Bridge put-in.

Bridge. Enter the Wolf bordered by swamp hardwoods and lily pads. The waterway repeatedly divides into channels and gathers again as it flows westerly. Prepare to work your way around fallen trees and partially submerged logs that occasionally alter the river course. In some areas the route passes through tupelo and cypress swamps where these trees rise from the water. Luckily for paddlers the way is signed. The canoe trail signs do not detract from the experience but rather put you at ease in an otherwise extremely confusing area.

River Overview

The Wolf River begins in Mississippi's Holly Springs National Forest, just a few miles south of the Tennessee state line. Here the Wolf wanders westerly, leaving the national forest, aiming for the Volunteer State, then says goodbye to Mississippi near the hamlet of Michigan City. The river then enters Fayette County, creating part of the 40,000 some odd acres of bottomland that lie along the river between this point and its confluence with the Mississippi River. The Wolf makes a serious northward jog, coming close to the town of LaGrange. Here it turns west and flows within the protected corridor of the Ghost River State Natural Area where it wanders westerly in many incarnations while bordered by hills to its north. The Wolf then speeds toward Moscow to pick up the North Fork Wolf River, significantly increasing its flow from waters that drain eastern Fayette County and extreme western Hardeman County. The bottomland strip continues west, passing near Rossville. It becomes hemmed by habitation upon entering Shelby County and the greater Memphis area. The river still meanders until it meets Grays Creek, where this tributary and the Wolf are both channelized, done in the 1960s. The Wolf continues to remain channelized the duration of its length. Some wildness remains due to adjacent bottoms, especially where it passes through the protected Shelby Farms Park. The Wolf continues to be fed by municipal streams and becomes muddier and a victim of urban litter before meeting the Mississippi River just north of downtown Memphis. Paddlers can enjoy the river from LaGrange all the way to Memphis even though the channelized area is less appealing. Public accesses are springing up all along the river as the corridor is being recognized as a vital natural resource for West Tennesseans.

The Paddling

The put-in is above Bateman Bridge. The ramp leads into a swift section with scattered cypress trees and is a scenic spot in its own right. After hopping in your boat you will speedily flow under Bateman Bridge. The Wolf River is quite shallow here as it surges over a tan sand bottom. A beach is located on river left just a little ways below the bridge. It is a popular gathering spot for locals. Lily pads and grasses border the river, as well as river birch, tupelo, ironwood, and sycamore. Watch for occasional canoe trail markers nailed to trees. These trail markers will be more closely spaced in areas that may prove confusing. Also watch for saw marks on fallen trees to help guide you when the river braids around islands. If you dare to take a channel at random, chances are you may not get through since it will be overgrown, too shallow, or simply a dead end.

Occasional sandbars will be exposed along the shore, as will the knees of cypress trees by the hundreds. The undercurrent often flows around swamp trees standing in the middle of the river. The Wolf continues dividing and coming back together. The overhead tree canopy widens and narrows with the changing channels. At lower water levels expect to scrape over the ever-shifting shallow sand bottom in places.

Keep an eye peeled for beaver lodges. You will see large piles of stacked branches and limbs. You may also see muskrats and will certainly see ample birdlife from herons to ducks. The paddling remains exciting and you never know what to expect around the corner, whether it be a tight channel, a wide swamp, or something in between. At 3 miles the river begins aiming north for Moscow, though it does so in a convoluted fashion as it did when heading westerly.

At 5.1 miles, the marked paddling trail splits. Here, you can head right for the quickest way to the takeout or head left and take the scenic route. The scenic route takes you on a wider channel, which curves to enter a full-blown cypress swamp where you will be paddling among trees and knees. At 5.5 miles, the route works its

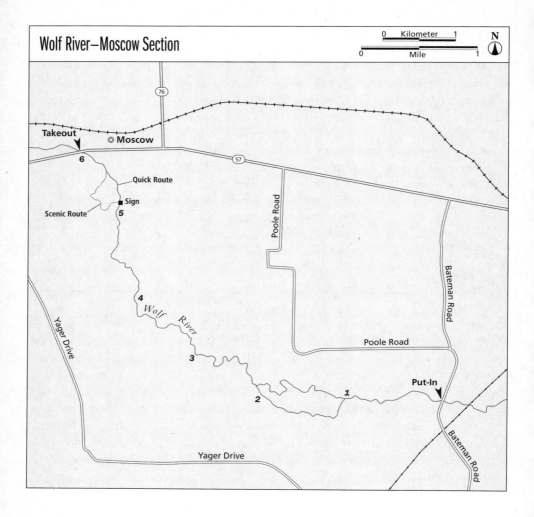

0   Kilometer   1

0   Mile   1

N

Takeout

◎ Moscow

76

57

6

Quick Route

Sign

Scenic Route

5

Poole Road

Bateman Road

4

Wolf River

Poole Road

3

Put-In

Yager Drive

1

2

Bateman Road

Yager Drive

way into a channel that leads away from the old public boat ramp, no longer in use due to lack of water. Roam close enough to where you can see the hill on which Moscow sits and shortly come to the TN 57 bridge. Just beyond the bridge look right for a linear straight channel heading away from the river. It may be partially blocked with lily pads. This channel leads to dry ground at a point within walking distance of the shopping center parking area. This channel was dug by volunteers in order to make this paddle possible after the Wolf River rerouted itself and made the nearby public boat ramp obsolete. Such things happen with swamp rivers. Your paddle ends at the terminus of the dug channel at 6.1 miles.

Paddler prepares to guide the boat in swift section narrowed by cypress. ▶

SHELBY FARMS

In eastern Shelby County the Wolf River flows through what is known as Shelby Farms Park. The 4,500-acre plot is now in the heart of the greater Memphis metroplex. As a kid growing up in Memphis, I always knew Shelby Farms Park as the Penal Farm, though by the time I got old enough to comprehend what a penal farm was, the area had reverted more to a simple holding facility surrounded by extensive fields and wild land.

The penal farm—established in 1929—was a place where prisoners worked the land, growing their own food and selling the surplus to pay their way. The penal farm was a thriving operation and drew other prison operators to copy its methods. Over time the farm became less successful as the prisoners became more reluctant to work. The prison's farming operations were abandoned in 1964. Inmates continued to be incarcerated and are held on part of the property to this day.

Shelby County investigated numerous plans to shed the property. However, by this time citizens had begun using the waters and lands of the penal farm for outdoor recreation. The population of Memphis had begun to shift east as well, putting pressure on the land for development while simultaneously leading citizens to realize the value of the land as green space. Over the past several years the park model has come to fruition, despite political and business pressures to make it otherwise. Today, you can enjoy a 3.5-mile Wolf River paddle through Shelby Farms, from Germantown Parkway to Walnut Grove Road. Other developed recreation ranges from hiking, mountain biking, horseback riding, and bird watching to fishing and disc golf. Paved and unpaved trails course through the park. More than thirty bodies of water are open to anglers. Runners have designated 3-mile and 10K courses. Kayaks and paddleboats can be rented for paddling on Patriot Lake. No matter your activity, Shelby Farms has something for you. For more information visit www.shelbyparkfarms.org.

Middle Tennessee

7 Yellow Creek

This swiftwater gravel-bottomed creek makes for a fun spring paddle.

County: Houston, Montgomery
Start: Williamson Branch Road near Ellis Mills, N36° 17.786', W87° 33.264'
End: McFall Road near Lake Barkley, N36° 22.841', W87° 32.777'
Length: 9.9 miles
Float time: 4 hours
Difficulty rating: Moderate
Rapids: Class I-I+
River type: Big creek
Current: Moderate to swift
River gradient: 5.1 feet per mile
River gauge: Yellow Creek at Ellis Mills, minimum runnable level 120 cfs

Season: Winter, spring, early summer, and after heavy rains
Land status: Private
Fees or permits: No fees or permits required
Nearest city/town: Cumberland City
Maps: USGS: Ellis Mills, Needmore; *DeLorme: Tennessee Atlas and Gazetteer,* Page 51 B6
Boats used: Canoes, kayaks
Organizations: Cumberland River Compact, P.O. Box 41721, Nashville 37204, (615) 837-1151, www.cumberlandrivercompact.org
Contacts/outfitters: Tennessee Clean Water Network, 123A S. Gay St., Knoxville 37902, (865) 522-7007, www.tcwn.org

Put-in/Takeout Information

To takeout: From the intersection of TN 46 and TN 149 near Cumberland City, take TN 149 east for 2.6 miles to Old Highway 13. Turn right and drive north on Old Highway 13 and follow it 2.1 miles to McFall Road. Turn left on McFall Road and follow it 1.7 miles to the bridge over Yellow Creek. Parking and access are on the southwest side of the bridge, before the stream crossing.

To put-in from takeout: Backtrack on McFall Road to Old Highway 13. Turn left on Old Highway 13 and follow it south 3.5 miles to TN 13. Turn left on TN 13 north and follow it 1.4 miles to Ellis Mills Road. Turn right and head south on Ellis Mills Road. Stay with Ellis Mills Road as it jogs left at 3 miles. At 3.7 miles, Ellis Mills Road meets Williamson Branch Road at a T intersection. Park here. The stream access is just south of this intersection.

Paddle Summary

This fast water paddle winds its way through an agricultural valley, gathering in narrow channels and sometimes spreading wide as it slides over huge gravel bars for which it is known. The stream will also pass around islands aplenty. The shifting bed of the stream changes during high water. This change sure makes for an interesting float, and you must be on your toes to avoid tree strainers and extensive shallows. The scenery is pleasing to the eye, though you are never far from farm buildings and

Yellow Creek runs swift in spring.

other signs of civilization. Fast-moving shoals can be found where tributaries enter the stream, and tributaries are plentiful. Yellow Creek does make a couple of short classic drops where the river is constricted by rock. Bluffs occasionally ascend from the waters.

River Overview

Yellow Creek flows off the Tennessee Valley Divide near the Dickson County town of Dickson. Here, Yellow Creek flows north into the Cumberland River and the Piney River, also detailed in this guidebook in chapter 20 (page 116) and chapter 8 (page 55), flows south to the Duck River, which flows into the Tennessee River. Yellow Creek begins its northbound journey quickly gaining volume. Major tributaries of note are Salmon Branch and Leatherwood Creek. After flowing under the McFall Road Bridge and the end of this paddle, Yellow Creek slows its flow and becomes an embayment of Lake Barkley. Here, water enthusiasts can do some slack water paddling. A boat ramp is located on TN 149 just before Yellow Creek enters the main body of Lake Barkley and the Cumberland River. From the Houston/Dickson county line to Lake Barkley, paddlers can float some 15 miles of the stream. At high flows paddlers could pick up additional mileage in Dickson County. TN 46 roughly

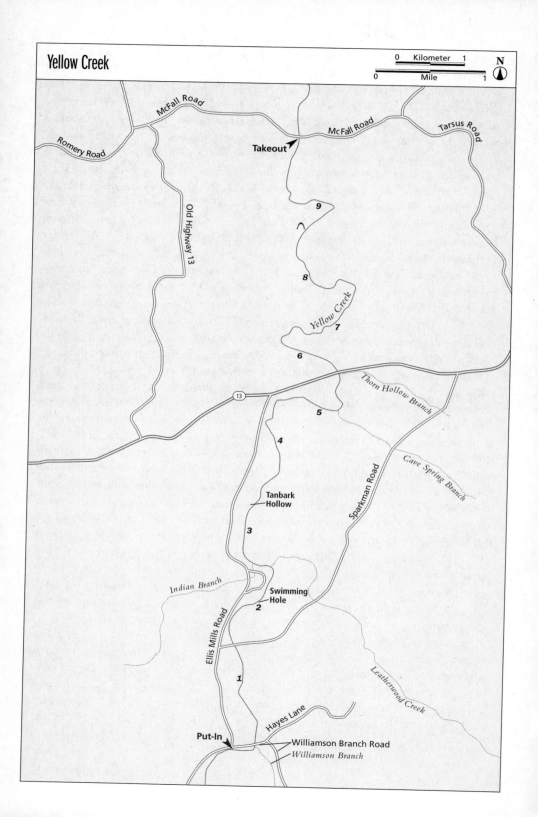

parallels Yellow Creek on this upper stretch, availing access and allowing paddlers to make on-site determinations as to paddleability.

The Paddling

The put-in can be challenging, as you must descend over a short but steep bank to the stream. Unfortunately, the Williamson Branch Road Bridge just to the east has been closed off to river access. Yellow Creek flows about 40 to 50 feet wide here as it travels easterly, meeting Williamson Branch, then curves north under the Williamson Branch Road Bridge. The stream immediately reveals its shallow swift character, traveling over a wide tan gravel bed for which it is known. However, deep pools will form in spots and against bluffs. Don't count on this stream being like it was the time you paddled it before, as it is a dynamic ever-changing ribbon of water.

This creek will braid where the bed widens. Timber will pile up in high flows, making you wonder what it would be like when the water is high enough to stack fallen trees above a man's head. Pass under a power line at 0.6 mile, near a white bluff pocked with cedar. At 1.0 mile, note where a landowner has placed riprap on the shore to prevent Yellow Creek from claiming more land. The stream primarily wanders through the agricultural valley, only occasionally banking against a hill or bluff. Float under the Sparkman Road Bridge at 1.4 miles.

Most of the rapids are Class I riffles or speedy long shoals as it keeps a generally north course. However, about 100 yards below the Sparkman Road Bridge, a single drop occurs where Yellow Creek is constricted by rock outcrops to a width of 30 feet. Other times the banks will be sheer soil walls or rock. At 2.0 miles, Yellow Creek banks against a low bluff. Here, locals jump off the bluff into a deep hole below. A gravel bar stands across the bluff, making this area a good stopping/swimming spot. At 2.4 miles, Leatherwood Creek flows in on river right. At 2.6 miles, smaller Indian Branch comes in on your left. By now you will have noticed the extensive beaver activity on this stream—limbs shredded of their bark and chewed-down trees.

At its widest Yellow Creek will extend 120 feet bank to bank, then narrow again. The waters are usually shallow where wide, and much gravel is exposed. At 3.3 miles, an unnamed branch flows out of Tanbark Hollow. Pass another transmission line at 3.8 miles. These power lines are distributing electricity created at the Tennessee Valley Authority (TVA) Cumberland Steam Plant in nearby Cumberland City. At 5.1 miles, the river once again constricts and forms a single drop rapid. Pass under the transmission line again shortly after this. Cave Spring Branch comes in on your right at 5.2 miles. Yellow Creek curves back north to pass under the TN 13 bridge at 5.7 miles. Thorn Hollow Branch comes on river right at the bridge as a small waterfall.

The stream has widened to around 80 feet by this point and continues curving in its bed and carving the valley, creating many a gravel bar and island, some covered with brush. At 6.7 miles, come along an alluring white bluff on river right. The agrarian valley reveals more fields, barns, and even a few houses. Come along another partly exposed white bluff at 8.2 miles. Watch for a cave in the bluff on river left at 8.5 miles. At 8.9 miles, a stream comes out of Bushwhacker Hollow on river right. Reach the McFall Road Bridge at 9.9 miles. Take out on river left before you reach the bridge. It is best to work around the riprap banked against this newer span.

FORT DONELSON BATTLEFIELD

Fort Donelson National Battlefield is located a few miles west of where Yellow Creek flows into Lake Barkley/Cumberland River. This battlefield was the site of an important Civil War encounter, and you can visit it today. Fort Donelson and nearby Fort Henry were built by the Rebels to hold sway over the Tennessee and Cumberland Rivers, thwarting the Union from using these waterways for troop or supply movements. Fort Henry was poorly located in a low area subject to flood by the Tennessee River and, in February 1862, was easily bombed into submission by Federal ironclad gunboats. The Rebels escaped east to Fort Donelson, securely located on a hill with a sweeping view of the Cumberland River. The soldiers of Fort Henry reached Fort Donelson already protected by earthworks, then built an outer perimeter of trenches beyond the fort. These earthworks were stretched along high ground from Hickman Creek in the west to the tiny town of Dover in the east. Federal gunboats couldn't do much against the well-placed Rebel artillery at Fort Donelson, but while the water war was going on, Federal troops amassed around the Rebel perimeter. The Union successfully attacked the Rebels. Most Confederates escaped southeasterly to Nashville, leaving too few to defend Fort Donelson, which was surrendered to General Ulysses S. Grant the next day.

On hiking trails and by road you can travel along the Confederate earthworks. Pass a tall monument to Confederate soldiers. Drop to the shores of Lake Barkley, where river batteries look over a stunning sweep of the Cumberland River. It is easy to see that well-placed Confederate cannons could control the Cumberland River at this point. What you see today is Lake Barkley, formed by the downstream damming of the Cumberland River. Visit replicas of the log huts that housed Confederate troops, and enjoy a woods walk on hiking trails. For more information, visit www.nps.gov/fodo.

8 Piney River

This fun run drops 8 feet per mile! Before you imagine big rapids, wrap your brain around a fast creeklike waterway sliding over frequent gravel shoals.

County: Hickman
Start: Big Spring Creek, N35° 55.909', W87° 28.024'
End: Pinewood Canoe & Camp, N35° 53.416', W87° 28.965'
Length: 4.8 miles
Float time: 2.5 hours
Difficulty rating: Moderate
Rapids: Class I
River type: Winding creeklike waterway
Current: Moderate to swift
River gradient: 8.0 feet per mile
River gauge: USGS Piney River at Vernon, TN, minimum runnable level 75 cfs
Season: Year-round

Land status: Private
Fees or permits: Put-in/takeout fee unless using outfitter shuttle
Nearest city/town: Centerville
Maps: USGS: Texas Hollow; *DeLorme: Tennessee Atlas & Gazetteer,* Page 35 B6
Boats used: Canoes, kayaks
Organizations: Duck River Watershed Association, P. O. Box 141, Duck River 38454, www.duckriverwatershed.org
Contacts/outfitters: Pinewood Canoe & Camp, 2011 Cash Hollow Rd., Nunnelly 37137, (931) 670-4230, www.pinewoodcanoecamp.com

Put-in/Takeout Information

To takeout: From the town square in Centerville, take TN 100/TN 48 north. At 5.1 miles, stay left with TN 48 as TN 100 continues forward. Cross the Piney River at 11.2 miles. At 12.3 miles, reach Cash Hollow Road and turn left. (From exit 148 on I-40 take TN 48 south for 6.8 miles to Cash Hollow Road. Turn right on Cash Hollow Road and continue directions.) You may see a sign for Pinewood Canoe and Camp. Coming from Centerville, make an acute left on Cash Hollow Road. At 1 mile on the left, reach Pinewood Canoe and Camp and takeout.

To put-in from takeout: To reach the put-in, backtrack on Cash Hollow Road to TN 48. Turn left and follow TN 48 for 1.8 miles and turn right on Piney River Road. Bridge the Piney River at 0.4 mile. Climb the hill and reach a road split. The put-in is to the right, on private property owned by Pinewood Canoe and Camp.

Paddle Summary

Hold on and enjoy this shallow, swift stream. Single steep drops are rare in these parts. The swift current carves ever-changing channels over ample gravel bars partially covered in sycamores. It will also carve out new stream bank, leaving the Piney subject to strainers, where the current will run you into fallen trees. Don't fear the Piney—it's one of my five favorite rivers in the state. Just think of it this way: If you want to hone

Fallen boulders crowd a slow section of the Piney River.

your paddling skills, come to the Piney River—it's like an obstacle course. Though the rapids are only Class I–I+ at normal water levels, expect to duck your head, slide by fallen trees, and make a few sharp turns among fleet waters.

The ride on the turquoise-tinted water is mostly over shallows, where aquatic life is abundant. Expect clarity even in the occasional deep pools. Gravel bars often spread many times the width of the river. Pass bluffs rounded over by erosion over time, including "The Faces," an area of carved promontories where you may see human mugs in the rock above you. The only bummer of the trip is that it is a little short at just under 5 miles, but accesses on the Piney are limited and mostly private, therefore an outfitter is your best bet.

River Overview

The Piney may be the smallest river in Tennessee or its largest creek. A river by name, this major tributary of the Duck River is born in Dickson County, just south of the town of Dickson. The West Fork Piney and East Fork Piney merge just north of I-40. It is below this confluence where the Piney enters Hickman County and becomes paddleable and then only in winter and spring. Numerous spring branches and clear creeks continue to feed the river, with Big Spring Creek becoming the final piece of the watery puzzle to make the Piney paddleable year-round 8 miles below I-40.

The river continues winding southbound through agricultural country until it meets the Duck in the western reaches of Hickman County. Including the upper sections the Piney does offer 35 miles of paddling. Trips can be extended by floating on to the Duck River and using access points on the Duck.

The Paddling

Your run actually starts on shallow and clear Big Spring Creek. In about 500 feet Big Spring Creek meets the Piney River, flowing shallow with an interesting blue-translucent color. Willow trees, ironwood, and sycamores grow along the river. The Piney spreads 30 to 40 feet over an easily visible gravel bottom. The banks—where bluffs aren't present—range from 4 to 15 feet high. When you come upon shoals, which will be immediate, the river divides around gravelly islands topped with syca-more and narrows to canoe-width—10 or 15 feet. Occasional houses border the river. Sometimes fields encroach the Piney. Mud banks rise vertically from the water near fields. In between the shoals—primarily fast-moving gravel riffles—will be wider pools. Sometimes, the channel leaving the wide pool will be so narrow as to not be visible until you are up close. However, there's always a channel. River grasses line slender sections of the Piney. Trees will overhang the waterway, which helps with shade. However, since the river is small, it also results in overhead obstructions.

At 0.6 mile, Beaver Creek comes in on your right. You may not see it if you go down a channel on the east side of the river. At 1.3 miles, the Piney River cuts through open fields bordered by sheer mud banks with huge gravel bars. The water resembles an aquarium. Its clarity allows for viewing of all that's under there: sub-merged logs, rocks, minnows, fish of all types, crawdads, and other living and nonliving subsurface items.

At 1.7 miles, Little Spring Creek comes in on the left. Immediately shoot a rapid, then pass under the Pinewood Road Bridge. Little Spring Creek is another example of the many crystalline streams that lace this part of Hickman County. At 1.9 miles, pass the water intake for Centerville. At 2.1 miles on river right, look for a large outcrop about 30 feet up. An overhanging rock forms a cave/shelter. The river turns left and begins sharp bends. Stacked rock bluffs—eroded roundish over time—begin emerging among trees that grow on the rising shoreline. Huge boulders, many par-tially submerged, crowd the river. At 2.6 miles, overhanging bluffs become common. Many are undercut. Some are as high as 50 feet and extend 20 feet over the Piney. At 3.4 miles, reach a series of overhanging bluffs known as "The Faces." Depending on where you are in the river, imaginative paddlers can see shapes of faces in the eroded rock.

At 3.5 miles, within sight of "The Faces," pass under a power line. Keys Branch comes in on the left just before the TN 48 bridge at 3.9 miles. More interesting bluffs rise on river left just beyond the bridge. The rock soon gives way and the Piney

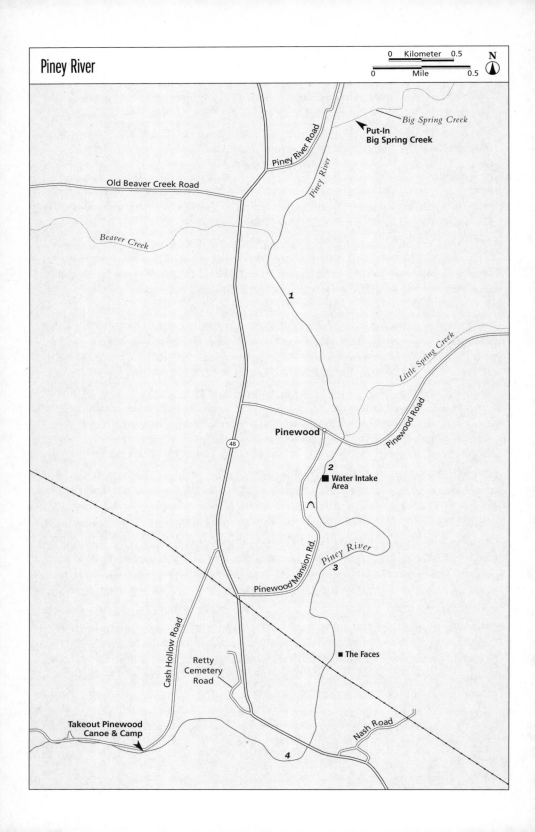

Piney River

0   Kilometer   0.5

0   Mile   0.5

N

Big Spring Creek

Put-In
Big Spring Creek

Piney River Road

Piney River

Old Beaver Creek Road

Beaver Creek

1

Little Spring Creek

Pinewood Road

Pinewood

48

2

■ Water Intake
Area

Piney River

3

Pinewood Mansion Rd.

Cash Hollow Road

Pinewood Mansion Rd.

Retty
Cemetery
Road

■ The Faces

Takeout Pinewood
Canoe & Camp

Nash Road

4

speeds downward, dividing islands with channels. At 4.6 miles, Mill Creek, a major feeder stream, comes in on the left. You are almost to the end. Take out at 4.8 miles at the large gravel bar on the right at Pinewood Canoe and Camp.

GORDON HOUSE AND FERRY SITE

The Natchez Trace Parkway runs on the eastern edge of Hickman County, not far from the Piney River's confluence with the Duck River. The Natchez Trace crosses the Duck here. It is at this crossing you can explore the interesting Gordon House and Ferry site.

In the early 1800s, the United States realized the economic importance of the path and improved it to encourage trade. Along the way, many inns, or "stands" as they were known, were established to feed and house travelers. Around 1803 John Gordon obtained 600 acres along the Duck River in a land grant and began operating a ferry across the Duck astride the Trace. In 1817, Gordon built himself and his wife a brick home, one of the few original buildings associated with the Old Trace. A hiking trail explores the home and the river area. On the way to the Duck, the trail bridges Fattybread Branch. The name origin of this translucent and attractive watercourse has been lost to time. Pick up the Old Trace on the far side of Fattybread Branch. Think of all the travelers who, either coming or going, had the crossing of the Duck River on their mind at this point. Follow the Old Trace as it leads toward the Duck River. Reach a final level spot, which was the staging area for the ferry. Many a traveler, horseman, and farmer waited here. The dirt path continues down to the banks of the Duck. Decades of off-and-on flooding have obliterated signs of the ferry operation here. The ferry operated from the early 1800s to 1896, when a bridge was built over the Duck. Today, the Duck is easily crossed on the Natchez Trace Parkway and numerous other bridges. Life sure has changed over the past 200 years. The Gordon House is located at mile 407.7 on the Natchez Trace Parkway. For more information, visit www.nps.gov/natr.

⑨ Big Swan Creek

This Duck River tributary is a first-rate swift creek paddle in a bucolic valley.

County: Hickman
Start: Sunrise Road, N35° 40.933', W87° 25.750'
End: Raleigh Chapel Road, N35° 43.844', W87° 24.900'
Length: 5.3 miles
Float time: 2.5 hours
Difficulty rating: Moderate
Rapids: Class I+
River type: Shallow braided gravel stream
Current: Moderate to fast
River gradient: 4.9 feet per mile
River gauge: Piney River at Vernon, minimum runnable level 150 cfs

Season: Winter, spring, early summer, and after heavy rains
Land status: Private
Fees or permits: No fees or permits required
Nearest city/town: Centerville
Maps: USGS: Sunrise; *DeLorme: Tennessee Atlas and Gazetteer,* Page 35 C7
Boats used: Canoes, kayaks
Organizations: Duck River Watershed Association, P. O. Box 141, Duck River 38454, www.duckriverwatershed.org
Contacts/outfitters: Tennessee Clean Water Network, 123A S. Gay St., Knoxville 37902, (865) 522-7007, www.tcwn.org

Put-in/Takeout Information

To takeout: From the intersection of TN 48/100 and TN 50 just south of Centerville, take US 50 east for 1.5 miles to Swan Creek Road (this turn is on a hill, so be watchful). Turn right on Swan Creek Road and follow it for 1.5 miles to intersect Raleigh Chapel Road. Turn left on Raleigh Chapel Road and follow it for 1.3 miles to reach the bridge over Big Swan Creek. Park on the northeast side of the bridge.

To put–in from takeout: Backtrack to Swan Creek Road, and turn left, southbound, and drive for 4.7 miles to Sunrise Road. Turn left on Sunrise Road and follow it 0.6 mile to the bridge over Big Swan Creek. The parking and put-in are on the northwest side of the bridge.

Paddle Summary

This is a classic swift stream paddle. Flowing boldly in spring, Big Swan Creek cuts an ever-changing path north to make the Duck River. As the water levels rise, the river rushes around curves and often braids to form islands and leave old channels behind. The wide valley that Big Swan Creek creates contains some of Tennessee's finest agrarian scenery, with quaint barns bordering fields guarded by wooded hills.

The creek is narrow and fast, necessitating good judgment when the water is high enough to be paddled. Fallen trees will form strainers, and Big Swan Creek changes year to year with the floods. By the way, the most helpful gauge is the Piney River at Vernon,

Bluff view of Big Swan Creek.

another tributary of the Duck River, which is just north of Big Swan Creek and therefore is an inexact indicator. In normal years Big Swan runs too low by July. Gravel bars are numerous, allowing for ample stopping places. Rapids consist of fast shoals, and the difficulties are limited to strainers and midstream logjams. Don't be afraid to jump out and walk your boat around difficult areas. Also, if you want to extend your trip, put in upstream of the Sunrise Bridge at the Horse Branch Road Bridge.

River Overview

Big Swan Creek begins in Lewis County, named for the famous American explorer Meriwether Lewis. It flows northwesterly at first, cutting sharp bluffs through hills to meet Little Swan Creek a few miles east of Hohenwald. Now a fairly large and swift gravel-bottomed stream, Big Swan Creek enters Hickman County and is considered paddleable in higher water at this point. It then begins a tortured northerly course where it acquires numerous small tributaries while creating a gorgeous valley. The river continues carving deeper into hills before dumping its contents into the Duck River a few miles upstream of Centerville. Including the uppermost section at the confluence with Little Swan Creek, Big Swan Creek offers about 20 miles of

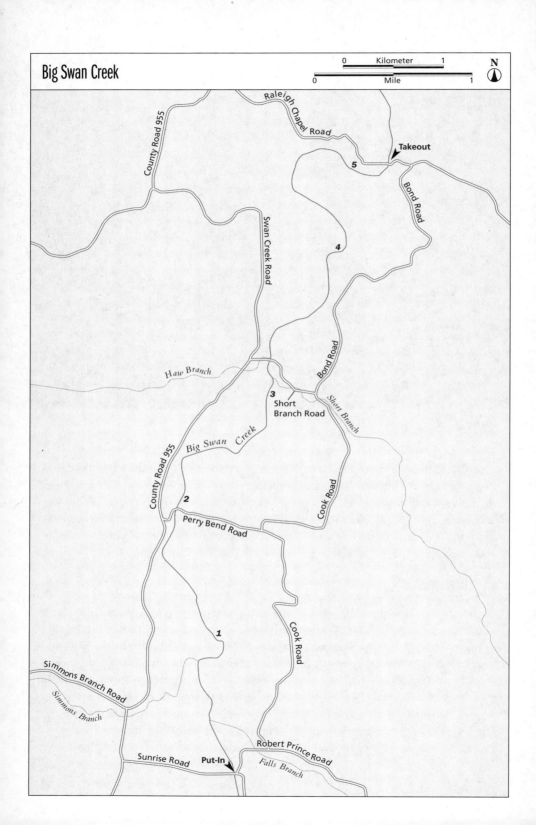

Big Swan Creek

0   Kilometer   1

0   Mile   1

N

Raleigh Chapel Road

County Road 955

Swan Creek Road

Takeout

Bond Road

5

4

Bond Road

Haw Branch

3

Short Branch Road

Short Branch

Big Swan Creek

County Road 955

Cook Road

2

Perry Bend Road

1

Cook Road

Simmons Branch Road

Simmons Branch

Sunrise Road

Put-In

Robert Prince Road

Falls Branch

paddling, though most floating is done from the Horse Branch Road Bridge to the Duck.

The Paddling

Put in across from a gray bluff to which the Sunrise Bridge is attached. Still blue-green waters and clear shallows speed over the ever-shifting gravel bottom. Big Swan Creek averages 30 to 40 feet wide. Where the banks are stable and bluffs are absent, river birch and sycamore overhang the waterway. The center of the stream is usually open to the sun overhead.

Falls Branch comes in on river right at 0.4 mile. The color and clarity of the tributaries is even more alluring than Big Swan. Falls Branch drains the ridge upon which the Natchez Trace travels and also Devils Backbone State Natural Area (see sidebar for more). Smart paddlers will be looking downstream in order to follow the most prudent course, as the swift water will take your boat into partially submerged logs or wide shallows. In other places, the stream will cut into vertical soil walls, rerouting itself. This bank cutting sometimes leads to more deadfall in the waterway. To complicate matters, beavers are active in the watershed and fell trees on their own. Finally, since cattle are run in the valley, watch for barbed-wire fences crossing the creek, though this practice is diminishing.

Simmons Branch comes in on river left at 0.7 mile. Big Swan Creek runs generally shallow but does have occasional deep holes. A screen of trees flanks the waterway as it courses amid fields. Gravel bars flank the stream, usually on bends or where tributaries enter Big Swan Creek, are quite large relative to the size of the waterway. Pass one such bar at 1.0 mile, where the river makes an extended bend. Depending upon the water level, the creek breaks up into braids, making you choose the proper route. When in doubt go with the strongest flow.

At 1.6 miles, the waterway banks up against Swan Creek Road and continues its northerly journey. Pass by a white church on river left just before floating under the Perry Bend Road Bridge at 1.9 miles. At 2.2 miles, the river is slow and deep as it abuts a bluff on river left, near Swan Bluff Spring. Watch for a cave in this bluff. Big Swan Creek continues to divide around gravel bars and small islands. Wooded bottoms will be heavy with wildflowers in spring. Pass under the Short Branch Road Bridge at 3.1 miles. There is a nice landing at the confluence of Big Swan Creek and Short Branch. The gravel spot is popular with locals for fishing and swimming. Haw Branch flows into the creek just downstream on river left.

At 4.2 miles, saddle alongside a wooded bluff on river right. At 4.7 miles, a stone citadel rises on river left a bit back from the banks. This is the lower end of Grimmett Hill, over which Raleigh Chapel Road travels. Grimmett Hill forces an easterly turn as Big Swan Creek widens then splits around an island before coming back together at the Raleigh Chapel Road Bridge, which you meet at 5.3 miles. Be very careful at this low water bridge that doesn't avail room to paddle under. Scout it out while placing the take-out vehicle here. At this point you may wish you had started higher up the valley. If you want to lengthen the paddle, continue 1.8 miles up Swan Creek Road beyond Sunrise Road to put in at Horse Branch Road Bridge, which offers easy access to boot. This will extend your float by a little over 2 miles.

THE DEVILS BACKBONE

Devils Backbone State Natural Area is located in the upper Big Swan Creek watershed, just a few miles from this paddle. A 2.7-mile hiking trail loops the 950-acre woodland. The name Devils Backbone conjures up an array of images in your mind—a hellish maze of rocks or maybe a menacing ridge of stone. This name was actually inspired by the adjacent Natchez Trace, which bridges Big Swan Creek. In the early 1800s, during the heyday of traveling the Trace from Natchez, Mississippi, to Nashville, an arduous trip was virtually assured. Flooded streams, robbers, bad weather, hostile Indians, and the rigors of day-after-day, self-propelled travel made the journey challenging. The perils that befell Natchez Trace travelers were said to be the work of the devil, and the "Devils Backbone" sprang up as a nickname for the Trace.

The Devils Backbone Trail descends into Spring Hollow, reaching Fall Branch, a Big Swan tributary by which you paddle. The path is one of exploration, not expediency. Climb out of Spring Hollow by switchbacks, returning to the oak-dominated ridgeline. The seemingly endless forest and distant hills radiate a wildness that belies the size of the state natural area.

To combine a hike here with your paddle, take Swan Creek Road south beyond Sunrise Road to reach US 412. Head east on 412 to intersect the Natchez Trace. Drive north a few miles on the Trace to milepost 394, on your left. Also, visit Fall Hollow Waterfall at milepost 391.9. A short paved trail leads to the top of this cascade. Swan View Overlook is at milepost 392.5.

As you travel the Devils Backbone remember these words beside a section of the Trace in Mississippi: "This is the Natchez Trace. For many years it served man well, but as with many things when its usefulness past, it was abandoned. Over the years, this timeworn path has been a silent witness to honor and dishonor. It bears the prints of countless men. Walk down the shaded trail—leave your prints in the dust, not for others to see but the road to remember."

10 Buffalo River

The Buffalo River is perhaps the most celebrated canoeing river in the Volunteer State.

County: Wayne, Perry
Start: Bell Bridge, N35° 27.465', W87° 46.564'
End: Slink Shoals, N35° 27.929', W87° 50.827'
Length: 10.7 miles
Float time: 4.5 hours
Difficulty rating: Moderate
Rapids: Class I–I+
River type: Prototype canoer's river
Current: Moderate
River gradient: 4.4 feet per mile
River gauge: USGS Buffalo River near Flat Woods, TN, minimum runnable level 160 cfs

Season: Year-round
Land status: Private
Fees or permits: Launch fee at Bell Bridge put-in
Nearest city/town: Waynesboro
Maps: USGS: Leatherwood; *DeLorme: Tennessee Atlas & Gazetteer,* Page 19 A5, 18 A4
Boats used: Canoes, kayaks, johnboats
Organizations: Tennessee Clean Water Network, 123A S. Gay St., Knoxville 37902, (865) 522-7007, www.tcwn.com
Contacts/Outfitters: Crazy Horse Canoe, 2505 Waynesboro Hwy., Waynesboro 38485, (800) 722-5213, www.crazyhorsecanoe.com

Put-in/Takeout Information

To takeout: From exit 143 on I-40, take TN 13 for 33 miles to Flatwoods (you will see canoe liveries here). Turn right on Horseshoe Bend Road and follow it for 0.9 mile to Slink Shoals Road. Turn right on Slink Shoals Road. Follow it past a few cabins before dropping off onto the riverside gravel bar at 0.7 mile.

To put-in from takeout: To reach the put-in, backtrack to Flatwoods and TN 13, then continue on TN 13 south for 4 miles to intersect TN 48. Continue south on TN 13 for 1.6 miles farther to bridge the Buffalo River and reach Crazy Horse Canoe.

Paddle Summary

This particular run reflects the popularity of this waterway. Numerous outfitters operate this general area, therefore summer weekends can get busy, but they provide shuttles, too. Having said that, there are many more days where the river is quiet and a great paddling destination. On this trip, paddlers will be in store for a special treat of a riverside waterfall and also a bluff that swimmers use as a jumping/diving platform. After leaving the busy Bell Bridge area, the river settles down and you travel over gravel shoals where the river speeds and also beneath high bluffs for which the river is known. The river will often divide into separate channels as it comes to a rapid. At the tail end of rapids, shallow gravel areas drop off into deep holes. Be wary of strainers on this river, as the current will take your boat directly into fallen trees. Otherwise, the

The Buffalo is a free-flowing river throughout its distance.

shoals are Class I. Occasional islands are scattered on the river and are more notable at high water. Often one of the channels around these islands will dry up at normal flows, and you won't even recognize these islands as islands. Clear creeks continuously feed the Buffalo, adding to its transparency. Ample gravel bars allow for stops.

River Overview

The Buffalo River is free flowing in its entirety, a rare thing these days for a river that offers in excess of 100 miles of paddling pleasure with the capacity for multi-day trips. I have floated the entire Buffalo, and it lives up to its billing as a fantastic paddling destination. This waterway starts in the northeastern tip of Lawrence County. Tributaries gather and the Buffalo becomes paddleable by the TN 240 bridge near Henryville. Logs can extend across the waterway here, forcing a pull-over. The river's beauty is evident with bluffs and gravel bars already present. It then enters Lewis County and passes under the Natchez Trace at historic Metal Ford. The Little Buffalo River joins the main Buffalo, which then enters Wayne County and continues curving westerly as a first-rate paddler's mecca. It is in this area that the river is its most busy. However, by the time it begins its big north turn into Perry County, the river is much less used.

It passes directly by the town of Linden and winds still north. Riverside bottoms increase in size as it passes under I-40 to meet the Duck River just before the Duck joins the Tennessee River.

The Paddling

Leave Bell Bridge at a large gravel bar. The area can be busy with outfitters loading and unloading their canoes and customers. The alluring clear-green waters flowing over a gravel bottom harbor many fish. This waterway is considered to be one of the state's finest river fisheries. At this point, the Buffalo is around 80 to 100 feet wide but will narrow to as little as 30 to 40 feet at shoals. Conversely the waters can spread wide, in excess of 160 feet, and become extremely shallow. The shoreline is generally wooded except where the numerous gravel bars occur around rapids or where bluffs rise. Ironwood is plentiful along the shore. Sycamore, river birch, and box elder—the usual suspects—also line the shore. Willows rise from the shallows in bushlike fashion.

A few shoals initiate the paddler. By 0.7 mile, the river slows a bit. Start making Choate Bend about 1.2 miles. Here, the Buffalo hastens and begins to demonstrate its propensity to flow strongly through strainers, fallen trees which will dunk the unsuspecting canoeist. Alluring gravel bars form in the bend. As you continue the bend, at 1.5 miles, keep an ear peeled for a waterfall entering the river on the right. It's a multitiered 50-foot fall flanked with greenery as it trips over a sheer bluffline. A trail leads up along the fall.

Beyond Choate Bend, the Buffalo begins to widen. At 2.5 miles, the river makes another big bend as Choate Branch comes in on the left. Despite the additional water the Buffalo narrows as it curves back to the north. If bluffs are not present, the banks can range anywhere from 6 to 20 feet high and are usually vegetated. On bends without trees, the river cuts sheer dirt bluffs.

At 3.5 miles, on the left, you'll see a private horse camp. At 3.8 miles, the river curves left, revealing the first large exposed rock bluff that is undercut at water level. A partially wooded gravel sandbar across from the bluff draws paddlers to a stop—including litterbugs. Many of them also stop to see paddlers jump off the bluff here. On the upstream end of the bluff, you will see a dirt trail leading up to a small cave and the jump-off point.

At 4.7 miles, Bridge Branch comes in on the left and the Buffalo begins curving around Bastin Bend. Note the undercut nature of the low bluffs on this bend. At low water the current will take you directly into these undercut bluffs, so be on the look-out. You may see turtles galore in the Buffalo—at least until they dive off fallen trees into the water as you paddle near them. At 6 miles, begin the long curve of Stone Bend. Pine Bluff rises on the outside of this curve with an attractive gravel bar on the inside. Watch and listen for a dripping waterfall falling off the bluff.

A transmission line crosses the river at 8.4 miles, near the old Bunch Ford. Another bluff rises on river right just beyond the transmission lines. At 8.9 miles, the river begins curving around Horseshoe Bend. A white bluff, partially obscured by beech

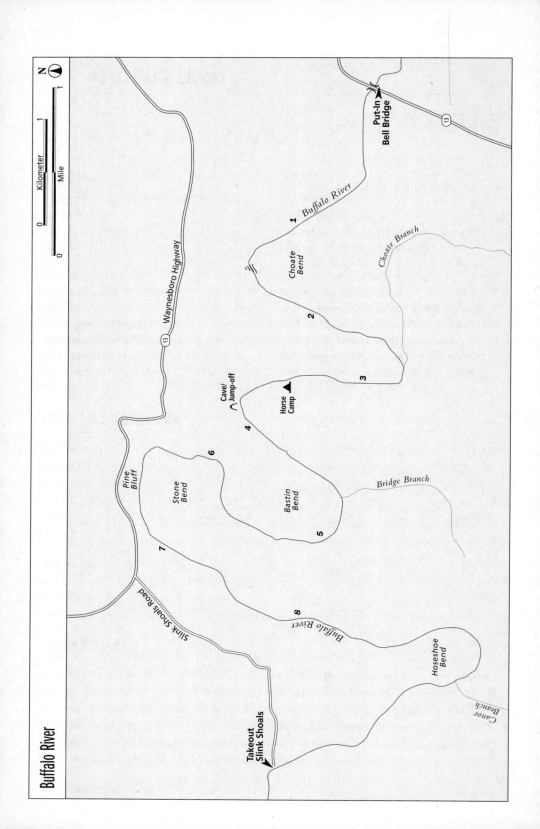

Buffalo River

trees among others, forces this turn. The north-facing bluff creates a cooler, moister environment conducive for beech trees. At 9.6 miles, the bluff gives way as aptly named Canoe Branch comes in on river left. Low wooded shores border the river as it works around high water islands. Keep your eye peeled for the painted rock on river right and a gravel landing. This large gravel bar is commonly used as a takeout and may have cars and canoes within sight. This is Slink Shoals.

MERIWETHER LEWIS MONUMENT

On my way to the Buffalo River, I often cruise the Natchez Trace Parkway, stopping and camping at Meriwether Lewis Monument. There I can see a historic site but also hike trails, fish, and enjoy an added bonus—free camping! Meriwether Lewis Campground lies on a ridgetop in oak-hickory woods. The campsites are well maintained, well spaced, and offer decent privacy. Campers can get a site almost any time of year.

The original Natchez Trace came to be in the early 1800s when boatmen, returning from delivering crops and other goods down the Cumberland, Ohio, and Mississippi Rivers, began returning to their homes via a buffalo and Indian path running from Natchez, Mississippi, to Nashville, Tennessee. The federal government then commissioned roadwork, improving the path. The Natchez Trace became one of our first western roads. Portions of this old road are actually preserved to this day and can be walked on here at Meriwether Lewis.

Here, near the campground, is the actual monument to Lewis, the leader of the famous Corps of Discovery expedition, as in Lewis and Clark, that went up the Missouri River and overland to the Pacific in the early 1800s. After the expedition, Lewis died here under circumstances that remain one of the great mysteries in American history. He is buried at the monument.

Several miles of trails run along the ridges and hollows of the immediate area. You can follow part of the original Trace, preserved for over 200 years. Check out the picnic area at Little Swan Creek, also near the campground, an attractive stream with little bluffs running alongside its clear waters. Meriwether Lewis Monument is located at mile 385.9 on the Natchez Trace Parkway. For more information, visit www.nps.gov/natr.

11 Shoal Creek

This paddle is a fun run down a swift and clear stream that flows off the Highland Rim.

County: Lawrence	**Season:** Year-round
Start: Old Bromley Ford on Factory Creek, N35° 6.091', W87° 32.227'	**Land status:** Private
End: Iron City Park, N35° 1.386', W87° 34.744'	**Fees or permits:** No fees or permits required
Length: 8.2 miles	**Nearest city/town:** Iron City
Float time: 4.5 hours	**Maps:** USGS: Saint Joseph; *DeLorme: Tennessee Atlas & Gazetteer,* Page 19 D6
Difficulty rating: Moderate	**Boats used:** Canoes, a few kayaks and johnboats
Rapids: Class I–I+	**Organizations:** Tennessee Clean Water Network, 123A S. Gay St., Knoxville 37902, (865) 522-7007, www.tcwn.com
River type: Shallow gravel-bottomed creek	
Current: Moderate to swift	**Contacts/outfitters:** Shoal Creek Canoe Run, 470 Iron City Rd., Iron City 38463, (888) CANOE-80, www.shoalcreekcanoerun.com
River gradient: 5.3 feet per mile	
River gauge: USGS Shoal Creek at Iron City, TN, minimum runnable level 100 cfs	

Put-in/Takeout Information

To takeout: From the intersection of TN 227 and TN 242 in Iron City, take TN 227 east just a short distance and turn right into Iron City Park, which is on the west side of the TN 227 bridge over Shoal Creek.

To put-in from takeout: Return to the intersection of TN 227 and TN 242, then turn right, north, on TN 242, and travel for 3.4 miles. Turn right at Railroad Bed Road. Go just a short distance, then stay left on Railroad Road. Take Railroad Road northeasterly for 3.8 miles to turn right on Hardin Loop Road. Immediately bridge Factory Creek and reach the put-in.

Paddle Summary

Start your trip on Factory Creek, a scenic tributary, before it merges with Shoal Creek. The run is shallow more often than not, with infrequent deeper holes. You will enjoy seeing ample aquatic life easily visible in the stream. Gravel bars of all sizes are located along the river and make for good picnic or relaxation spots. Occasional bluffs crowd the clear stream and add to the scenery. Be prepared to negotiate narrow speedy sections with occasional small drops. The stream difficulty is easily managed, however. It is often so shallow that if any problems arise downstream, all you have to do is step out of your boat, stop, and assess the situation. Clear tributaries feed and widen the creek throughout its journey.

Shoal Creek occasionally stretches wide and shallow.

River Overview

Shoal Creek begins just east of Lawrenceburg. Springs and tributaries slowly add to the flow, namely Little Shoal Creek, which flows through David Crockett State Park (see sidebar). From Lawrenceburg, Shoal Creek winds southwesterly absorbing springs and more tributaries, Long Branch among others. Here, Shoal Creek becomes paddleable most of the year. The addition of Factory Creek, where this paddle begins, marks the year-round paddling beginning of Shoal Creek. It continues working south amid a pastoral valley to pass Iron City before leaving the Volunteer State and entering Alabama. Once in the Heart of Dixie, the stream flows free for another 8 miles before being stilled by Wilson Lake a little below Goose Shoals, adding up to around 28 miles of creek paddling. The next 10 miles of the stream are a long embayment before Shoal Creek meets the Tennessee River, which at this point is backed up at Wilson Lake.

The Paddling

The trip actually starts on Factory Creek, a crystal-clear, 30-foot-wide feeder branch of Shoal Creek that runs over a rock bed. Immediately pass under the Hardin Loop

Bridge. The channel may narrow to 15 to 20 feet where it runs rapid. Tan, rocky gravel bars and river grasses flank the moving water areas. The flat bottom looks almost as if it were a single rock slab in places. Sycamore, water maple, and river birch overhang much of the quick stream. Ironwood crowds low moist shores. Small ledges noisily tumble over a rock.

Occasional houses on stilts are situated on Factory Creek. At 0.9 mile, pass under a power line. Shoal Creek is not far ahead. Continue speeding over gravel areas along with the flat rock slabs. A sizable gravel bar from which grows sycamore and willow forms just before Factory Creek's confluence with Shoal Creek. Interestingly, the exact meeting point is subject to change, as rising and falling water levels alter the banks and gravel bars here. On some shores, you'll see this in evidence with exposed earth from cut stream channels.

Reach the confluence at 1.4 miles. Here, Shoal Creek and Factory Creek are nearly equal size. Shoal Creek immediately widens to 40 or more feet. Just downstream of this confluence, another unnamed creek comes in noisily as it spills over a ledge. Alert paddlers will notice numerous small clear creeks spilling into Shoal Creek. Ahead, the stream widens to in excess of 100 feet but will be just inches deep in places. In these clear shallows, you'll see many rough fish in the waters, such as darters and suckers, finning away from you. A pattern of pools and fast riffles/foot-high drops develops. Railroad Road borders on the right as you paddle toward Iron City. Gravel banks are prevalent along one side or another, with the opposite bank rising 20 feet or more.

Pass under another transmission line at 2.6 miles. At 3 miles, the river curves sharply to the right and turns westerly with a tall bluff to its left along with a wide gravel bar. The bluff gives way to lowlands. Gravel bars are sometimes covered with grasses, willows, even sycamores. At 3.9 miles, the river turns to the south with another bluff rising to the right. Despite the shallows, deep holes occur often enough to make for good swimming spots. Rock striations are often visible in the creek bed. The pool/riffle pattern continues. At 5 miles, Brewer Branch comes on the right. Shoal Creek widens and begins running alongside TN 242. The stream remains shallow. At 5.7 miles, a low rock bluff exposes itself on the right-hand bank. But this is nothing compared to Mackey Bluff, reached at 5.9 miles. The wooded rampart rises over 200 feet above Shoal Creek. An equally superlative gravel bar spreads across from this bluff.

Beyond Mackey Bluff, the stream widens considerably to 120 feet or more. Fields come down to the water's edge in this lower area. Shoal Creek remains wide with numerous changing gravel bars with multiple channels. A bluff rises on river right before giving way to Holly Creek, which comes in at 7.7 miles. Pass under the TN 227 bridge. Make sure and paddle to the right-hand side of the stream, as the takeout is on river right, at Iron City Park.

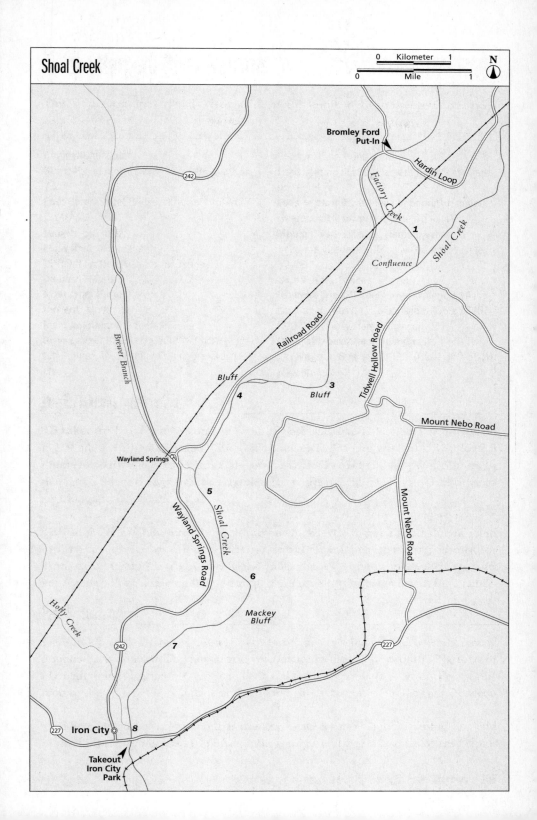

Shoal Creek

0 Kilometer 1

0 Mile 1

N

Bromley Ford
Put-In

Hardin Loop

Factory Creek

1

Confluence

Shoal Creek

2

Railroad Road

Tidwell Hollow Road

Bluff

3

4

Bluff

Mount Nebo Road

Wayland Springs

Brewer Branch

5

Shoal Creek

Mount Nebo Road

Wayland Springs Road

6

Mackey
Bluff

Holly Creek

242

7

227

Iron City

227

8

Takeout
Iron City
Park

DAVID (NOT DAVY) LIVED HERE, TOO

It seems that few of David Crockett's real life adventures and accomplishments overshadow the myths imparted by the Disney television shows of the 1950s about our Tennessee hero. The main myth is that he went by "Davy" Crockett. His name was David and he went by David, and Mr. Crockett may well have been put off being called Davy. That was just one of the many things I learned while visiting the museum at David Crockett State Park, located on Little Shoal Creek, that also offers outdoor recreation and some pretty decent camping.

Little Shoal Creek is the centerpiece of the park. It is along this creek that Crockett had a gristmill, a powder mill, and a distillery. This spot has seen many changes through the years. A flood in 1821 washed away Crockett's creekside "empire," then he left for West Tennessee. Nowadays, Shoal Creek flows through the park and borders the main camping area.

I like the wide variety of activities in which to engage both inside and outside the park. Developed park facilities include an Olympic-size swimming pool and park restaurant, which overlooks forty-acre Lake Lindsey. This impoundment offers anglers a chance to catch bass, bream, or catfish. If you don't want to fish from shore, rent a park paddleboat or johnboat. Private boats and motors are not allowed, making for a quiet and rustic experience. I particularly enjoyed the park museum, which, of course, features David Crockett and times gone by in this slice of the Volunteer State.

Traditional outdoor pursuits include hiking on the park trails. My favorite is the one traveling along Little Shoal Creek. Speaking of Little Shoal Creek, you can fish it, too. Trout are stocked here in the spring. Many people like to head into Lawrenceburg, which is only 2 miles away, or eat in the park restaurant. History buffs will check out the James D. Vaughan and David Crockett museums in Lawrenceburg. Crockett is worth two museums of history and maybe more. This experience will round out your Shoal Creek/Crockett Country adventure. Just remember, it's David Crockett, not Davy.

12 Richland Creek

This underutilized stream flows through the agricultural heart of Giles County.

County: Giles
Start: Clear Creek Road off US 31, N35° 18.776', W87° 1.740'
End: Annie Wade Road near TN 166, N35° 15.104', W87° 5.078'
Length: 9.9 miles
Float time: 4.5 hours
Difficulty rating: Easy
Rapids: Class I
River type: Valley river through agricultural lands
Current: Moderate
River gradient: 2.7 feet per mile

River gauge: Richland Creek at US 64 near Pulaski, minimum runnable level 120 cfs
Season: Winter, spring, early summer, and after heavy rains
Land status: Private
Fees or permits: No fees or permits required
Nearest city/town: Pulaski
Maps: USGS: Walterhill; *DeLorme: Tennessee Atlas and Gazetteer,* Page 20 B3
Boats used: Canoes, a few kayaks, johnboats
Organizations: Tennessee Clean Water Network, 123A S. Gay St., Knoxville 37902, (865) 522-7007, www.tcwn.org
Contacts/outfitters: None

Put-in/Takeout Information

To takeout: From the intersection of US 31 and US 64 in Pulaski, take US 64 west for 3.1 miles to TN 166. Turn right on TN 166 north for 2.7 miles to intersect Annie Wade Road. Park on the shoulder near this intersection.

To put-in from takeout: From TN 166 and Annie Wade Road, take Annie Wade Road north for 3.7 miles to US 31. Turn left and take US 31 north for 5 miles to the intersection with Clear Creek Road, just before the bridge over Richland Creek. Turn right on Clear Creek Road and immediately park.

Paddle Summary

This high water season run, primarily done in spring, offers a gorgeous canopied stream meandering through the main valley of Giles County. The normally clear-green stream wanders under woodland bordering alternating fields, bluffs, and wooded flats. Occasional shoals and riffles keep you moving, but current speed is highly dependent upon water levels, which generally pick up with the fall rains and remain high through winter and spring. By mid-June Richland Creek is often too low to paddle. The river frequently twists and turns on its way to the community of Wales. A railroad runs down the valley and bridges Richland Creek twice.

Since the river is but 30 to 40 feet wide, occasional deadfalls will have to be paddled around or even pulled over. Gravel bars are often submerged by the high water necessary for floating, though lucky paddlers will catch Richland Creek when the water is high enough to float yet low enough to expose gravel bars. Numerous clear branches feed Richland Creek, and easy shoals are where the tributaries come in. The shuttle is easy.

River Overview

Richland Creek is a tributary of the Elk River, which in turn flows into the Tennessee River down Alabama way. Richland Creek begins on the south side of Elk Ridge in Marshall County. It flows westerly into Giles County, taking out numerous small tributaries before Robertson Creek adds significant flow just above this paddle. At this point Richland Creek turns south, aiming for the Elk River as it carves a rich agricultural valley amid the hills of southern Middle Tennessee and becomes the central geographic feature of Giles County. Big Creek, aptly named, adds more flow, as does Weakly Creek. At this point, Richland Creek flows through the town of Pulaski, then once again enters more remote terrain until it meets the Elk River near the Tennessee-Alabama state line. From the point of this put-in to the Elk River, paddlers can enjoy 45 miles of Richland Creek in season.

The Paddling

Immediately pass under the US 31 bridge. An island forms just below the bridge. Richland Creek is running 30 to 40 feet wide bordered by a line of trees beyond which lies agricultural lands. Steep banks about 10 feet high are populated with sycamore, hackberry, ash, and maple. Stands of cane crowd together. Watchful paddlers read the gravel stream bottom, aiming for the deeper, faster channels. Fallen trees are a regular feature of this waterway, so expect to work around them. Pass the first low rock bluff at 0.6 mile. Richland Creek is turning south and flows under the narrow Milky Way Drive Bridge at 1.2 miles. Despite being in cultivated lands, the small stream and high banks keep the setting natural. The streamside maple trees are impressive in size. At 1.5 miles, a wooded bluff rises on river left.

Pass an odd, square concrete structure on the right bank at 1.8 miles, perhaps an old water gauging station. A wooded hill rises downstream of it. Pass under the Tennessee Southern Railway bridge at 2.5 miles. Note the cut stone pilings still in use. Shortly come within earshot of US 31. Richland Creek will be in the road corridor for the next 2 miles.

At 3 miles, an unnamed creek comes in on river left, near where Shady Lane meets US 31. This is an alternate put-in if you want to shorten your paddle. Shady Lane is 3.1 miles north of the intersection with US 31 and Annie Wade Road. Watch out for your first rapid of note just ahead. Here, Richland Creek flows over an old low water bridge. It will be a fun drop when the stream is running at 300 or more cubic feet per second (cfs) but will be a scraper at low flows. At 3.5 miles, Haywood Creek comes in on your left. US 31 is nearby, and this could also be a potential put-in. A gravel bar forms at this confluence.

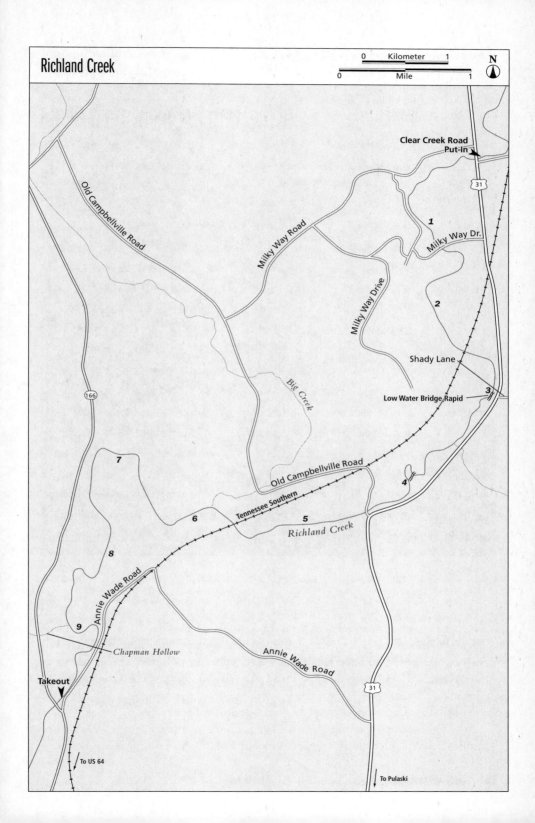

Richland Creek

0 Kilometer 1

0 Mile 1

N

Clear Creek Road
Put-In

31

Old Campbellville Road

Milky Way Road

Milky Way Dr.

1

Milky Way Drive

2

Shady Lane

166

Big Creek

Low Water Bridge Rapid

3

4

7

Old Campbellville Road

6

Tennessee Southern

5

Richland Creek

8

Annie Wade Road

9

Chapman Hollow

Annie Wade Road

31

Takeout

To US 64

To Pulaski

A bank of Giles Creek doubles as a dripping spring.

At 3.9 miles, Richland Creek narrows at a rock shelf and forms a shoal. An island stands here as well. Pass under the Old Campbellsville Road bridge at 4.4 miles. Here, Richland Creek and US 31 separate. An unnamed branch comes in on river left. Pass under the Tennessee Southern Railway a second time at 5.6 miles. The stream slows in a pool as clear Big Creek, draining northwest Giles County, comes in on your right at 5.8 miles. Richland Creek widens to 80 feet before narrowing. It now stays wide enough to have a corridor of sunlight between the wooded banks.

At 6.3 miles, the stream rams against a hill and turns north. The creek resumes its southbound ways after pinballing into a wooded bluff with prominent citadel rocks at 7.2 miles. The bluff recedes and a few houses appear. Downstream, watch for low mossy bluffs over which water spills. Richland Creek continues twisting and turning southerly, creating gravel bars. At 8.9 miles, a stream flows out of Chapman Hollow on river right. Old bridge pilings flank the tributary. Shortly you will saddle alongside quiet Annie Wade Road. When you see the TN 166 bridge ahead, slide over to the left-hand bank and look for the takeout well upstream of the bridge.

REMEMBER THE LIGHTNING CROUCH

The spring day started bright as my tall friend Steve Grayson and I paddled Richland Creek on a floating and fishing foray. We met some success, tossing back a few redeye (rock bass), while primarily vying for smallmouth. The sky slowly clouded over as morning became afternoon. We heard dull thuds of thunder somewhere beyond Richland Creek, but our streamside position—hemmed in by woods and hills—afforded limited view of the sky. We donned our rain jackets, continuing to fish and float toward Annie Wade Road. The rain finally came in torrents, followed shortly by sharp bolts of lightning and wind so strong it was downing branches from trees.

Steve and I pulled onto a gravel bar and got under a tree grove. We shuddered with every nearby crackle and flash of ensuing lightning bolts. Lightning can strike paddlers, and with fatal results. However, the odds are better that you will be injured in a car wreck on the way to the paddling destination rather than by lightning. Play it smart. When you sense a storm coming, have a plan as to what you will do when it hits.

Lightning does kill. It is the number one weather killer in the state of Florida. However, the odds of an average Tennessean being struck by lightning in a given year is 280,000 to 1. In determining whether lightning is dangerous, use the 30-30 rule. If you see lightning, count the time until you hear thunder. If you hear thunder before you reach 30, then seek shelter. Height, shape, and isolation of a given object, whether a tower, tree, or person, are the three factors that affect where lightning will strike. If you are paddling, get out of your boat and away from water. Avoid being the tallest object. If your skin tingles or your hair stands on end, squat to the ground on the balls of your feet. Put your head between your knees, making yourself into the smallest target possible. It's called the "lightning crouch." You are getting as low as you can, yet touching the ground as little as possible. Lying down on the ground actually increases your chance of getting hit by the electric current of lightning. So next time you are out there and hear thunder or see lightning, look around for shelter and be prepared to do the lightning crouch. It may save your life.

13 Duck River

The entire paddle is within the 37-mile section of the Duck that is a designated state scenic river.

County: Maury
Start: Carpenter Bridge, N35° 37.082', W86° 51.959'
End: Leftwich Bridge, N35° 34.237', W86° 52.306'
Length: 8.6 miles
Float time: 5 hours
Difficulty rating: Easy
Rapids: Class I
River type: Pastoral river
Current: Slow
River gradient: 1.5 feet per mile
River gauge: USGS Gauge Duck River at Columbia, minimum runnable level 180 cfs

Season: Year-round
Land status: Public—TVA land
Fees or permits: No fees or permits required
Nearest city/town: Columbia
Maps: USGS: Verona, Glendale; *DeLorme: Tennessee Atlas & Gazetteer,* Page 37 D5
Boats used: Canoes, kayaks, a few johnboats
Organizations: Duck River Watershed Association, P.O. Box 141, Duck River 38454, www.duckriverwatershed.org
Contacts/outfitters: Yanahli Kayak & Canoe Company, 1253 Iron Bridge Rd., Columbia 38401, (931) 840-9808, www.tennesseepaddler.com

Put-in/Takeout Information

To takeout: From exit 46 on I-65, take TN 99, Sylvester Chunn Pike, east to US 431. Turn right and take US 431 south about 6 miles to reach Jordan Road. Turn right on Jordan Road (the left turn at this intersection is Wiles Lane). Follow Jordan Road west. Along the way, Jordan Road becomes Sowell Mill Pike, crossing the Duck River at 2.5 miles. Look for the immediate left turn to reach the takeout.

To put-in from takeout: Backtrack on Sowell Mill Pike east toward US 431, reaching the intersection with Old Sowell Mill Pike at 1.0 mile. The Antioch Church of Christ is at this intersection. Turn left, north, on Old Sowell Mill Pike. At 0.5 mile, Tom Littlejohn Road veers right; stay left. At 0.8 mile, make a sharp right, now on Carpenter Bridge Road. At 2.3 miles, reach a stop sign and stay left on Carpenter Bridge Road and follow it to cross the Duck River after 4.4 miles. The put-in is on the left after crossing the Duck.

Paddle Summary

This part of the Duck River passes through Tennessee's Central Basin, and therefore has gentler gradient than the sections that pass through the Eastern Highland Rim and the Western Highland Rim. Expect to do some work when the water is low and

A canoe camper paddles past one of the Duck's signature bluffs.

slow; however the scenery won't disappoint. Funny how things work out. At one time TVA was considering building a dam near the town of Columbia, backing up and flooding this section of river. The dam was built. In the meantime, researchers found endangered mussels in the river and what was to be Columbia Lake was never filled. However, TVA had already purchased the land to be flooded and now this remains in public hands as part of the 12,800-acre Yanahli Wildlife Management Area, through which this paddle goes. Therefore the banks are primarily wild.

However, civilization has been a part of the Duck for thousands of years. Along just this paddle you will see the remains of Indian fish traps and old mill sites used by early Tennessee settlers. Other sections of river reveal more mill sites, dams, fords, and ferry locales. Natural features include bluffs, islands, and occasional rapids, and over eighty-four species of fish, purportedly more than the entire European continent.

River Overview

The Duck River is a Tennessee jewel. For starters, it is the longest river contained entirely within the state's borders at 270 miles in length. From its humble beginnings in "The Barrens" of Coffee County, it is soon dammed in Manchester, then descends in impressive falls at Old Stone Fort State Park, where a hiking trail loops between the Little Duck River and the Duck River, circling around a 2,000-year-old stone wall built by ancient American natives. The Duck is soon slowed at Normandy Lake and then is freed—and paddleable—for the duration of its 250-mile journey, save for a few small dams.

It meanders westerly passing through the horse country of greater Shelbyville, passing historic Henry Horton State Park, where camping facilities are available. It then enters the lake area of forsaken Columbia Dam and the not-to-be-drowned public lands of this paddle before passing through the heart of the town of Columbia. Beyond Columbia, the river becomes remote again and meets the Natchez Trace, where a ferry operated to shuttle weary travelers walking the "Devils Backbone," the moniker given the Natchez Trace by those who traveled between Nashville and Natchez. West of the Trace, the river enters Hickman County. Here, the now-large Duck enters remote country, becoming briefly civilized as it passes through Centerville. The Piney River, also detailed in this book in chapter 8 (page 55), flows into the Duck as the Duck turns north toward the Tennessee River. Interestingly, the Duck absorbs the flow of the Buffalo River—also in this book in chapter 10 (page 65)— just before meeting the mighty Tennessee River near Cuba Landing.

The Paddling

A gravel road leads down to the southeast side of Carpenter Bridge where there is a put-in, part of the Yanahli Wildlife Management Area. The greenish-tinted river is about 100 feet wide as it flows under the bridge. The span is built on a bluff, the first of many bluffs that you shall see during the paddle. Sycamore and river birch are the primary shoreline species. The banks run around 10 feet high, but are often higher where rock faces are

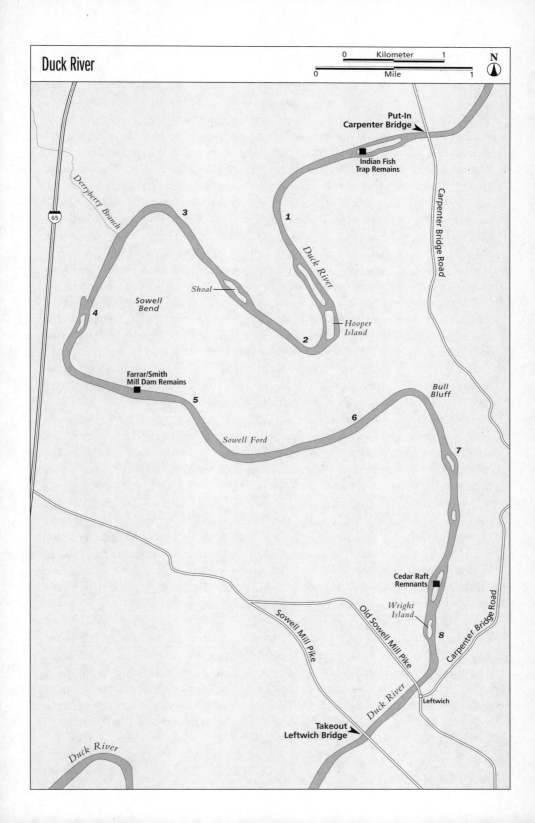

present. Grasses, wildflowers, and brush grow thickly along the shore where trees aren't present. River clarity is limited. Recent rains can muddy the Duck. Patches of sycamore will grow along shoals, along with river grasses. Tan-colored gravel and shiny mussels will reveal themselves in the shallows. Estimates vary, but the Duck contains around forty freshwater mussel species and many are endangered. The Duck River's numerous islands are subject to overflow and flooding and the trees that grow on them have limited size, stripped branches, and/or face downstream, giving them a ragged appearance.

The initial faster-moving water is within sight of the put-in, beside a long, unnamed island. The left channel around this island flows only at higher water levels. At 0.4 mile, look for the remains of an old Indian fish trap near the lower end of this island. At 0.7 mile, the river makes its first bend, exposing low bluffs above rising ranks of oak trees along with a few scattered cedars. Note the preponderance of cane on the shoreline, as well as broken rock that has tumbled to rest at the water's edge. At 1 mile, the current speeds and you pass islands, the lowermost of which is named Hooper Island. These long, narrow isles run parallel to the Duck's flow. Wooded hills climb sharply as the river curves back to the northwest and begins the miles-long curve of greater Sowell Bend. At 2.6 miles, the river speeds into a shoal. Heavy water flow has undercut the riverbank here, toppling trees into the river. At certain water levels the river will take you directly into the fallen trees, so be mindful. Consider walking or lining your boat around this spot.

At 3.0 miles, the Duck turns southwest at a bluff. Despite the river being in a wildlife area, you will hear the sounds of I-65 as it runs nearly parallel to the river. Cedars grow atop the promontory here. A gravel bar forms on the inside of the bend. Derryberry Branch flows in on river right at bluff's end. Turn away from I-65 at 4.2 miles. The slower water gives way as you speed over the remnants of the Farrar/Smith mill dam. It's barely recognizable now, but you may see rock and timber on river right. The spot creates a river-wide shoal with a small, unnamed island to your right. Just below the dam remains, look for a small cave on river right—at lower water levels. The cave emits water working through the limestone labyrinth that is much of Middle Tennessee.

Pass the Sowell Ford and dam site at 5.3 miles. The Duck speeds here, too, while flowing over remains of yet another timber/rock dam. The natural highlight of the river is reached at 6.5 miles. Here, on a right bend, Bull Bluff rises high. It is mostly wooded, but it is easily the highest hill here along this stretch of the watercourse. Note the rock outcroppings amid the craggy cedars. Its lower end is pure rock promontory overhanging the Duck. A large gravel bar lies across the bluff.

The Duck now travels southbound the entirety of the remaining paddle. At 7.7 miles, the Duck River speeds up and splits around an island. Stay right to see remnants of an old cedar raft, its planks embedded into the far right bank. At higher water it will be completely submerged. Pass Wright Island then bend to the right, passing under the Old Sowell Mill Road Bridge at 8.3 miles. Timber may be piled up against the bridge, so approach with caution. A couple of small islands lie between this bridge and the Leftwich Bridge. Make sure and go around to the right side of these last islands, as the takeout is on the right.

CHEEKS BEND STATE NATURAL AREA

Just a mile from the takeout on Sowell Mill Road, off Cheeks Bend Road, you can explore a recent addition to the Tennessee State Natural Area's holdings, Cheeks Bend. Part of the 2,135 acre, six-unit Duck River State Natural Area Complex within the greater Yanahli Wildlife Management Area, the Cheeks Bend Vista Trail travels along a bluff overlooking the Duck River and includes a special surprise—a side trip through a cave, where you can enter on a blufftop and emerge near the Duck at the base of the bluff.

If you are afraid of the dark, bring a flashlight, though one is not necessary. The Cheeks Bend Vista Trail follows a singletrack path into oak-hickory-cedar woods among pale rock outcrops, as it works to the top of a bluff. Reach the loop portion of the trail at 0.6 mile. Keep forward here, still stair-stepping up the bluff, gaining obscured views of the river below. Ferns and mosses offer green contrast to the white outcrops. Cedars cling to shallow soils on the bluff. Reach the edge of the bluff and you can look downriver to the southwest toward I-65, which isn't visible but is audible.

The bluff levels off and reaches a junction. Watch carefully here for a cedar tree banded with both blue and red stripes. To reach the cave turn right here, following the red blazes away from the river and down to a cave entrance *not visible* from where you stand. The cave entrance is nearly square and big enough for a man to stand. Follow the cave at a downhill angle as the passage narrows and the world darkens. In summer, the cave here could be 20 to 30 degrees cooler than outside. At this point, give your eyes time to adjust and you will be able to see, as light is coming from the passage that you just entered and also from the passage through which you will emerge, if you are tough enough to continue. While keeping downward you will see other smaller water-carved passages merging into the main cave. The cave opening down here is far taller than wide. You literally went under the bluff that you walked to get here. The Duck is still a good 30 feet or so below the lower cave opening.

Backtrack up the cave, returning to the main trail along the bluff, where fields and woods are visible across the river. At 0.8 mile, the trail turns away from the Duck, passing through a good spring wildflower area before stair-stepping over more outcrops to reach a high point. From there, work downhill while passing linear sinks. Complete the loop portion of the hike at 1.2 miles, then backtrack to the trailhead. To reach the trailhead, follow the directions to the takeout, then continue for 0.8 mile beyond the Duck River Bridge on Sowell Mill Road to reach Cheeks Bend Road. Turn left on Cheeks Bend Road and follow it for 0.9 mile to dead-end at the trailhead.

14 Elk River

This paddle shows off the beauty of the Elk, a mostly swift waterway traveling over scattered fun Class I shoals.

County: Lincoln
Start: Shiloh Bridge, N35° 8.357', W86° 22.967'
End: Cowley Bridge, N35° 8.196', W86° 28.572'
Length: 8.8 miles
Float time: 3.5 hours
Difficulty rating: Easy to moderate
Rapids: Class I-I+
River type: Dam-controlled valley river
Current: Moderate to swift
River gradient: 2.2 feet per mile
River gauge: Check Tims Ford Dam at www.tva .com for release schedule, or call (800) 238-

2264, then press 4, then 50.
Season: Year-round
Land status: Private
Fees or permits: No fees or permits required
Nearest city/town: Fayetteville
Maps: USGS: Mulberry; *DeLorme: Tennessee Atlas & Gazetteer,* Page 22 C1
Boats used: Canoes, kayaks, johnboats
Organizations: Keep Fayetteville/Lincoln County Beautiful, 208 Elk Ave. S., Fayetteville 37334, (931) 433-8208, lctnrecycles.com
Contacts/outfitters: Kelso Canteen and Canoe Rental, 2167 Winchester Hwy., Kelso 37348, (931) 438-4402, (800) 933-2827

Put-in/Takeout Information

To takeout: From the intersection of US 64 and US 231 on the east side of Fayetteville, take US 64 for 6.3 miles to Champ Road. Turn left on Champ Road. There is a sign here for Kelso Canoe Rental. Follow it for 0.3 mile to reach an intersection. Turn left here, still on Champ Road. Go for 0.1 mile and turn left just past a bridge over a small creek, into the Kelso Canoe Rental Campground. It's about a mile down to the Cowley Bridge access. You will seemingly dead-end at the old iron Cowley Bridge, but veer left at the bridge to access the river just downstream.

To put-in from takeout: Backtrack to Champ Road and turn left, north. It's 1.1 miles down Champ Road to Dickey Bridge. There is a public boat access here. Cross Dickey Bridge and stay on Champ Road for 5.7 miles—and then turn right on Tucker Creek Road. Go for 0.7 mile on Tucker Creek Road to reach Shiloh Bridge. However, keep straight instead of turning right to cross Shiloh Bridge, to shortly reach a put-in with steps leading down to the Elk River.

Paddle Summary

The release from the Tims Ford Dam keeps a steady flow, about 1.5 miles an hour without paddling, as it passes through a wide valley where hills occasionally crowd the river. The shoreline in this valley is normally wooded but occasionally fields encroach all the way to the river.

Paddler's eye view of the Elk River.

Paddlers need to be wary as the waters will sometimes speed up and rush past strainers—submerged trees through which the river will flow. Crystalline feeder branches enter the Elk throughout the paddle. You will see an occasional house or a fish camp along the shore but not too many. A couple of outfitters operate on the stretch of river and it could be busy with canoes on summer holiday weekends.

River Overview

The Elk, another of Middle Tennessee's "critter rivers" (as in Duck River, Buffalo River, and Big Swan Creek), is a fine paddling destination. It starts fast in the Cumberlands atop lofty Grundy County, flowing out of Burrow Cove near the community of Elkhead. Before the Elk is allowed to gain too much steam, it is stilled as Woods Reservoir. From here, the Elk flows just a short distance before once again being dammed at Tims Ford, a large TVA impoundment used by boats of all stripes.

It is below Tims Ford Dam where river enthusiasts can enjoy nearly 100 miles of Volunteer State paddling. A coldwater fishery for many miles, the river supports trout. By the time it reaches this paddle, trout are still present but smallmouth bass are king. In the future this river may be restored back to a warmwater stream, as TVA is

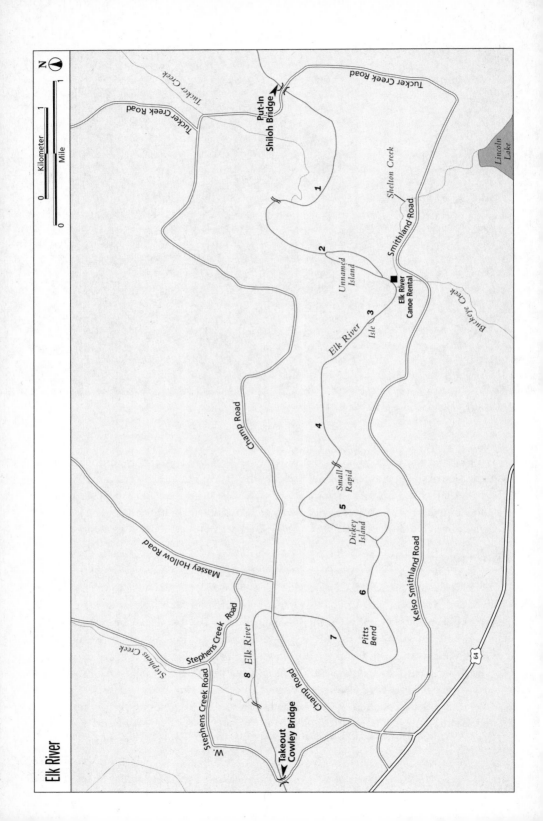

Elk River

Put-In
Shiloh Bridge

Tucker Creek Road

Tucker Creek

Tucker Creek Road

Shelton Creek

Lincoln Lake

Smithland Road

Elk River Canoe Rental

Buckeye Creek

Unnamed Island

Elk River

Isle

Champ Road

Small Rapid

Dickey Island

Kelso Smithland Road

Massey Hollow Road

Stephens Creek Road

Stephens Creek

W. Stephens Creek Road

Pitts Bend

Champ Road

Elk River

Takeout
Cowley Bridge

64

N

0   Kilometer   1
0   Mile   1

1 2 3 4 5 6 7 8

considering warming the waters back up to restore the endangered cracking pearly-mussel populations in the river.

Its westerly course leads through Franklin County, Lincoln County, and past the town of Fayetteville. Here the pastoral winding river continues west into Giles County, slowing its flow but getting nearer and nearer the state of Alabama until it turns south at Prospect, then crosses the state line where it continues to wind its way through north Alabama to soon join the Tennessee River just west of Athens.

The Paddling

Immediately pass under Shiloh Bridge. Translucent green waters flow cool from beneath the upstream Tims Ford Dam. Tims Ford Dam usually generates in the evening, but no matter the generation schedule, TVA keeps a minimum flow rate on the Elk River of 160 cfs at all times. The banks are gravel or mud where not vegetated. But it's mostly trees bordering the shore—box elder, silver maple, river birch, and sycamore. The river is about 60 to 80 feet wide at this point. Expect to occasionally work around deadfall, and be wary of the sometimes swift current running you into a strainer. At 0.5 mile, an unnamed creek comes in on the left. At 0.7 mile, a wooded hill rises on the south shore.

At 1 mile, a low bluff makes the river curve to the right. Gravel bars are frequent enough to make for convenient stopping points. Later in summer the gravel bars will partially grass over. Tucker Creek flows in on river right at 1.3 miles. A speedy shoal pushes downriver at 1.5 miles as the Elk curves west. Occasional logjams will crowd one side or other of the river. At 2.1 miles, the Elk quickens as it moves around an unnamed island. The primary channel is on the left. At 2.7 miles, on a fast-moving curve, you will see Elk River Canoe Rental, as well as Shelton Creek and Buckeye Creek contributing their waters to the Elk.

Beyond the outfitter, a low bluff forms on river left with a spring branch noisily dripping over it. At 3 miles, the Elk hastens around a small wooded isle. Low rock bluffs continue to rise on one side of the river or the other. The waterway relaxes but eventually meets a small rapid at 4.3 miles. Reach Dickey Island at 4.9 miles. The river splits here. Stay with the left channel, though the right channel is larger. Both channels around Dickey Island speed and are significantly more narrow than what you've been paddling, therefore be watchful for the channels flowing into strainers and deadfall. A gravel bar awaits at the base of Dickey Island where the channels join. Just a little ways downstream, the Elk divides again into multiple shallow and swift channels amid small, sycamore-covered islands.

The Elk slows and deepens after the channels regather. The now-wider river slowly curves north around Pitts Bend at 6.4 miles and resumes a hasty current at 6.9 miles. Reach Dickey Bridge at 7.4 miles. The public access is on river left, as well as an old cut stone abutment from the former bridge. Shoot a fun rapid just below the bridge. Another shoal takes you downriver at 8 miles, where clear Stephens Creek flows in from the north. One last rapid leads to the old iron Cowley Bridge. The takeout is on a gravel bar on the left side of the Elk.

FOSTER FALLS

The south end of the Cumberland Plateau has some of the wildest, roughest country in Tennessee. Sheer bluffs border deep "gulfs"—what natives call gorges. In these gulfs flow wild streams strewn with rock gardens hosting a variety of vegetation. Intermingled within this is a human history of logging and mining that has given way to the non-extractive use of nature: ecotourism.

Foster Falls Recreation Area, near the headwaters of the Elk River, is operated by the Tennessee Valley Authority. It offers a safe and appealing base for experiencing the South Cumberland Mountains, whether you are paddling the Elk or just exploring this slice of the state.

The likable campground is situated on a level, wooded tract near the actual Foster Falls. Your camping companions may be rock climbers, for Foster Falls has quietly emerged as a premier rock-climbing area in the Southeast. For hikers, a connector trail leaves the campground to Foster Falls. Take the short loop trail that leads to the base of 120-foot Foster Falls or intersect the south end of the Fiery Gizzard Trail and see Foster Falls from the top looking down. If you take the Fiery Gizzard Trail, views await of Little Gizzard and Fiery Gizzard gulfs. Trail signs point out the rock bluffs where rock climbers ply their trade. The first 2.5 miles offer many vistas and small waterfalls where side creeks plunge into the gorge below. My favorite view is from the Laurel Creek Gorge Overlook, where rock bluffs on the left meld into forested drop-offs beyond, contrasting with the flat plateau in the background. It is but a short drive to Grundy Forest and Grundy Lakes. Grundy Forest contains about 4 miles of the most feature-packed hiking you can ask for: waterfalls, rock houses, old trees, old mines, and strange rock formations. Just remember to watch where you walk, as the trails can be rough. Grundy Lakes is on the National Historic Register. Once the site of mining activity, this area has seen prison labor, revolts, and the cooling down of the infamous Lone Rock coke ovens. The Lone Rock Trail will lead you to all the interesting sites. So after your paddle on the Elk, consider heading east to Foster Falls. For more information visit www.tva.gov.

15 Red River

The Red is a classic Tennessee paddle and has been a favorite for decades. Travel down a bluff-lined valley with an added waterfall flowing into the main stream. The river makes for a casual float and is serviced by an outfitter.

County: Robertson, Montgomery
Start: TN 256 bridge near Adams, N36° 35.264', W87° 5.358'
End: Port Royal State Historic Area, N36° 33.287', W87° 8.506'
Length: 7.6 miles
Float time: 3.5 hours
Difficulty rating: Easy
Rapids: Class I
River type: Pastoral river
Current: Moderate
River gradient: 2.1 feet per mile
River gauge: Red River at Port Royal, minimum runnable level 140 cfs

Season: Year-round except for drought years
Land status: Private
Fees or permits: No fees or permits required
Nearest city/town: Adams
Maps: USGS: Adams, Sango; *DeLorme: Tennessee Atlas and Gazetteer,* Page 64 D3
Boats used: Canoes, kayaks, johnboats
Organizations: Red River Watershed Association, P.O. Box 1185, Springfield 37172, www .redriverwatershed.org
Contacts/outfitters: Red River Canoe Rental, Hwy. 41, Adams 37010, (931) 696-2768

Put-in/Takeout Information

To takeout: From exit 11 on I-24, Adams/Clarksville, take TN 76 east for 3.4 miles, then turn left onto Old Clarksville Springfield Road (there will be a sign here for Port Royal State Park). Follow Old Clarksville Springfield Road for 1.7 miles to TN 238/Port Royal Road. Keep forward to drop into Port Royal State Historic Area at a boat landing at the confluence of Red River and Sulphur Fork.

To put-in from takeout: From Port Royal, turn right on TN 238/Port Royal Road, crossing the bridge over Red River to follow it 0.9 mile to Sadlersville Road. Turn right on Sadlersville Road, and drive 4 miles to US 41. Turn right on US 41 and follow it, bridging the Red River and traveling a total of 2.2 miles to turn right into Red River Canoe Rental, then veer left, leaving the pavement. A gravel road leads to the put-in by the river.

Paddle Summary

With an outfitter on one end and a state park on the other, this is a classic Middle Tennessee river run. The Red River not only draws paddlers but also fishermen who like to make a lazy float at low water—when the water is at its clearest—to catch bass, bream, and redeye. Others will be relaxing on the numerous gravel bars or swimming when the weather is warm. It all adds up to a fun recreational river that paddlers of all abilities can enjoy. Class I riffles and shoals push paddlers along yet do not cause

The confluence of Red River and Sulphur Fork at Port Royal.

concern even for novices. So if you're looking to break into a new river or want to bring along some friends and get them into paddling, the Red River is a good choice.

River Overview

The Red River is a product of the Volunteer State and its neighbor Kentucky. The most easterly tributaries of the Red extend into Sumner County, then flow west as a small stream entering the Bluegrass State. It is generally considered paddleable around the hamlet of Prices Mill, Kentucky, as it wanders westerly out of Simpson County into Logan County where it meets the South Fork Red River. The South Fork also begins in Tennessee and flows into Kentucky to join the main Red at the town of Dot. From here to its confluence with the Cumberland River, the Red is considered paddleable year-round. A few miles below Dot, the Red returns to Tennessee, coming near the town of Adams, where Elk Fork Creek adds significant flow. At the historic Port Royal, Sulphur Fork, a canoeable stream detailed in this guidebook in chapter 16 (page 95), comes in. Below Port Royal, the Red bisects Montgomery County while entering Clarksville and its populated areas. Just prior to reaching the Cumberland it meets the West Fork Red River. The main Red offers 20 miles of seasonal paddling in Kentucky to Dot. From Dot down, year-round paddlers can ply over 50 miles of water, including urban Clarksville.

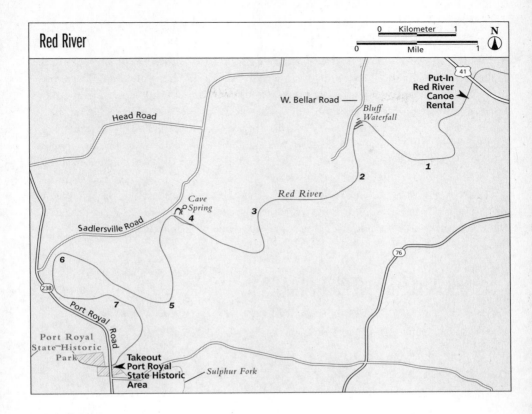

Red River

0 Kilometer 1

0 Mile 1

N

Put-In
Red River
Canoe
Rental

W. Bellar Road

*Bluff
Waterfall*

41

Head Road

1

2

Red River

*Cave
Spring*

4

3

Sadlersville Road

76

6

238

7

5

*Port Royal
Road*

Port Royal
State Historic
Park

Takeout
Port Royal
State Historic
Area

Sulphur Fork

The Paddling

Leave the outfitter landing and join the tan–clear waters, which can become quite stained during floods and high flows, hence the name Red River. The current varies seasonally but will push enough to keep you moving any time of year. Pass an old bridge abutment at 0.2 mile. This river has many bluffs, the first of which you pass on your left at 0.6 mile. A large gravel bar is situated inside the bend and makes for a good stopping spot, especially if you hastily loaded yourself and your gear into your boat. Grass and mud banks 10 to 20 feet high border the waterway unless rock palisades are present. Sycamores, maple, ash, and ironwood border the stream. Oaks stand on higher, drier ground.

At 1.4 miles, as the Red River curves left, a bluff rises on river right. Get the cotton out of your ears and tune in for falling water. Here, a waterfall drops down the bluff in multiple stages. Just like the Red River, it roars in the spring and babbles in autumn. Locals simply refer to this as "the falls," when talking about the Red River. A convenient gravel bar is located across from the falls, so you can stop and admire the scenery or have a picnic lunch.

With each curve a bluff rises on the outside bend, keeping the scenery at a high level and the river turning. At 2.8 miles, the Red runs into another palisade and turns south, cutting ever deeper toward the Cumberland River. At 3.2 miles, another rock wall emanates from the Red on river left. Pass around an island at 3.9 miles, just before banking against—guess what—another bluff on river right. Paddle alongside this bluff and you will see a water-level cave spring at 4.1 miles. The cave opening is about 3 feet high and 7 feet wide and is another major highlight of a Red River run.

The bluffs briefly give way to farmland, but you are coming alongside another stone rampart on river left at 4.8 miles. The bluffs just keep on coming! Soon pass under a major power line. The river turns northwest and begins a 180-degree elongated turn that lasts for 2 miles, yet you end up 400 feet from where you were before—separated by a massive bluff! At 5.8 miles, a bluff on river right forces the actual U-turn. Nearly return back to where you were at 7.1 miles, then curve southwesterly for Port Royal and Sulphur Fork. Pass the outfitter's takeout on river right just before meeting Sulphur Fork. The Port Royal Road Bridge is dead ahead, and the takeout is on river left just below the confluence with Sulphur Fork.

CLARKSVILLE'S RIVERSIDE TRAIL

The Red River meets its mother stream—the Cumberland River—in Clarksville. The town was born at this confluence, and the two waterways have shaped its path and continue to do so to this day. Clarksville is making the most of these watery assets by developing the McGregor Park Riverwalk, a 1-mile greenway. McGregor Park also offers a museum, overlooks, stages, picnic areas, and walkways.

Back in 1989, then-mayor Don Trotter appointed the River District Commission to develop a master plan for economic, recreational, and historic development along the Cumberland River corridor through Clarksville. Problem was, the river was eroding the land along its banks. Austin Peay State University professor and geologist Philip Kemmerly came up with a plan to save the riverbank. What is known as geotextile was placed along the bank, both above and below water level. The geotextile, a fabriclike mat, allows water to pass through it without taking the soil. The geotextile was then covered with conventional rock riprap. Fill was added to restore the shoreline, and the bank was secured.

Before you travel the Riverwalk, take a moment to look inside the Riverwalk Museum. It tells the intertwined history of Clarksville, the Red River, Cumberland River, and the people who made the area come alive. Then let your imagination wander as you walk along the Cumberland. The walkway is primarily concrete but is punctuated with brick and other ornamentation to make it both stylish and functional. Lights line the path, allowing for walking in the dark. A line of eastern cottonwoods grows between the Riverwalk and Riverside Drive, otherwise the trail is exposed to the sky. Enjoy.

16 Sulphur Fork

This scenic creek is serviced by an outfitter and makes for a great outing with numerous waterfalls and cave springs along its banks.

County: Robertson, Montgomery
Start: TN 256 bridge near Adams, N36° 30.944', W87° 3.401'
End: Port Royal State Historic Area, N36° 33.287', W87° 8.506'
Length: 10.5 miles
Float time: 5.5 hours
Difficulty rating: Easy to moderate
Rapids: Class I
River type: Pastoral creek
Current: Moderate
River gradient: 5.0 feet per mile
River gauge: Red River at Port Royal, minimum runnable level 500 cfs

Season: Winter, spring, early summer, and after heavy rains
Land status: Private
Fees or permits: No fees or permits required
Nearest city/town: Adams
Maps: USGS: Springfield North, Adams, Sango; *DeLorme: Tennessee Atlas and Gazetteer,* Page 64 D3
Boats used: Canoes, kayaks
Organizations: Red River Watershed Association, P.O. Box 1185, Springfield 37172, www .redriverwatershed.org
Contacts/outfitters: Red River Canoe Rental, Hwy. 41, Adams 37010, (931) 696-2768

Put-in/Takeout Information

To takeout: From exit 11 on I-24, Adams/Clarksville, take TN 76 east for 3.4 miles, the turn left onto Old Clarksville Springfield Road (there will be a sign here for Port Royal State Park). Follow Old Clarksville Springfield Road for 1.7 miles to TN 238/ Port Royal Road. Keep forward to drop into Port Royal State Historic Area at a boat landing at the confluence of Red River and Sulphur Fork.

To put-in from takeout: From Port Royal, turn left on Port Royal Road, away from the bridge over Red River, and drive for 1.2 mile to intersect TN 76. Turn left and take TN 76 east for 0.7 mile, then keep forward on Harmony Church Road as TN 76 goes left. Travel for 0.5 mile on Harmony Church Road and reach Harmony Church. At the church, keep forward on narrow Toby Darden Road. It looks more like a driveway than a road. Follow Toby Darden Road for 1.4 miles to turn left on Edd Ross Road. Follow Edd Ross Road for 2.6 miles to reach TN 256. Turn left on TN 256 and follow it for 1.2 miles to reach the bridge over Sulphur Fork. The parking and put-in are on the left before crossing the bridge.

Paddle Summary

Sulphur Fork carves a valley in which some of Middle Tennessee's earliest settlements took place. Settlers came from back east to till the rich soil here. Today you can float through this still quiet part of Robertson County, meandering on a winding river

Author at a gravel bar composite on Sulphur Fork.

bordered with bluffs and bottoms. Streamside habitation is very limited, and you will enjoy the intimate waterway as it alternates between quiet pools and fast shoals. Numerous water features include cave springs and cascades that flow into Sulphur Fork.

An outfitter operating on the Red River also runs trips on Sulphur Fork, eliminating the hassle of a shuttle. Most paddlers—and there aren't many—will be locals and fishermen vying for smallmouth bass. The gauge used to determine paddleability is for the Red River and is therefore not exact. Also, consult the outfitter whether you can get on Sulphur Fork or not.

River Overview

Sulphur Fork has its beginnings north of Nashville, where Sumner County, Davidson County, and Robertson County converge. Here, spring branches drop north off these dividing hills, gathering and picking up more tributaries before the creek curves west to wander around the north side of Springfield. Keeping west, Sulphur Fork once again enters quiet farm country, curving and carving its way to meet the Red River at Port Royal State Historic Area. From Springfield to the mouth of the Red River, paddlers can ply nearly 25 miles of stream, though the lower you go the longer the paddle season. In normal years, Sulphur Fork will be too low by the end of June.

The Paddling

Leave the TN 256 bridge. Sulphur Fork is in the middle of a 180-degree bend. The water flows normally clear-tan, though it will stain in high water. Sycamore, ash, and oak overhang the 40-foot-wide stream. Cedar grows atop rock outcrops that border bends. The stream often divides around russet gravel bars, lying inside bends and near tributaries. Brushy islands are frequent. Cane grows thick on the shoreline. Even when you have agricultural fields, a screen of trees divides the waterway from the fields and partially shades the creek.

Pass an old water gauging station on river left then back up against a bluff. A nice gravel bar lies across the bluff and makes for a good stopping point in case you need to regroup. Herons will fly away as you round the bends. Wildlife is abundant in the valley, including beaver, muskrat, and deer. Note the old bridge pilings at 0.3 mile, made from cut block. A wooded hill culminating in sheer rock ramparts rises on river right at 1.1 miles. The bluff gives way and you pass a second set of bridge pilings at 1.4 miles. At 1.8 miles, a bluff rises on river left. It seems with every bend a new bluff rises and a gravel bar settles in across it. This begs the question: Which came first, the bluff or the bend? Bluffs are not continuous by any means, and you do have river segments that have fields on both sides.

At 3.7 miles, Brush Creek adds significant clear flow on river left. Shortly beyond here a bluff rises on river left and you reach Slide Cascades flowing off it at 4.1 miles. Just downstream, at 4.2 miles, is Cave Cascades. This series of waterfalls emerges from the side of a bluff and spills down mossy rocks into Sulphur Fork. Flow rates obviously depend upon rainfall, but when Sulphur Fork is up and floatable, Cave Cascades will be a highlight of the trip. This fall is as wide as it is tall. An old pipe and a concrete box remain from efforts to harness this reliable water source.

Sulphur Fork has widened to 80 or more feet here. Continue curving downstream to come alongside a water-level cave spring vent on river left at 4.4 miles, where you can hear the water spilling through hollow rocks to emerge at the stream's edge. Pass another cave spring below a bluff on river right at 4.8 miles. This collection of springs and caves demonstrates the interrelationship between rock and water in the Sulphur Fork Valley. The stream cut the bluffs and also slowly wore away underground, creating a honeycomb of passageways through which rainwater travels and continues to erode the above and below ground strata.

Split around a noteworthy island as you pass beneath a bluff on river left at 5.5 miles. Pass Triple Cascades—three side-by-side drops—emerging from a bluff on river left at 5.6 miles. Pass under a power line at 5.9 miles. The creek is slowing thanks to the Halls Mill Dam ahead, which you reach at 6.9 miles. It was a hammer mill operation used to grind wheat and corn. Portage on river left. The river speeds as if trying to catch up for the slow flow as you pass beside pilings of a defunct bridge.

Sulphur Fork

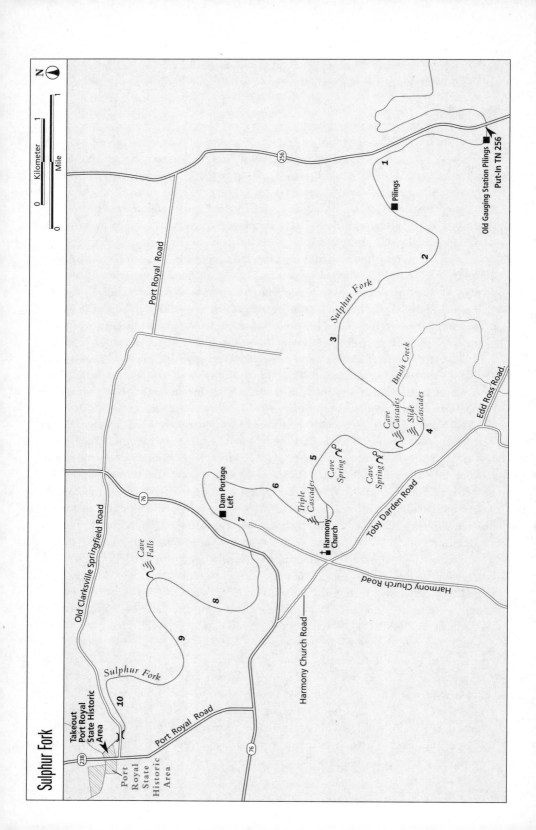

N

Old Gauging Station Pilings
Put-In TN 256

Pilings

1

2

Sulphur Fork

3

Brush Creek

Cave
Cascades

Slide
Cascades

4

Cave Spring

Cave Spring

Edd Ross Road.

Toby Darden Road

5

Triple
Cascades

6

Cave Falls

7

Harmony
Church

Dam Portage
Left

Harmony Church Road

Harmony Church Road

8

9

10

Sulphur Fork

Takeout
Port Royal State Historic
Area

Port Royal State Historic Area

Port Royal Road

Old Clarksville Springfield Road

Port Royal Road

76

256

238

76

0   Kilometer   1

0   Mile   1

Pass under the TN 76 bridge at 7.3 miles and join a high bluff. The river curves again and nears a bluff on river right at 8.5 miles. Here, Cave Falls tumbles a ways back from the river. Two more big curves pass big bluffs before passing under the Old Clarksville Springfield Road Bridge to enter Port Royal State Historic Area. Meet the Red River and take out on river left just a few feet down the Red River.

PORT ROYAL: ALMOST THE STATE CAPITAL?

The state of Tennessee generally settled east to west. However, some pockets of Middle Tennessee grew faster than others did. One such place was French Lick, now known as Nashville. Another place was Port Royal, which happened to be the head of navigation on the Red River. Located at the confluence of Sulphur Fork and the Red River, this was a natural point of passage for years, as an aboriginal American trail passed this way and was used by hunters exploring what was then the Wild West for furs and land speculation. Later, commercial boat traffic, primarily steamboats, became more important and trading and transportation communities sprang up along riverways, all claiming to be the best spot for boat traffic. Port Royal grew because it was also on a stagecoach route as well as the Red River, and was considered as the potential capital of the state after it was moved from Knoxville. Nashville won out, but Port Royal chugged on with the addition of manufacturing. The reprieve was short lived as the economic downturn following the Civil War combined with railroad access to towns other than Port Royal doomed the place. It further dwindled, and finally the post office left, the official end to a town that might have been the capital of Tennessee.

17 Sycamore Creek

Often overlooked by paddlers, this Cumberland River tributary has bluffs aplenty, waterfalls, a lake—and a dam portage. The only thing it doesn't have is year-round water.

County: Cheatham
Start: Old Clarksville Pike, N36° 20.752', W87° 1.721'
End: TN 12 west of Ashland City, N36° 18.659', W87° 7.197'
Length: 10.4 miles
Float time: 5.5 hours
Difficulty rating: Moderate
Rapids: Class I–I+
River type: Big creek
Current: Moderate to swift
River gradient: 6.1 feet per mile
River gauge: Harpeth River near Kingston Springs, TN, minimum runnable level 500 cfs

Season: Winter, spring, early summer, and after heavy rains
Land status: Private
Fees or permits: No fees or permits required
Nearest city/town: Ashland City
Maps: USGS: Ashland City; *DeLorme: Tennessee Atlas and Gazetteer,* Page 52 B3
Boats used: Canoes, kayaks
Organizations: Cumberland River Compact, P.O. Box 41721, Nashville 37204, (615) 837-1151, www.cumberlandrivercompact.org
Contacts/outfitters: Tennessee Clean Water Network, 123A S. Gay St., Knoxville 37902, (865) 522-7007, www.tcwn.org

Put-in/Takeout Information

To takeout: From the intersection of TN 12 and TN 49 in downtown Ashland City, take TN 12 west for 4.9 miles to the bridge over Sycamore Creek. Just beyond the bridge, turn right on Maconwall Road. Travel just a few feet to turn right on a gravel stream access road that leads down to Sycamore Creek. Note the lowermost part of the access road may be muddy/flooded when Cheatham Lake is high. When parking, do not block the gravel road.

To put-in from takeout: Backtrack to downtown Ashland City, then take TN 49 north for 7.1 miles toward Pleasant View to Old Clarksville Pike. Turn right on Old Clarksville Pike and follow it for 1.8 miles to the bridge over Sycamore Creek. The parking/access is on the northwest side of the bridge, before you cross Sycamore Creek.

Paddle Summary

Paddlers who make their way to this underutilized stream don't seem to be spreading the word. Granted, Sycamore Creek is a late fall through spring run, but it simply doesn't get the traffic or accolades that it deserves. With a gradient of over 6 feet per mile, the stream swiftly courses its way past bluffs aplenty—some with waterfalls spilling over them—and southwest past a mix of woodland and civilization to meet the backwaters of Cheatham Lake and the Cumberland River.

One of many waterfalls that drop into Sycamore Creek.

Gravel bars are ample for stopping and the green-tinted water—when running high—will absolutely fly. At lower water levels ample shoals will keep you flowing between slack pools. The nearest stream gauge is on the north side of the Cumberland, on the lower Harpeth River. And if the Harpeth is flowing boldly, chances are you can float Sycamore Creek. However, the Harpeth River drains a large area and thus using this gauge for floating Sycamore Creek is a crapshoot. Spring is undoubtedly the best time to come here—waterfalls are running and the wildflowers are blooming. Be apprised you must portage Powder Mill Dam 2 miles into the adventure.

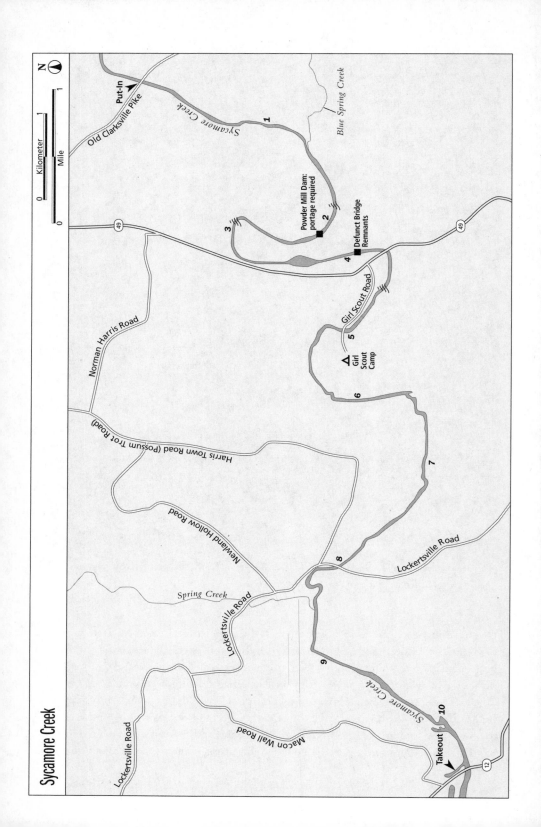

Sycamore Creek

N

Old Clarksville Pike

Put-In

Sycamore Creek

1

Blue Spring Creek

Powder Mill Dam: portage required

2

3

4

Defunct Bridge Remnants

Girl Scout Road

5

△ Girl Scout Camp

6

Norman Harris Road

Harris Town Road (Possum Trot Road)

Newland Hollow Road

7

8

Lockertsville Road

Spring Creek

Lockertsville Road

Macon Wall Road

9

Lockertsville Road

Sycamore Creek

10

Takeout

12

49

49

0   Kilometer   1

0   Mile   1

River Overview

Sycamore Creek becomes a full-blown stream where the counties of Robertson, Cheatham, and Davidson converge. Its branches gather below Dividing Ridge and Paradise Ridge. From the tri-county area, Sycamore Creek flows west, dividing Robertson and Cheatham Counties before flowing under I-24. The addition of Jones Branch and Holts Creek precede the conventional uppermost paddling at Old Clarksville Pike. Two miles downstream, the historic Powder Mill Dam slows the stream as it circles past a golf course. The stream twists and turns its way to eventually make the backwaters of Cheatham Lake roughly across from the mouth of the Harpeth River. A U.S. Army Corps of Engineers ramp is located on the lower Sycamore Creek embayment. Including the Cheatham Lake backwaters, paddlers can ply about 14 miles of water here.

The Paddling

Immediately pass under Old Clarksville Pike Bridge and the stream draining Slick Hollow on your right. Sycamore Creek runs about 40 feet wide at this point. The gravel bottom is bordered by mud banks about 10 feet high. Ash, hornbeam, river birch, and of course sycamore border the translucent green waters. Spring freshets will dinge the water. Cane grows in streamside stands. Wooded bottomlands will be colored with wildflowers in spring. It isn't long before you reach the first of many islands and shoals. Your southwesterly journey takes you under a power line at 0.7 mile.

Tan gravel bars take their place on the insides of stream bends. Even when the stream travels by flat fields, hills rise in the distance and continually run close enough to the stream to form magnificent bluffs and alter the course of Sycamore Creek. Pass some landowner-placed riprap along the creek to prevent erosion.

Simple Class I riffles keep the boat moving. Watch for occasional partially submerged trees and for the current to run you into partly submerged snags. Since Sycamore Creek is infrequently paddled, fallen trees are not kept cut back. At 1.4 miles, Blue Spring Creek flows in on your left. The stream begins to slacken as you curve around a golf course to your right. At 1.9 miles, a four-tiered waterfall drops from the bluff to your left. The bluff rises its sharpest just before giving way. At 2.3 miles, reach Powder Mill Dam. You can portage it on the right or left banks—just allow yourself plenty of distance between you and the dam crest before reaching the shore. This mill dam, originally built of wood in 1835, used waterpower to make gunpowder. During the Civil War, the Confederacy worked the mill and made large quantities of powder. The current dam was built in 1891 but the water power hasn't been harnessed for a century.

Below the dam a lower bluff continues on river left and the creek speeds at a single drop rapid. At 2.9 miles, Sycamore Creek runs smack dab into a high bluff, forcing the stream into a 180-degree turn. A slender ribbonlike waterfall spills over the bluff. Float under the TN 49 bridge at 4.3 miles and resume a westerly direction. Watch out for debris piled against the bridge abutments here. Come along another bluff with a waterfall at 4.5 miles. At 5.0 miles float under the bridge leading to the Girl Scout camp on river left. At 5.2 miles, an unnamed stream comes in on your right. At 5.3 miles, a high swinging footbridge spans the creek. This is part of the Girl Scout camp. Impressive bluffs continue to flank the outside river bends as another unnamed stream comes in on your right at 5.6 miles. Riffles and shoals occur where these tributaries enter southbound Sycamore Creek.

At 6.4 miles, pass an island and a nameless tributary as Sycamore Creek turns west again and divides around numerous islands. Pass under the Lockertsville Road Bridge at 8.0 miles. Spring Creek joins Sycamore Creek at 8.6 miles. At 8.9 miles a massive bluff stands streamside and turns the waterway southwest. By 9.5 miles, you may be feeling the current slow as Cheatham Lake exerts its influence. Shoals have ceased unless the lake is low. As you near the TN 12 bridge, drift to the right bank to make the gravel access road and takeout before passing under the bridge at 10.4 miles. A finger embayment extends toward Maconwall Road.

CUMBERLAND RIVER BICENTENNIAL TRAIL

Bicyclers and hikers take note of the Cumberland River Bicentennial Trail, which crosses lower Sycamore Creek just downstream of the paddle's takeout. The trail traces the bed of the Tennessee Central Railroad. Steep bluffs to the north and a vast floodplain to the south border the trail. The Cumberland River is just out of sight. However, the embayment of Sycamore Creek, which flows into the Cumberland, lies along much of the rail trail, lending a watery aspect. The railroad-turned-greenway passes over small creeks that have cut their way through the riverside bluffs. Here, trestles bridge the creeks, offering a bird's-eye view of the surroundings. In places, the right-of-way has been elevated to keep the former tracks level. A hardwood forest of sycamore, oak, and sweetgum trees shade the path. Look for railroad ties and occasional steel rails near the greenway. In places, the yellow-tan bluffs to the right of the trail were blasted to make room for the tracks. Cedar trees hang precariously from atop the bluffs. The Cumberland River Bicentennial Trail continues northwest, traversing multiple trestles. Farm country is visible around you—old wooden outbuildings, fields, and rows of trees. Hills rise on the far side of the Cumberland River. The trestle spanning Sycamore Creek is curved and has a steel-frame span in its center. It is by far the largest bridge on the rail trail. Reach the Eagle Pass trailhead at the 4-mile mark. The path continues for 3 more miles as a gravel track. Four additional miles of railbed have been acquired and are slated for opening down the line. The trail can be accessed off TN 12 by way of Chapmansboro Road. For more information visit www.cumberlandrivertrail.org.

18 Harpeth River Narrows

This is the most user-friendly river paddle in this entire guidebook—you don't need a shuttle to do it!

County: Cheatham
Start: Harpeth Narrows, N36° 8.864', W87° 7.258'
End: Harris-Street Bridge, N36° 9.135', W87° 7.149'
Length: 5.5 miles
Float time: 2.5 hours
Difficulty rating: Easy to moderate
Rapids: Class I
River type: Pastoral river
Current: Moderate
River gradient: 2.9 feet per mile
River gauge: USGS Harpeth River near Kingston Springs, TN, minimum runnable level 120 cfs

Season: Year-round
Land status: Public—Harpeth River State Park, private also
Fees or permits: No fees or permits required
Nearest city/town: Kingston Springs
Maps: USGS: Lillamay, Harpeth Valley; *DeLorme: Tennessee Atlas & Gazetteer,* Page 52 C3
Boats used: Canoes, kayaks
Organizations: Harpeth River Watershed Association, P.O. Box 1127, Franklin 37065, (615) 790-9767, www.harpethriver.org
Contacts/outfitters: Tip A Canoe, 1279 Hwy. 70, Kingston Springs 37082, (800) 550-5810, www.tip-a-canoe.com

Put-in/Takeout Information

To takeout: From exit 188 on I-40 west of Nashville, take TN 249 north and follow it 2.3 miles to a T intersection with US 70. Turn left, heading west on US 70 for 2.3 miles to Cedar Hill Road. Turn right on Cedar Hill Road and follow it 3 miles to the Harris Street Bridge over the Harpeth River. Turn right just before the bridge to a parking area above the river.

To put-in from takeout: To reach the put-in, backtrack just a short distance and turn right on Narrows of Harpeth Road. Travel for 0.1 mile at the signed turn for TUNNEL AREA AND CANOE RAMP. At 0.4 mile, you'll see the canoe launch on your left, leading down a steep hill. The parking area is a short distance beyond the ramp.

Paddle Summary

Here in Cheatham County, the Harpeth River makes a huge bend where it nearly doubles back on itself. The put-in and takeout are in the confines of the Narrows of Harpeth unit of Harpeth River State Park. Hiking trails connect you from the beginning to the end. Before you balk at the hiking part, realize it is but 0.5 mile between the put-in and takeout.

The paddle itself is just about as friendly. Leave a canoe launch, passing one end of the historic tunnel used to power an iron forge, and begin a series of easy rapids

Even snakes like this section of the Harpeth River.

bordered by large, tan gravel bars. The scenery alternates between bluffs and tree-lined fields. As you make the curve of Bells Bend, rock walls rise prominently over the waters, and the water continues dropping over Class I–I+ rapids. Finally, come near the other end of the iron forge tunnel, which makes for an interesting stop. Massive cottonwoods tower overhead here. The takeout is not far beyond this, and you can utilize the hiking trails not only to complete the shuttle but also to climb to a high rock outcrop with a view of the Harpeth River.

River Overview

The Harpeth State Scenic River begins in southwest Rutherford County, only to enter Williamson County before it gains any real steam. It continues into the heart of fast-growing Franklin. The West Harpeth joins the main stream before it flows into the Bellevue area of Davidson County. Ahead lies Cheatham County. Here the Harpeth's numerous bends become more pronounced and the river cuts a course back in time. This is where the bulk of Harpeth River State Park's numerous holdings are, including Mound Bottom, an ancient Indian town site. Petroglyphs can be found at Mace Bluff. Then comes the Narrows of Harpeth, where this paddle takes place. As it curves toward the Cumberland River, paddlers enter the most remote stretches of waterway left. It finally reaches Cheatham Reservoir and an Army Corps of Engineers campground that makes for a good final takeout. The upper stretches of the Harpeth, from Franklin to the confluence with the West Harpeth, and the West Harpeth itself offer 20 or so paddleable miles during winter and spring. Below the confluence of the streams, the main Harpeth becomes paddleable most of the year. It is about 60 miles from the confluence to the mouth of the Cumberland River, though it takes the South Fork Harpeth's flow, in Cheatham County, to make the main stem paddleable year-round. The most popular stretches begin in this area around Kingston Springs, where outfitters are stationed. Stay tuned as river accesses continue to multiply and the Harpeth River Blueway is developed.

The Paddling

The put-in can be challenging, as you head down some steep steps with a built-in canoe slide. If the water is low, you will have to drop your boat below the last step, so be prepared to help one another. Within the first hundred yards on your right is Montgomery Bell's tunnel, used to harness water power for an iron forge. This was one of Tennessee's earliest industries. Even though water flows through the tunnel, do not be tempted to try this, as it is often clogged with boulders and logs.

The Harpeth stretches 80 feet shore to shore at this point. However, where it narrows around islands or fast-moving shoals, it can be merely 40 to 45 feet wide. Willow, river birch, and sycamore border the river. Immediately pass below a high bluff on your right. Rock outcrops stand bold against the sky. After your paddle consider hiking up to this outcrop where you can look down upon the river. Class I riffles are broken by slow pools. The river is dotted with ample deadfall. Expect to work around these fallen trees, especially at low water. Leave the bluffline and begin the grand loop, curving around Bells Bend. At lower water levels enjoy the large gravel bars favorable for stopping, picnicking, or relaxing. The Harpeth is also popular for anglers vying for smallmouth bass, among other species.

The first 0.75 mile has several shoals. Note the large cottonwoods along the river here, usually a little way back from the water, but in the riparian zone. The river will continually tighten, then shoot over tan gravel bars, speeding your boat, then widen and slow. At 1.3 miles, the river bends to the right and yet another gravel bar forms. A wooded bluff rises on river left at 1.5 miles. At 1.7 miles, an unnamed creek comes in on your left. Beyond here a line of trees screens farm fields on both sides of the Harpeth. As you begin making the main curve around Bells Bend, an exposed bluff downstream rises beyond the fields. Trace Creek flows in on river left at 2.6 miles. Meet a rapid at the confluence of Trace Creek and the Harpeth River. Shoals continue as you make the Bells Bend. At 3 miles, pass directly under the bluff seen earlier in the curve. It's a tan overhanging promontory topped with craggy cedars. The rocky arid ecosystem contrasts with the lush riparian zone through which you paddle.

Bluffs continue throughout the rest of Bells Bend as the Harpeth cuts an ever-deeper valley trying to meet the Cumberland River. Pass another impressive bluff at

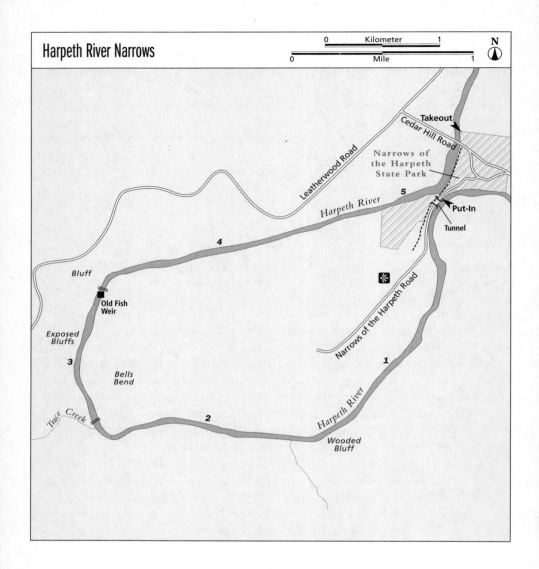

0   Kilometer   1

0   Mile   1

N

Takeout

Cedar Hill Road

Leatherwood Road

Narrows of
the Harpeth
State Park

Harpeth River

5

Put-In

Tunnel

4

Bluff

Old Fish
Weir

Narrows of the Harpeth Road

Exposed
Bluffs

3

Bells
Bend

1

Trace Creek

2

Harpeth River

Wooded
Bluff

3.4 miles. The Harpeth speeds below this outcrop and down a shoal that is perhaps an old Indian fish trap. Note the obvious V shape of the rapid rocks. This is your biggest drop of the paddle. The river is now swinging northeasterly, aiming for the endpoint. The pattern of a pool and shoal keeps the boat moving.

At 5 miles, reach the Narrows and the outflow of the tunnel. It is not immediately visible at lower water levels. You will have to park your boat and walk a trail to the mouth of the tunnel. At higher water levels you can paddle over to the outflow. An island forms—a result of the tunnel outflow. Tall cottonwoods thrive in this area. The Harris Street Bridge shortly comes into view. Pass under the bridge and reach a gravel bar dead ahead. The takeout is on the gravel bar, which is accessible by auto from the takeout parking area.

HIKING THE NARROWS OF HARPETH

This state historic area, part of the greater Harpeth River State Park, is a lesser-known gem of the Tennessee state park system. Here, visitors can not only float the Harpeth River but also hike its trails, including trails that connect the takeout to the put-in. Back in the early 1800s, as Montgomery Bell developed the iron ore industry in Middle Tennessee, he searched for a place to build a water-powered mill. He noticed the location where the Harpeth River made such a bend it nearly doubled back on itself, separated only by a tall bluff a mere 200 feet in width. In those 5 miles, the Harpeth dropped 15 feet. It was here that Bell saw the chance to harness waterpower for his iron ore industry by diverting water from the river through a tunnel—if he could cut through that bluff.

Using slave labor, Bell started the project in 1819, boring an 8 foot high, 16 foot wide, 290-foot tunnel through the limestone bluff. Just think of the skill and fortitude needed to complete such a project using the tools available then! The ironworks, known as Patterson Forge, around the Narrows are long gone, but water still flows through the tunnel.

Start your hike at the takeout parking area, heading upstream to pass under the Harris Street Bridge. Hike upstream above the Harpeth in a cedar, oak, and maple wood. Beard cane crowds the understory. Look out on the river, where turtles may be lazing in the sun on logs. Soon come to a rocky ravine. Uphill to the left is a small rock house. Ahead, traverse the base of a bluffline with many small rock houses. Shortly reach a gap and trail junction at 0.4 mile. To your left, one trail leads a short distance to the canoe put-in. Another trail heads to the Narrows overlook. A third trail leads right, downhill on an old wagon road toward the tunnel. Turn right and descend on the old wagon road into a flat where huge eastern cottonwoods and sycamores tower over lush underbrush. Soon reach the pool created by the outflow from Montgomery Bell's tunnel. This is a popular fishing hole. You can peer into the tunnel and appreciate the hard work it took to make it.

Backtrack to the previous trail junction, heading uphill to the overlook. Several wooden steps take you to the blufftop, traveling among shortleaf pine and cedar to a clear overlook 0.3 mile distant. Here, look down on the Harpeth River and the farm and hill country through which it flows. For more information about the state historic area, visit www.tnstateparks .com.

19 Harpeth River near Kingston Springs

This pleasant float on the Harpeth State Scenic River utilizes accesses of the greater Harpeth River State Park, a multiparcel recreation destination for hikers and paddlers alike.

County: Cheatham
Start: Kingston Springs, N36° 6.36', W87° 6.243'
End: Gossett Tract off Cedar Hill Road, N36° 8.101', W87° 6.42'
Length: 6.4 miles
Float time: 3 hours
Difficulty rating: Easy to moderate
Rapids: Class I
River type: Pastoral river
Current: Moderate
River gradient: 2.9 feet per mile
River gauge: USGS Harpeth River near Kingston Springs, TN, minimum runnable level 120 cfs

Season: Year-round
Land status: Public—Harpeth River State Park, private also
Fees or permits: No fees or permits required
Nearest city/town: Kingston Springs
Maps: USGS: Kingston Springs, White Bluff, Lillamay, Harpeth Valley; *DeLorme: Tennessee Atlas & Gazetteer,* Page 52 C3
Boats used: Canoes, kayaks
Organizations: Harpeth River Watershed Association, P.O. Box 1127, Franklin 37065, (615) 790-9767, www.harpethriver.org
Contacts/outfitters: Tip A Canoe, 1279 Hwy. 70, Kingston Springs 37082, (800) 550-5810, www.tip-a-canoe.com

Put-in/Takeout Information

To takeout: From exit 188 on I-40 west of Nashville, take TN 249 north and follow it 2.3 miles to a T intersection with US 70. Turn left, heading west on US 70 for 2.3 miles to Cedar Hill Road. Turn right on Cedar Hill Road and follow it 0.8 mile to the left turn into the signed Gossett Tract of Harpeth River State Park. Once in the tract, veer right to the boat launch. Take note that the parking is located away from the launch area.

To put-in from takeout: Backtrack on Cedar Hill Road to US 70. Turn left and take US 70 east and drive for 0.5 mile to Pinnacle Hill Road. Turn right on Pinnacle Hill Road and follow it for 1.8 miles, then turn right into Kingston Springs City Park. Finally look left for the gate and boat launch, which is part of Harpeth River State Park.

Paddle Summary

This section of the Harpeth River is part of the Lower Harpeth Blueway, an established paddling trail with many put-ins and takeouts that are part of Harpeth River State Park. The state park comprises several different parcels of land located along the Harpeth, a state scenic river. The put-in and takeout for this paddle are both on state

Bluffs like this add beauty to the Lower Harpeth River Blueway.

park lands, including the newer Gossett Tract. This section of the river is fairly user friendly—I have walked the shuttle. Also, several outfitters are located in the vicinity should you want a pay shuttle or boat rental. The float leaves Kingston Springs and begins curving past bluffs as mild shoals bordered by river grasses push you deeper into the Harpeth River Valley. The waterway makes a very deep bend, then passes under US 70. From here the Harpeth makes yet another big bend and enters the Gossett Tract, a designated state natural area. The paddle ends at a large limestone outcrop forming a natural dock. Steps lead away from the dock to the auto-accessible area of the Gossett Tract. When at the takeout, make sure to physically look at the takeout point. The rock slab isn't immediately evident as a takeout, especially compared to concrete boat ramps or spots located adjacent to bridges. The shoals here are primarily Class I, with a few pushing Class I+. Alluring tan gravel bars are located inside bends, while bluffs border hilly sections. Meadows extend away from the river and flatter areas, beyond the screen of trees that lined the Harpeth.

River Overview

The Harpeth State Scenic River begins in southwest Rutherford County, only to enter Williamson County before it gains any real steam. It continues into the heart of fast-growing Franklin. The West Harpeth joins the main waterway before it flows into the Bellevue area of Davidson County. Ahead lays Cheatham County. Here the Harpeth's numerous bends become more pronounced and the river cuts a course back in time. This is where the bulk of Harpeth River State Park's numerous holdings are, including Mound Bottom, an ancient Indian town site. Petroglyphs can be found at Mace Bluff. Then comes the Narrows of Harpeth. As it curves toward the Cumberland River, paddlers enter the most remote stretches of waterway left. It finally reaches Cheatham Reservoir and an Army Corps of Engineers campground that makes for a good final takeout. The upper stretches of the Harpeth, from Franklin to the confluence with the West Harpeth, and the West Harpeth itself offer 20 or so paddleable miles during winter and spring. Below the confluence of the streams, the main Harpeth becomes paddleable most of the year. It is about 60 miles from the confluence to the mouth of the Cumberland River, though it takes the South Fork Harpeth's flow, in Cheatham County, to make the main stem paddleable year-round. The most popular stretches begin in this area around Kingston Springs, where outfitters are stationed. Stay tuned as river accesses continue to multiply and the Harpeth River Blueway is developed.

The Paddling

Steps lead to the river and canoe launch, set just below the bridge leading into the town of Kingston Springs. Immediately drift into a Class I, grass-lined riffle typical of the Harpeth River. The waterway narrows at these shoals, then widens out again in the slower sections. These variations stretch from 40 to 120 feet along this paddle. Burns Park is on river left, keeping the river natural. However, the corridor here stays natural throughout most of the paddle. River birch, sycamore, and willows border the greenish-clear water flowing over a rocky bed. Beech trees, maple ash, and cane also find a place along the shoreline. Fallen trees occupy the river's edge but generally don't pose an obstacle. The river is generally too wide for a continuous canopy, but live trees often overhang the waterway, providing shade for the shoreline paddler.

At 0.2 mile, a gently sloping gravel bar extends into the water and offers a chance for you to pull over and get organized in your boat. It isn't long before a hallmark tan bluff rises from the water's edge. These sentinels of craggy repose where cedars cling precariously to the cliff's edge rise as much as 200 feet above you. This one comes on river right at 0.4 mile as the Harpeth makes a bend to the left, now heading southwest. Gravel bars continue to be ample for stopping. River distance is easy to calculate as mile markers—set in 0.5-mile increments—are nailed to riverside trees. The river mileage is noted in descending order, counting down the distance to the confluence of the Harpeth River and the Cumberland River, west of Ashland City.

At 0.9 mile the Ashland City water discharge flows in on river left. The free-flowing Harpeth River is subject to rainfall for its paddleability, but this section is generally doable year-round except during periods of drought. You may have to pull your boat over a shoal or two in late summer or early fall. However, this section is

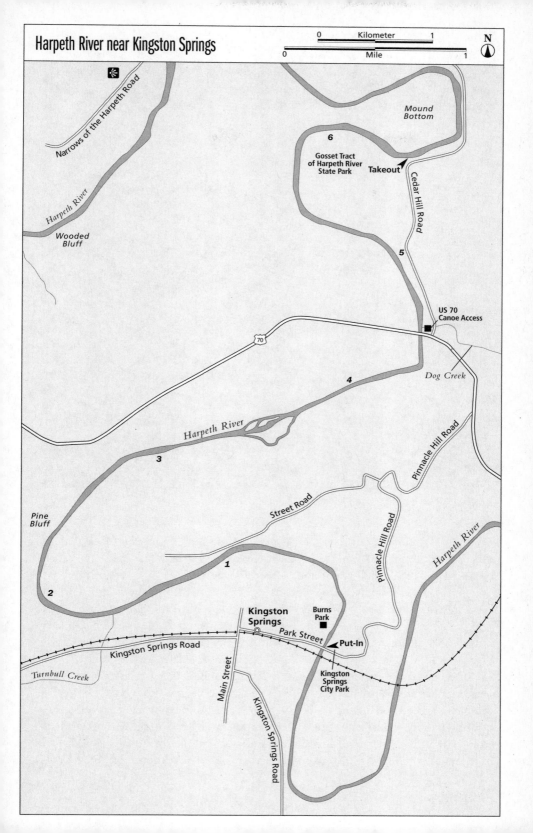

Harpeth River near Kingston Springs

0 Kilometer 1

0 Mile 1

N

Narrows of the Harpeth Road

Mound Bottom

6

Gosset Tract of Harpeth River State Park

Takeout

Cedar Hill Road

Harpeth River

Wooded Bluff

5

US 70 Canoe Access

70

Dog Creek

4

Harpeth River

3

Pine Bluff

Street Road

Pinnacle Hill Road

Pinnacle Hill Road

1

Harpeth River

2

Kingston Springs

Burns Park

Put-In

Park Street

Kingston Springs Road

Kingston Springs City Park

Turnbull Creek

Main Street

Kingston Springs Road

Scenic shoals such as this speed paddlers along the Harpeth.

aided by the inflow of Turnbull Creek, a springtime paddling stream that enters on river left at 1.6 miles. Its water also adds clarity to the Harpeth. Extensive gravel bars are found where Turnbull Creek and Harpeth River meet.

In shallows you will see large and flat rock slabs that form the riverbed where rocks aren't present. At 1.8 miles the waterway begins a sweeping bend to the right. A high rock rampart known as Pine Bluff stands sentinel over the Harpeth. Look up and you will see that the bluff actually overhangs the river at its apex. At 2.2 miles on river left look for a low flow waterfall spilling down a break in Pine Bluff.

An unnamed stream enters on river left at 2.7 miles. At 3.6 miles, pass by some very large partially vegetated gravel bars. The river splits into channels. Class I riffles continue to speed you downriver between slower sections. Brush can crowd the river at shoals, leaving but slender waterways for paddlers. The river sidles alongside a bluff on river right with many fallen boulders just before passing under the US 70 bridge at 4.6 miles. The US 70 state park river access is located at the bridge. Dog Creek comes in on river right just below the span. A few houses are located along the shore before the natural setting resumes.

The Harpeth slows a bit before making a final bend. At 5.4 miles, a soil bluff rises on river left with a large gravel bar on river right. The Harpeth River completes its bend, then begins heading easterly. Pass through one final riffle just before the takeout on river right at 6.4 miles. Look for a slightly sloped limestone outcrop on river right before a bend to the left.

HIDDEN LAKE—ANOTHER GEM OF HARPETH RIVER STATE PARK

This paddle uses two parcels of Harpeth River State Park. Another newer parcel—Hidden Lake—offers a hiking destination through transitioning fields before entering woodland to reach bluffs above the Harpeth River. The trail then straddles the bluffs with the Harpeth on one side and Hidden Lake on the other before looping around a wooded knob past an old abandoned resort. The Hidden Lake parcel also offers a canoe launch.

The double loop hike at Hidden Lake enters a field, following a grassy track toward Hidden Lake. A separate route heads downhill toward the Harpeth River and is a canoe/kayak access. At 0.2 mile reach a trail junction. Here, the Bluebird Loop heads right through the field. For now, keep forward into woodland, ambling on an old roadbed. At 0.4 mile the trail abruptly curves left and uses an old bridge to cross the creek along which you've been walking.

Reach a trail intersection at 0.5 mile. Stay left, heading toward Hidden Lake. Just ahead, a spur trail leads right and uphill to a small quarry pond. Watch for a high bluff on your right that is actually exposed stone from another quarry. Reach Hidden Lake at 0.7 mile. The trail ascends a rocky ridgeline dividing the Harpeth River from Hidden Lake, a large quarry pond. Reach a rock prominence offering views into Hidden Lake. You are literally walking a stacked rock spine that drops off in both directions. Finally, the trail begins circling Hidden Lake, passing a vista looking south into Hidden Lake. Watch for cactus growing in the dry rocks. At 0.8 mile, reach a four-way junction. To your far right, stone steps lead down to the water. To your right, a trail shortcuts the main loop. Keep straight, making the longest loop possible, tracing a roadbed to reach the remains of an old 1940s resort. Shortly complete the main loop and begin backtracking toward the trailhead. Reach the Bluebird Loop at 1.4 miles. Turn left here, meandering through the field near McCrory Lane before completing the loop at 1.6 miles. To reach Hidden Lake from exit 192 on I-40, take McCrory Lane north for 0.9 mile, crossing the Harpeth River, then immediately look left for the trailhead parking.

20 Cumberland River

Float on Tennessee's other big river below Old Hickory Dam. The verdant scenery and lack of use will surprise.

County: Davidson
Start: Old Hickory Dam, N36° 17.552', W86° 39.491'
End: Peeler Park, N36° 11.411', W86° 39.386'
Length: 9.8 miles
Float time: 4 hours
Difficulty rating: Easy
Rapids: Class I
River type: Dam-controlled wide river
Current: Moderate, dependent on generation schedule
River gradient: 1.4 feet per mile
River gauge: TVA Old Hickory release schedule, www.tva.com/river/lakeinfo/index—Old Hickory, check release schedule or call (865) 632-2264. Runnable year-round; best run during dam generation

Season: Year-round
Land status: Private except around put-in and takeout
Fees or permits: No fees or permits required
Nearest city/town: Hendersonville
Maps: USGS: Goodlettsville, Nashville East; *DeLorme: Tennessee Atlas and Gazetteer,* Page 53 6C
Boats used: Canoes, kayaks, johnboats, pleasure craft
Organizations: Cumberland River Compact, P.O. Box 41721, Nashville 37204, (615) 837-1151, www.cumberlandrivercompact.org
Contacts/outfitters: U.S. Army Corps of Engineers, No. 5 Power Plant Rd., Hendersonville 37075-3467, (615) 822-4846, www.lrn.usace.army.mil/op/old/rec/

Put-in/Takeout Information

To takeout: From exit 14A on Briley Parkway on the north side of Nashville, take US 31E north, Gallatin Pike, to Neely's Bend Road. Turn right on Neely's Bend Road and follow it for 6 miles to turn left into Peeler Park, then dead-end at the trailhead and a boat ramp on the Cumberland River.

To put-in from takeout: Backtrack to US 31E, Gallatin Pike, and turn right, northbound, to reach TN 45W after 0.6 mile from Neely's Bend Road. Turn right on TN 45W and follow it for 2.5 miles to bridge the Cumberland River. Keep on TN 45W for 0.1 mile farther, then turn left on Bridgeway Avenue. Follow Bridgeway Avenue for 0.1 mile, then turn left on Ensley Avenue. Follow Ensley Avenue for 0.2 mile, crossing railroad tracks and intersect Swinging Bridge Road. Turn left on Swinging Bridge Road, following it for 0.9 mile to reach Cinder Road. Turn right on Cinder Road and follow it for 0.9 mile, entering U.S. Army Corps of Engineers property. Veer left toward the Tailwater boat ramp, staying left again 0.5 mile farther to shortly reach the boat ramp.

Riverside beauty abounds along Middle Tennessee's big river.

Paddle Summary

The Cumberland River is often overlooked as a paddling destination. Most people thoughtlessly drive over it on bridges without regard to its paddling potential. However, the river can be enjoyed in many sections, even though it is dammed up as lakes in parts of the state. Other sections—like this one—have flow and are completely riverine in nature. This particular trek should appeal to Nashville area paddlers, as it has quality put-in and takeout points. Also, since the paddle starts below Old Hickory Dam, you can enjoy the push of water from power generation, easing the paddling burden. Furthermore, despite being in a populated area, the float offers a green corridor that will surprise, with its wooded banks and alluring waters that wildlife call home.

The paddle leaves the steep U.S. Army Corps of Engineers boat ramp below Old Hickory Dam. It then begins a southerly sweeping curve, flanked by occasional bluffs that border Hadley Bend. The river then passes under the TN 45 bridge. Ahead, the Cumberland offers a special treat as it divides around Hills Island. The narrow right channel offers an intimate paddling experience and an opportunity to see deer that call the island home. The river begins to border Peeler Park while making the westerly turn of Neely's Bend. The takeout is at Peeler Park. Interestingly, while

Old Hickory Lake will be packed with pleasure craft, Cumberland River below the dam will see little traffic. However, take note of the navigational buoys in the river designed to aid the nearly nonexistent barge traffic on this part of the Cumberland.

River Overview

The Cumberland River is one of Tennessee's two great waterways into which most rivers in the state flow. The other major river is the Tennessee. The Cumberland River is born in Kentucky amid steep-sided hollows where it gathers feeder branches to roar as the famous Cumberland Falls, before entering the Daniel Boone National Forest. Much of this segment is plied by Bluegrass State paddlers. Downstream, the Big South Fork of the Cumberland River, a national scenic river, adds its flow as the main Cumberland is slowed as Lake Cumberland.

The river finally enters the Volunteer State near the Tennessee town of Celina, where the dammed Obey River meets the Cumberland. From here, the Cumberland wanders westerly amid sharp and scenic hills until it is dammed as Cordell Hall Lake, near Carthage. The steep terrain keeps the Cordell Hall Lake riverine in appearance. Below Carthage the Cumberland continues west in sweeping bends into flatter terrain until it widens just east of Nashville as Old Hickory Lake. It then passes through Nashville and is slowed yet again as Cheatham Lake. Here, the river turns north and reenters the Bluegrass State as Lake Barkley, forming part of the recreation destination known as Land between the Lakes. It is here that the Cumberland connects to the Tennessee River via canal, but the Cumberland continues north to meet the Ohio River just east of Paducah. Recreational paddlers can enjoy many segments of the Cumberland including the exciting Kentucky sections above Lake Cumberland and flatwater sections at Land between the Lakes. Volunteer State paddlers will find the most pleasure in the section east of Nashville, notably the segments below dams such as this one.

The Paddling

Make sure to engage your parking brake while unloading at the bottom of the steep boat ramp. If the Corps is generating at Old Hickory Dam, the flowing water noise will be audible. The gravel shoreline at the ramp's base makes for a good loading spot. Barges will be few, but take note there is a lock at the dam. Immediately pass a couple of circular concrete structures below the ramp that straighten and stabilize barges before they enter the dam lock. Depending upon generation the water may be traveling slow or brisk. Try to time your paddle with the dam's generation, schedule. Try to ride the moving water and avoid the large eddies which form in this big river.

The Cumberland is at least 200 feet wide here. Hang along one shore or another. That way you can observe the natural setting along the bank as well as avoid any big boats and block winds which can be troublesome on bigger waters. The water is normally clear with a greenish tint. It tends to stay clearer since it is coming directly from

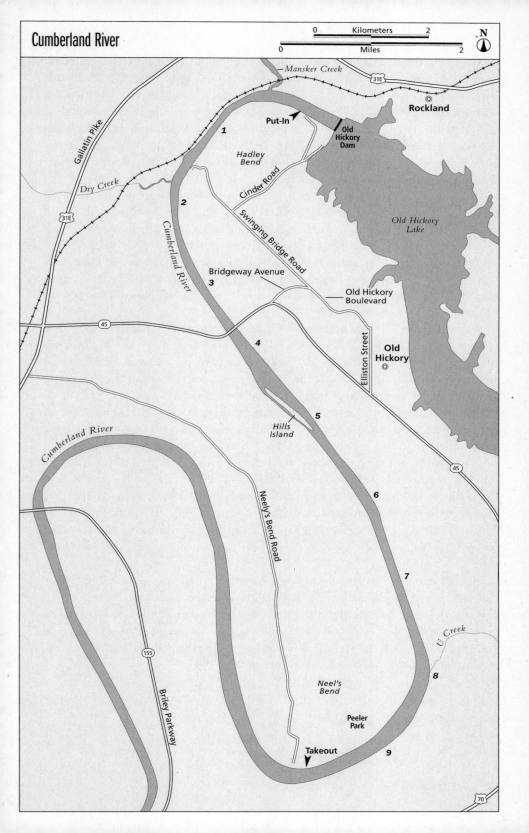

Cumberland River

0 — Kilometers — 2
0 — Miles — 2

N

Mansker Creek

31E

Rockland

Put-In

Old Hickory Dam

Gallatin Pike

1

Hadley Bend

Dry Creek

Cinder Road

Old Hickory Lake

31E

2

Cumberland River

Swinging Bridge Road

Bridgeway Avenue

3

Old Hickory Boulevard

45

4

Elliston Street

Old Hickory

Hills Island

5

Cumberland River

Neely's Bend Road

6

45

7

U Creek

155

8

Neel's Bend

Briley Parkway

Peeler Park

9

Takeout

70

the dam base. Rocks line the shore in most places—some are natural and some have been placed here by the Corps to prevent erosion from commercial river traffic that has never materialized. The red and green navigational buoys are here for the same reason. Other bank areas may be sand or mud and some limestone bluffs characteristic of Middle Tennessee. Thick wood of maple ash, willow, and sycamore, and thick brush rise from the water. Emerald ranks of oak and hickory stand atop the higher shores. Mansker Creek flows in on river right just a short distance into the paddle. It divides Davidson County from Sumner County.

The Cumberland begins its southerly turn of Hadley Bend. Since this is a big waterway, its turns are big as well. CSXT Railroad runs atop the right bank. At 1.8 miles Dry Creek comes in on your right and forms an embayment. You'll be surprised at the wild nature of the immediate river corridor even while the sounds of civilization drift over the water. Herons will be lurking on the shoreline; kingfishers will dart over the waterway as well. Other urban and suburban wildlife finds refuge here. Watch for springs seeps crowded with ferns along the blufflines, even as you see cell towers and power lines.

Pass under the TN 45W bridge at 3.7 miles. It is actually two distinct bridges, one old and one new. The pillars of the old bridge are of cut stone blocks, while the newer bridge is of concrete. Notice the decorative stone gates on the older bridge, which you will pass under first. Contrast the simple appearance of today's structures versus the more ornate way of doing things in days gone by.

The bluff accompanying you on river right finally gives way at 3.9 miles. Stay on river right to reach Hills Island at 4.3 miles. Take the slender channel to enjoy some intimate scenery astride the heavily wooded isle. The 60-foot-wide strait has plenty of deadfall and no rock on its shore, since the Corps didn't consider this a navigation channel. Look for large cottonwood trees on Hills Island, as well as deer. Rejoin the main river at 5.1 miles, and you will see a housing development on river left. However, the shoreline soon resumes its wooded nature. The curve of Neely's Bend becomes visible in the distance. Pass U Creek and an old private boat ramp on river left at 8.1 miles. Also, look for an unidentifiable abandoned structure rising from the river just downstream.

A bluff rises on river left as you begin curving to the right, westerly. This cedar- and oak-capped bluff is cut by occasional streams but also rises in excess of 150 feet. Peeler Park begins on river right. When you see the bluff receding and old cut block on the left shore, shift over to the right bank quickly to reach the takeout and boat ramp at Peeler Park at 9.8 miles. If in doubt, get to right-hand shore early, as the current in the Cumberland River can be quite strong.

TAKE A WALK ALONG THE CUMBERLAND

In addition to your paddle, you can also hike the 2.8-mile Peeler Park Greenway, located at the takeout. This hike is more proof that Nashville is once again turning to the Cumberland River, the reason for its location in the first place. The city first acquired the park property in 1963 from a farmer by the name of E. N. Peeler. The city held on to the land and subsequently bought the adjacent property of Sun Valley Swim Club in 1969, leasing out the plot for farming. More than a generation passed before the city began to develop the park and open it for use. Luckily for us paddlers the city built a boat ramp in addition to the asphalt path that traverses through a green area of fields and woods along the Cumberland.

Trail users will be greeted with a first-rate trailhead, complete with a shaded gazebo, metal benches, and a color map of Peeler Park. Join the asphalt track as it heads upstream on Cumberland. A line of thick trees, cane, and brush divide you from the water about 40 feet below. Travel under an open sky, walking the nexus between field and forest. Occasional spur paths lead to clearings overlooking the Cumberland. After 0.25 mile reach a park-built path leading to the river. The Stones River Greenway runs across the Cumberland. The Peeler Park Greenway turns away from the river at 0.6 mile, now drifting into woodland bordering a tributary. Shortly reach the loop portion of your hike and enter canopied woods. The path is forced back toward the river as it nears the 273-acre park's edge. The wetland boardwalk is just ahead, reaching a linear wetland, a mini-bayou that could be Louisiana. This swamp may have been part of the old Cumberland River channel, an overflow stream, or a dug area to drain the adjacent floodplain for crops. Trees grow directly from the water, standing on widely buttressed trunks. Complete the loop portion of the hike at 1.9 miles and backtrack to the trailhead.

21   Stones River below Percy Priest Dam

This year-round run in greater Nashville offers a scenic float in a surprisingly relaxed and scenic setting.

County: Davidson
Start: Percy Priest Dam, N36° 9.495', W86° 37.202'
End: Peeler Park on the Cumberland River, N36° 11.6419', W86° 39.6568'
Length: 7.1 miles
Float time: 3 hours
Difficulty rating: Easy
Rapids: Class I
River type: Dam-controlled coldwater river
Current: Moderate to swift
River gradient: 1.7 feet per mile
River gauge: Call (615) 883-2351 for Percy Priest Dam generation schedule, or on web at www.lrn.usace.army.mil/pao/lakeinfo/JPP.htm, scroll down to generation schedule

Season: Year-round
Land status: Public—Army Corps of Engineers and private
Fees or permits: No fees or permits required
Nearest city/town: Donelson
Maps: USGS: Hermitage, Nashville East; *DeLorme: Tennessee Atlas and Gazetteer,* Page 53 C6
Boats used: Canoes, kayaks, johnboats
Organizations: Cumberland River Compact, P.O. Box 41721, Nashville 37204, (615) 837-1151, www.cumberlandrivercompact.org
Contacts/outfitters: U.S. Army Corps of Engineers, Resource Manager's Office, 3737 Bell Rd., Nashville 37214, (615) 889-1975, www.orn.usace.army.mil/op/JPP/rec/

Put-in/Takeout Information

To takeout: From exit 14A on Briley Parkway on the north side of Nashville, take Gallatin/Madison/US 31E north to Neely's Bend Road. Turn right on Neely's Bend Road and follow it for 6 miles to turn left into Peeler Park, then dead-end at the trailhead and a boat ramp on the Cumberland River.

To put-in from takeout: Backtrack to Briley Parkway, then take it southbound to exit 214 on I-40. Take I-40 east to exit 219. From I-40 take Stewarts Ferry Pike south for 0.2 mile to Bell Road. Turn left on Bell Road and follow it to an intersection. The right turn is to the Percy Priest Lake Visitor Center. Take the left turn at this intersection, dropping down to a large level area below the dam.

Paddle Summary

This is a surprisingly underutilized paddle in the heart of metro Nashville. Flowing from Percy Priest Dam, the Stones River travels cold, clear—and swift when the dam is generating—through an area that offers more natural scenery than you would ever guess if you hadn't paddled it. The waterway travels northwesterly, then makes a series of two huge bends, traveling past streams, bluffs, bottoms, and parks, ultimately making its way to the Cumberland River. Here you must paddle upstream and against

Paddlers may see hikers on the Stones River Greenway river bluff bridge.

the current on the Cumberland River a short and doable distance to make a boat ramp located on the north side of the river at Peeler Park. Since the Stones is dam controlled, you can float it at any time of year, whether generation is occurring or not. Interestingly, the Stones River Greenway travels along much of the bank before turning away and returning to meet the Stones River at its confluence with the Cumberland River, availing a potential shuttle using your feet or a bicycle.

River Overview

The lower Stones River flows free only the length of this paddle, from Percy Priest Dam to the Cumberland River. The rest of the main body of the river has been submerged beneath Percy Priest Lake. The forks of the Stones River drain Cannon County and Rutherford County before entering Davidson County as the main Stones River. Percy Priest Lake is 42 miles long and has 213 miles of curving shoreline. Average lake depth is 29 feet. This engineering project was initiated after World War II as part of the Flood Control Act of 1946. Dam construction began in 1963 and took five years. The purpose of the lake is to control flooding on the Cumberland River, generate hydropower, and provide public recreation.

The placid waters of the lower Stones reflect riverside vegetation.

The Paddling

There is no designated boat ramp, so you can carry your craft to the water's edge. Avoid the rock riprap and look for a concreted area that extends down to the water. You are required to have your life vest on in the water this close to the dam. Begin drifting down the ultraclear waters and slip under roaring I-40. The Stones River Greenway is also beginning its journey to the Cumberland River on the left bank. The Stones extends around 120 feet bank to bank, and it is chilly to the touch. A low bluff rises just downstream of the I-40 bridges on river right. If bluffs aren't present, banks rise from 5 to 20 feet and are covered in soil or brush. Sycamore shades the shore. Oaks and cedars stand uphill from the banks. Herons and other bird life will be seen in this corridor of nature.

The roar of I-40 fades. A gas line clearing crosses the river at 0.7 mile. At 0.9 mile McCrory Creek comes in on your left. It is wide and slow—and attractive. You can

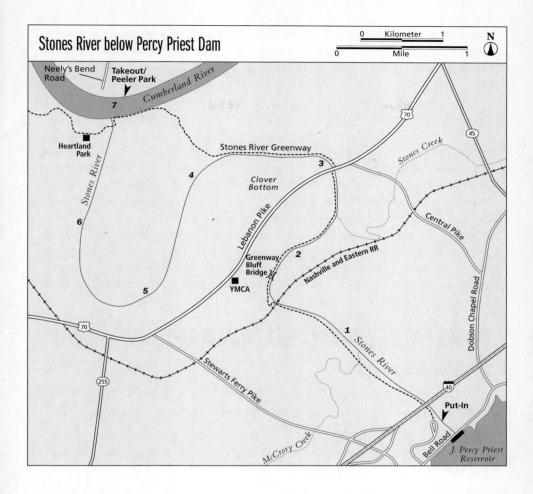

Stones River below Percy Priest Dam

paddle up a ways to see the greenway bridge spanning it. An old river gauging station is situated on the left bank just below the confluence with McCrory Creek. At 1.5 miles, pass old cut stone bridge pilings in the Stones. Note the cedar tree growing atop the pillar. Pass under the Nashville & Eastern Railroad bridge just below here.

The northwest river course is altered at a bluff and bends northeast at 1.7 miles. By this time you have probably seen joggers, bicyclers, and mothers with strollers along the Stones River Greenway. Houses and apartments were built atop this bluff, and the greenway was very difficult to integrate here. The city of Nashville built a bridge running along the bluff and above the river. Unlike other bridges, it doesn't cross a river but simply runs along the bluff before returning to more conventional banks.

Flats extend on both sides of the river. At 2.5 miles, Stones Creek comes in on your right. A small terraced bluff at the confluence of Stones Creek and Stones River makes for a good stopping spot. Pass under the Lebanon Pike/US 70 bridge at 2.8 miles. The old Lebanon Pike/US 70 bridge is now part of the Stones River

Greenway, which is now on the right-hand bank heading downstream. There is yet another abandoned bridge abutment below these two bridges. This short segment provides a study in the evolution of bridge building if you are interested in such things.

Turn west in bottomland while working around what was once known as Clover Bottom. At 3.9 miles, curve south as a big bluff rises on river right. Begin a second large bend at 5.0 miles, where a bluff rises on river left, the height of which is known as Todd Knob, reaching 360 feet above the Stones. The river widens as the bluffs recede. Heartland Park lies on your left as you pass under the Stones River Greenway Bridge at 6.8 miles. This is a potential takeout if you can carry your boat along the greenway to the Heartland Park trailhead. Ahead, the Cumberland River comes in sight. Slip over to the right-hand bank of the Stones and take a break to rest your arms before the crossing. Once at the Cumberland River, take note of the boat ramp at Peeler Park. This is your takeout. Turn upstream along the right-hand bank bordering a low rock bluff on the Cumberland. Try to get upstream of the boat ramp before you begin the crossing, look for motorboat and barge traffic, then make your dash to arrive at the boat ramp at 7.1 miles.

STONES RIVER GREENWAY OFFERS WALKING/PEDALING SHUTTLE POSSIBILITIES

The Stones River Greenway parallels much of this paddle, offering a two-for-one recreation experience and potential car-less shuttle. Both start in the same spot below Percy Priest Dam. The track, about 8 feet wide and paved, heads away from the dam then bridges McCrory Creek, a beautiful blue stream that still exemplifies the coloration of many creeks in Middle Tennessee. The trail also opens to fields.

The greenway passes under a railroad bridge before climbing a bluff astride the Stones. A highlight of the greenway is ahead as it works downstream along a bridge that runs parallel to the river bluffs—not across the river. From this bridge, walkers can gain great views up and down the Stones. Flood-proof pilings were sunk into the river's edge and the bridge built upon them directly beside bluffs. This cost a lot of money, so enjoy it.

The greenway keeps near the Stones, passing Lebanon Pike, then continues onward to border the Cumberland River near its confluence with the Stones at Heartland Park, where there is a trailhead. Unfortunately, no developed water access is on the Stones, but you could carry your boat from the river to the parking area and walk/ride back to the put-in, then pick up your boat. Check the carry distance from the river to the nearest parking area before you try this. For more information about the Stones River Greenway visit www.nashville.org /greenways.

22 East Fork Stones River

This paddle flows through public lands near Percy Priest Lake, providing a natural experience near Murfreesboro.

County: Rutherford
Start: Walterhill Dam, N35° 56.533', W86° 22.609'
End: Mona Boat Ramp, N35° 58.729', W86° 25.142'
Length: 5.8 miles
Float time: 3.5 hours
Difficulty rating: Moderate
Rapids: Class I
River type: Pastoral river with occasional shoals, partially dam affected
Current: Moderate
River gradient: 3.9 feet per mile
River gauge: West Fork Stones River at Murfreesboro, TN, minimum runnable level 160 cfs

Season: Late winter, spring, early summer
Land status: Public—U.S. Army Corps of Engineers
Fees or permits: No fees or permits required
Nearest city/town: Murfreesboro
Maps: USGS: Walterhill; *DeLorme: Tennessee Atlas and Gazetteer,* Page 39 A2
Boats used: Canoes, kayaks, johnboats
Organizations: Stones River Watershed Association, P.O. Box 2336, Murfreesboro 37133, www.stoneswatershed.org
Contacts/outfitters: U.S. Army Corps of Engineers, Nashville District, P.O. Box 1070, Nashville 37202-1070, (615) 736-7161, www.lrn.usace.army.mil/op/jpp/rec/

Put-in/Takeout Information

To takeout: From exit 61 on TN 840 north of Murfreesboro, take Jefferson Pike, TN 266, north for 1.7 miles to the right turn for the U.S. Army Corps of Engineers Mona boat ramp and the takeout. Be careful as this right turn comes quick. Alternate directions: From exit 238 on I-40, take US 231 south for 17.3 miles to TN 266, Jefferson Pike. Turn right on TN 266 and follow it westerly for 3 miles to the left turn to the Mona boat ramp.

To put-in from takeout: Return to Jefferson Pike, TN 266, and travel east for 3 miles to US 231, Lebanon Pike. Turn right on Lebanon Pike and follow it south for 0.5 mile, crossing the East Fork Stones River to turn left into Walterhill Park. Enter the park and put-in below at the gravel bar below the dam.

Paddle Summary

This run is quite scenic despite growth pressures from greater Nashville and Murfreesboro. Close enough to Percy Priest Lake to lie within the Army Corps of Engineers lake property boundaries, this lower run on the East Fork offers a natural wooded corridor through which the green-clear river flows over moderate shoals and easy riffles between slow pools. Occasional bluffs rise on one shore or the other, while unnamed feeder branches cut small tributary valleys.

Sycamores line the East Fork Stones River.

The shuttle is short and easy. Quick access off TN 840 makes this an easy spur-of-the-moment run for Music City residents. Be apprised the USGS gauge is for *West Fork Stones River* and therefore isn't perfectly accurate but will aid in determining paddleability. Other sections of the East Fork have old mill dams along them, both slowing the waters and forcing portages. Also, this is the lowest section of the river, which extends its paddling season the longest.

River Overview

Part of the Cumberland River watershed, the East Fork Stones River drains the hills of eastern Cannon County and wanders westerly into Rutherford County before meeting the Middle Fork and West Fork Stones River under the waters of Percy Priest Lake. Born where spring branches flowing off Short Mountain come together just east of the county seat of Woodbury, the East Fork becomes paddleable near the town of Readyville, at the Cannon-Rutherford county line. Here, Brawley's Fork joins East Fork Stones River. An old mill dam at Readyville slows the waters. Other mill dams stretch across the river as it rambles northwesterly. Use caution around the

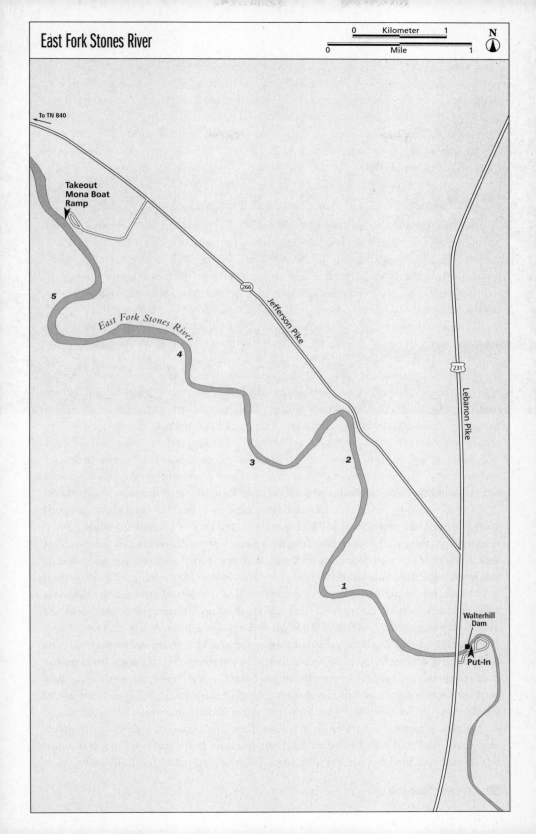

East Fork Stones River

0   Kilometer   1

0   Mile   1

N

To TN 840

Takeout
Mona Boat
Ramp

266

Jefferson Pike

East Fork Stones River

231

Lebanon Pike

5

4

3

2

1

Walterhill
Dam

Put-In

dams when portaging. Some of them have been breached and form challenging and perhaps dangerous rapids at high flows. Cripple Creek is a major tributary coming in from the south. Bradley Creek comes in just before the East Fork Stones River flows under the TN 96 bridge. The waters are slowed again at Walterhill Dam, just above the put-in for this paddle. The East Fork flows free until the influence of Percy Priest Lake is felt on the lower end of this paddle. All told, the East Fork offers 30 miles of paddling from Readyville to Percy Priest Lake.

The Paddling

A large tan gravel bar forms below Walterhill Dam. Anglers and sightseers will gather at this gravel bar, which makes for a good staging area. The East Fork loudly spills over the 15-foot-high concrete structure. A lively shoal pushes you downstream while passing under the US 231 bridge. The waterway, about 50 feet wide, is lined with stones and overhanging sycamores. Some of the older sycamores have massive contorted trunks, shaped from past floods. Maple, ash, and buckeye shade the shore as well. The banks generally range from 4 to 20 feet high and higher where stone bluffs ascend directly from the shore. Hills generally stand on one side of the stream or the other. The greenish waters speed over Class I riffles without noteworthy singular drops. White mussel shells color the tan gravel as you float through the riffles. At 0.4 mile, an unnamed stream comes in on the south, spilling over a rock slab just before reaching the river. Look for a cave spring coming in on river left just downstream from the unnamed stream. The first significant riverside bluff rises at 0.8 mile on river right. Cedars gain purchase where roots grasp breaks in the vertical walls. Large boulders, fallen from the bluffs into the river, stand still in the stream, forcing the water and paddlers to work around them. At 1.0 mile, the East Fork splits around an island. At 1.7 miles, pass a riverside flat rock shelf that is characteristic of the open rock glades that are common in this area. Cedars of Lebanon State Park harbors many such preserved glades. The river flows within earshot of TN 266 at 2.2 miles. Here, another unnamed feeder branch flows into the East Fork from a culvert. The river makes a sharp bend to the southwest and a bluff rises on river right. Here, you can take a break either on a gravel bar or a rock shelf.

The East Fork divides around another island at 3.2 miles. Depending upon the level of Percy Priest Lake, the current may be slowing. The river has widened also, making it more subject to winds. Another unnamed stream comes in on the right at 3.5 miles. The East Fork continues its westerly journey as another stream comes in on river left at 4.4 miles. A sheer stone bluff rises on river right at 5.3 miles. This vertical stone wall stands about 40 feet and is topped with cedars. Stay with the right-hand bank as you may begin to see shore fishermen near Mona boat ramp, which you reach at 5.8 miles.

CEDAR GLADES

For residents of Middle Tennessee, especially southeast of Nashville, cedar glades may seem a dime a dozen. A town called Gladeville lies in the East Fork drainage. However, when you view cedar glades and barrens from a global perspective, these plant communities are extremely rare and occur nowhere else on the planet. Cedars of Lebanon State Park and Cedars of Lebanon State Forest, just north of here, contain some of the largest intact glades. Other places, such as Vestas Glade and Flat Rock, are intact cedar glade preserves. Working in conjunction with the Tennessee State Natural Areas Program, The Nature Conservancy played a large role in protecting these glades, botanically known as a limestone outcrop glade. Barren in appearance, this habitat is home to very rare plants. One flower in particular, Pyne's ground plum, is found here and only three other known sites in the world. Pyne's ground plum was once thought extinct. Within these preserves are other rare plants, such as purple prairie clover and the sunny bell lily. As with other landscapes of this type, sinks, caves, and water seeps dot the seemingly dry landscape. This underground flow of water plays a large role in shaping the plants and animals that thrive in this harsh-looking country. Aboveground, wet-weather washes harbor endangered plant species such as Boykin's milkwort.

The Nature Conservancy invested in these sites not only because of Pyne's ground plum and the other rare plants but also because man had minimally impacted the sites. There is evidence of past use, but it doesn't detract from the beauty. At first glance, the glades resemble a parking lot grown over with weeds. But these "weeds" are actually some of the life that is so rare in this rare habitat. The flowers that grow in this barren area are best observed from mid-August to mid-September. Other alluring wildflower displays are from mid-April through mid-May. Wildflowers or no, the East Fork watershed is home to some of Tennessee's—and the world's—rarest plants.

23 Caney Fork River

This is a classic tailwater paddle, beginning below Center Hill Dam. Here, the waters of the impounded Caney Fork River are released and continue their journey toward the Cumberland River.

County: Dekalb, Smith, Putnam
Start: Center Hill Dam, N36° 6.024', W85° 49.731'
End: Betty's Island, N36° 8.835', W85° 50.287'
Length: 8.9 miles
Float time: 3.5 hours
Difficulty rating: Easy
Rapids: Class I
River type: Dam-controlled tailwater river
Current: Moderate to fast when dam is releasing
River gradient: 1.4 feet per mile
River gauge: TVA water release schedule, call (800) 238-2264, then select 4-37-# to get the release schedule for Center Hill Dam. Or

visit www.tva.com. Minimum water release at all times is 250 cfs.
Season: Year-round
Land status: Public below dam and at take-outs, otherwise private
Fees or permits: No fees or permits required
Nearest city/town: Gordonsville
Maps: USGS: Center Hill Dam, Buffalo Valley; *DeLorme: Tennessee Atlas & Gazetteer,* Page 55 C6
Boats used: Canoes, johnboats, kayaks, dories
Organizations: Caney Fork Watershed Association, P.O. Box 165, Cookeville 38503, www.cfwa-tn.org
Contacts/outfitters: Caney Fork Canoe, Big Rock 37023, (931) 858-0967

Put-in/Takeout Information

To takeout: From I-40 exit 268, Buffalo Valley, take TN 96 north for 1.7 miles, then turn left on St. Marys Road. Follow St. Marys Road for 4.1 miles then turn left into the Betty's Island access area. Follow the road until it drops onto gravel, but be careful by the water, as you may be stuck.

To put-in from takeout: Backtrack to exit 268 on I-40, and this time take TN 96 *south* for 3.7 miles to an intersection with TN 141, passing Edgar Evins State Park on your left. Continue forward on TN 96 for 0.2 mile farther, then veer right at the sign for Center Hill Dam Resource Manager's office. When the road splits again, follow the sign for Buffalo Valley to reach a put-in below Center Hill Dam.

Paddle Summary

The river offers different looks and flows depending upon whether TVA is generating. When TVA isn't generating the current is gentle. You will see moss covering rocks and downed trees above the water. Grassy gravel bars are exposed as well. The Caney Fork will be but a few feet deep with many scattered shallows. Rapids during this time will be fast riffles. However, when the generators are running, high water

Anglers and paddlers enjoy a summer afternoon on the Caney Fork.

covers the riverbed rocks and trees, and paddlers ride the swift deep river unimpeded. Despite the fast water, the level of difficulty is still Class I. The shoreline is wooded almost the entire way, and houses are few. The riverside scenery, a valley full of green meadows with wooded hills rising in the distance, is classic Tennessee. The Caney Fork offers fishing for brook, rainbow, and brown trout. After finding out the generation schedule, you may want to consider a paddle that starts before the generation and ends after generation, paddling for a while, then letting the river do the work for you. However, in spring, generation may continuously occur for weeks on end, pushing the winter rains downstream.

River Overview

The Caney Fork begins high on the western reaches of the Cumberland Plateau, near the town of Crossville in Cumberland County. The young river meanders west into White County, where it cuts a canyon through Scotts Gulf, a preserved Tennessee natural area. Leaving the canyon of Scotts Gulf, the river flows westerly before it is dammed up as Great Falls Lake at Rock Island State Park, a fine recreation destination and an early hydroelectric power plant. Below here, the river turns north before being dammed again, as part of Center Hill Lake, a gorgeous impoundment with steep hills, islands, and scenic recreation opportunities. The river flows free again its last 28 miles, including the section described here, until it meets the Cumberland River near the town of Carthage. This is the most popular section of river for paddlers, though sea kayakers sometimes ply Center Hill Lake and camp on the scattered islands. A few whitewater wildmen can be found during winter and spring flows doing some upper sections around the White-Cumberland county line where river gradients reach 80 feet per mile!

The Paddling

Center Hill Dam looms large above the put-in, a gravel bar/ramp that can be busy on weekends. You will immediately feel the chilly 52-degree year-round water, which cools summer breezes. A mandated 250 cfs minimum river flow ensures year-round floatable water. Anglers outnumber paddlers on weekends, vying for stocked tailwater trout. Be prepared to work your way around fishermen in the shallows when TVA is not generating. The Caney Fork is from 140 to 160 feet wide, bordered by sycamore and river birch. The lower trunks of standing trees are stained from the frequent inundation during generation cycles.

A shoreline angler area is on river right, and anglers will also be perched on river left, dropping down from Long Branch Recreation Area. Just downstream from the angler activity, on river right, reach the first of many bluffs on the river. At 1.5 miles, the river is soon forced right as it runs up against an incredibly steep wooded hill on river left. From this point on out, hills rise on one side of the Caney Fork or the other, making for a scenic backdrop above crystalline fishing holes.

The Caney Fork narrows and shoots past a sycamore-covered island. More islands lie downstream. You won't be able to tell they are islands, unless TVA is generating, as at lower flows the river generally goes around one island channel or another. Small islands can be found at the 2.9-mile mark. At 3.2 miles, the Caney Fork River makes a sharp right, turning easterly, after running into another high bluff. There's an alluring gravel bar here when not generating. Pass another island at 3.8 miles. Look for yet another sharp rising bluff on river right.

The river goes on a long straightaway beyond that last bluff. More islands are ahead. You'll know when you get close to Happy Hollow boat ramp by the weekend anglers standing in the water if they're not generating, and/or boats debarking the river, at 5.4 miles. The crowds drop off beyond Happy Valley, even on weekends. Enter Moss Bend, passing under two bridges. A railroad bridge precedes the I-40 bridge, both of which you pass under. Indian Creek flows in on the right between the two bridges. This is the first of three times you will go under I-40. By the way, you can also use the river access at the I-40 rest stop as a takeout point, located at 6.3 miles. This takeout point is just downstream of your first interstate intersection.

A cedar bluff rises on river right just beyond the bridges. The water is super clear and you can almost always see the bottom. The Tennessee Wildlife Resources Agency

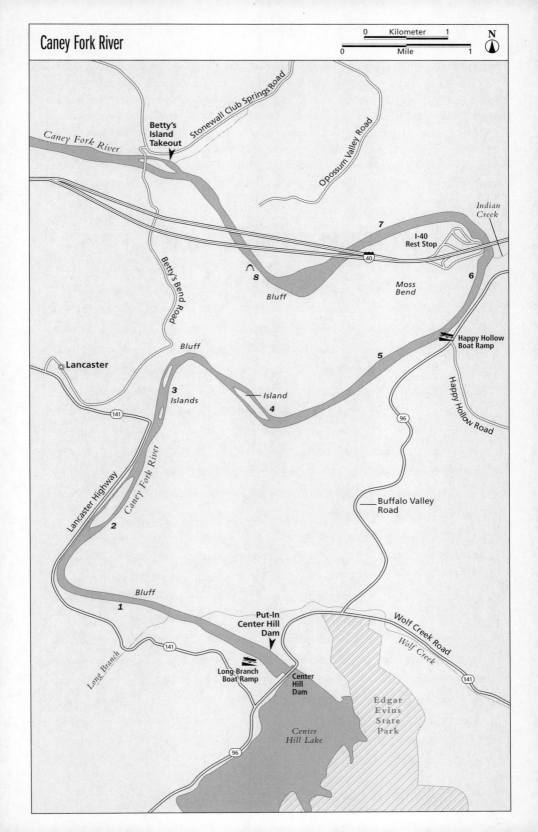

is trying to turn this into a fishery similar to that of the White River of Arkansas. Rock Springs Branch cuts through the bluff as it curves. A shoal accompanies your second passage under I-40 at 7.2 miles. A big bluff rises on river left beyond the second I-40 bridge. At 8.1 miles, watch for a cave in this bluff. A trail connects the river to the cave. Pass under I-40 a third and final time at 8.2 miles. Beyond this last crossing you may see more wading anglers, coming from your takeout point, Betty's Island, which is reached on river right at 8.9 miles. Make sure and check out the takeout before you begin your trip, as it will look different depending upon whether TVA is generating or not.

A CANEY FORK TREAT: EDGAR EVINS STATE PARK

While touring the state in search of the best paddles, the Caney Fork caught my attention. Very near the put-in, another outdoor destination also stood out: Edgar Evins State Park. Consider combining your paddle with a camping trip here. This recreation and campground is set on the shores of Center Hill Lake, where innumerable steep folded hills offer superlative scenery and also very little flat land. This lack of flat land forced campground designers to construct some of the most unusual campsites in the Volunteer State. Large, level wooden camping platforms—held up by concrete and metal poles—extend forth from the sloping terrain. Campers pitch their tent on a level platform while the ground recedes below. The picnic tables are on the platform, but the upright grills and fire rings are on the land, by the platform. Any smart camper wouldn't want to have their fire ring or grill on a wooden platform! This platform setup literally results in campers hanging out in the trees. The platforms are bordered by low wooden fences to keep you from falling off them. It is akin to camping on a deck looking upon the land below.

Edgar Evins State Park is primarily a warm weather summertime destination. The campground fills on summer holiday weekends. Many campers use this park to enjoy water-based recreation on Center Hill Lake as well as the Caney Fork River. The park has two lake boat launches, a boat dock, and marina. The marina rents boats and has a small store with limited items. There is no designated swim area—campers swim at their own risk on the lake. Don't forget landbased pursuits at Edgar Evins, for it has one of the best hiking trails in Middle Tennessee, the Millennium Trail. It offers a rugged, challenging hike through formerly settled land, atop rocky ridges, on lakeside bluffs, and through lush wooded hollows. This is a challenging hike, no doubt about it, so bring your game face. The Highland Rim Nature Trail is shorter at 2.4 miles, and it also has some steep ups and downs. But that is no surprise for a place where the campground had to have wooden platforms erected just to have some level land to camp!

24 Collins River

This river offers clearwater paddling at the base of the Cumberland Plateau.

County: Warren
Start: Myers Cove Road TWRA boat ramp, N35° 37.118', W85° 41.197'
End: Shellsford Road TWRA boat ramp, N35° 40.529', W85° 42.535'
Length: 8.3 miles
Float time: 4 hours
Difficulty rating: Easy
Rapids: Class I
River type: Pastoral valley river
Current: Slow to moderate
River gradient: 2.0 feet per mile
River gauge: USGS gauge—Collins at McMinnville, minimum runnable level 200 cfs
Season: Year-round

Land status: Private except for boat ramps
Fees or permits: No fees or permits required
Nearest city/town: McMinnville
Maps: USGS: Irving College, Cardwell Mountain; *DeLorme: Tennessee Atlas & Gazetteer,* Page 39 D7
Boats used: Canoes, johnboats, occasional kayaks
Organizations: Cumberland River Compact, P.O. Box 41721, Nashville 37204, (615) 837-1151, www.cumberlandcompact.org
Contacts/outfitters: Tennessee Wildlife Resources Agency, P.O. Box 40747, Nashville 37204, (615) 781-6500, www.state.tn.us /twra/

Put-in/Takeout Information

To takeout: From downtown McMinnville take TN 56 south 1.7 miles to TN 8. Veer left onto TN 8 and follow it for 0.8 mile to TN 127, Shellsford Road. Turn left on TN 127 and follow it for 1.8 miles to bridge the Collins River. Just beyond the bridge you will see the TWRA boat launch on the right. The launch does require a carry on a short trail connecting to the river.

To put-in from takeout: Backtrack on TN 127 for 0.3 mile then turn left on the Old Shellsford Road. Go for 1.2 miles, then cross TN 8. Continue forward, now on Fairview Road. Stay on Fairview Road for 1.8 miles, then turn left on TN 56 south. Go for 0.6 mile, then turn left on Myers Cove Road. Go for 2.6 miles and a boat ramp is on the left just before the bridge over the Collins River.

Paddle Summary

At the paddle's beginning the Collins River has dropped off the steepest parts of the plateau and is now carving a valley between Harrison Ferry Mountain to the east and Ben Lemond Mountain to the west. Clear waters flow swiftly down Class I riffles bordered by gravel bars, with stubby sycamores rising on the highest points. Big deep holes, great for swimming, set apart the shoals. The shore is mostly wooded and offers partial river canopy.

Looking downstream on the Collins during a lazy summer day.

Riverside bluffs are frequent but often rise a few feet above the Collins. Incoming springs are a regular feature on the river, as are caves. The whole area is underlain with pocked rock strata that makes for one complicated plumbing system. It's no surprise that an underground commercial tourist attraction, Cumberland Caverns, is located just a short piece off the river here in Warren County. Note in the information box that the minimum runnable level is 200 cfs. The Collins can be run as low as 150 cfs, but be prepared to scrape some and pull your boat over some shoals. At below 150 cfs, your trip will be a drag.

River Overview

Like most Middle Tennessee rivers, the Collins starts in the Cumberlands, this one beginning in one of the state's premier wildernesses, Grundy County's Savage Gulf State Natural Area. Here, Big Creek and Savage Creek meet the Collins River, the three gorges forming a giant crow's foot. Now a full-fledged river, the Collins flows north, exiting Savage Gulf near the Warren County line, evolving into a pastoral waterway offering 45 miles of quality paddling—the last 20 of which are riverine slackwater—before meeting the Caney Fork River at Great Falls Lake. Multiple access points, easy paddling, and a longer than expected paddling season for a free-flowing river add to the allure of the Collins.

The Paddling

The Collins is about 50 feet wide at the Myers Cove boat ramp, and is mostly canopied with river birch and sycamore. River grasses border the clear and gentle watercourse, with dark colored rocks below the surface. An overhanging bluff, partially obscured by woods, soon rises on river right. Fallen rocks line the waterway. Partially submerged timber is ample in the river but is generally not a hazard. You will generally have level wooded shoreline with the field beyond on one side of the river. During wetter times, many springs drip from bluffs into the water. In other places, the blufflines will rise just a few feet above the river.

At 0.5 mile, a chilly cave spring comes in on river right. A cool mist will drift from the cave on a warm summer day. A few gravelly Class I riffles begin where Panther Creek comes in on river right. The valley of Panther Creek, known as Myers Cove, inspires the name of the road used to access the put-in. Flats extend from both sides of the river here. However, overhanging trees almost always line the shoreline to offer some decent shade. Box elder is also a common species along the shore.

It isn't long before bluffs and rocky shorelines resume. Continue alternating between pools and riffles. The Collins River has seriously deep holes between shoals. In contrast, when the river is wide and shallow you can enjoy the clarity of it, seeing every rock on the bottom. Occasionally you'll gain glimpses from the river of the wooded ridgelines surrounding the river valley.

At 1.6 miles, on river right, flows a spring spilling over a low rock ledge. Its dripping sounds make it hard to miss. At 1.7 miles, another cave is exposed on river right. This may be submerged at higher water levels. A long, shallow, and straight stretch begins at 2.2 miles, where the Collins breaks up into narrow channels that wind among grassy isles. At higher water levels, you won't have a problem getting through, as there will be multiple floatable routes. However, at lower water levels you will have to pick the right channel or end up dragging your boat a little bit.

The straightaway ends at 3.1 miles and McGregor Creek adds to the flow. The water deepens and the river commences a 180-degree bend to the right. A bluff rises on river left. At 3.6 miles, shoot through remains of an old rock dam. The Collins River then deepens and slows before approaching TN 8 bridge at 4.5 miles, where the water shallows again. A small gravel bar forms here, which locals use to access the river. Elsewhere, low bluffs rise from the water. Broken rock from these bluffs has fallen into the water and provides good structure for the ample smallmouth bass and rock bass that live the Collins. At 4.9 miles, amid these broken rock overhangs, is an unusual structure on river right. A circular brick structure leads into a narrow cave. Its purpose and origin are lost to time, but my guess is that it was once used as a spring basin that was somehow piped up to the land above the river.

The Collins River remains slow and deep here, making for an easy paddle past rich agricultural bottomland. Shoals and bluffs resume at 6.0 miles, as the Collins River now begins a few bends. Rams Creek comes in on the right at 6.5 miles.

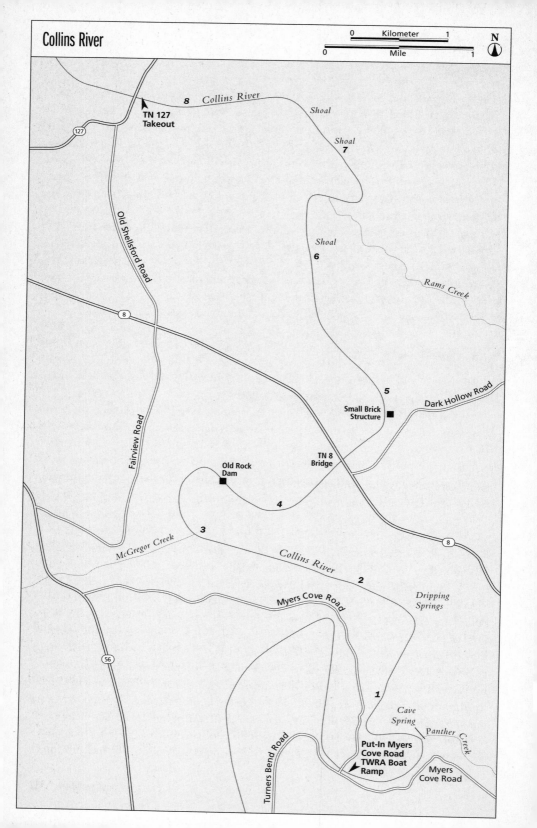

Collins River

0 — Kilometer — 1
0 — Mile — 1

N

Collins River

8 TN 127 Takeout

127

Shoal

Shoal
7

Old Shellsford Road

Shoal
6

Rams Creek

8

Fairview Road

5
Small Brick Structure

Dark Hollow Road

TN 8 Bridge

Old Rock Dam

4

3

McGregor Creek

Collins River

2

8

Dripping Springs

Myers Cove Road

56

1

Turners Bend Road

Cave Spring

Panther Creek

Put-In Myers Cove Road TWRA Boat Ramp

Myers Cove Road

Cumberland Caverns is less than a mile distant to the east, as the crow flies. Pass a couple more shoals before the Collins River aims westerly for the TN 127 bridge. This final due westerly push travels over a wide shallow area with an irregular rock bottom full of mild riffles. When the TN 127 bridge comes in sight, slip over to the right-hand side of the Collins, as the takeout isn't evident. Look for the dirt trail leading from the riverbank through woods to steps that lead to the parking area.

DON'T BE AFRAID OF THE SAVAGE GULF

Savage Gulf State Natural Area, on the wooded western edge of the Cumberland Plateau, harbors the Collins River headwaters and is one of Tennessee's finest hiking destinations. Savage Gulf offers 16,000 acres of rugged gorges, tumbling falls, stunning views, and human history. It is part of the larger South Cumberland Recreation Area, which covers ten wild parcels of land, all within easy striking distance of the Collins River.

Savage Gulf is not only botanically significant but historic as well. In the mid-1800s, an old stage road passed through the area, connecting McMinnville and Chattanooga. Part of this road has been incorporated into the Savage Gulf trail system. Also at the bottom of the gorge stands the Decatur Savage Cabin, a frail remainder of the tough life the settlers had in this land. His family name inspired the name of the state natural area, which came under state preservation in 1973.

Unusual watery features abound in Savage Gulf. Springs spew forth, then flow back underground and out of sight into what is known locally as a "sink." This geologically fascinating place of 300-million-year-old rocks is combed with sinks and springs that work their way to the Collins River. Trips to Ranger Creek Falls and Greeter Falls lend more evidence of the relationship between rock and water here. Contrastingly, the waters of Savage Gulf can nearly dry up in fall.

The Great Stone Door entrance to the park is nearest the Collins River Valley. This crack in the rim of the Big Creek Gorge was used by Indians as the way in and out of Savage Gulf as far back as pre-Columbian times. The term "gulf," used by local residents, refers to the gorges that cut deep swaths through the Cumberland Plateau here.

Horsepound Falls and Suter Falls are more water features. Suter Falls is a triple-tiered watery drop framed in a sylvan forest, spread over a 300-foot section of creek that curves beneath sandstone walls, fashioning an outstanding picture of Tennessee's unheralded beauty spots. A total of nine designated backcountry campsites in the park avail backpackers many camp choices and multi-day trip opportunities. Over 60 trail miles await those who want to combine some legwork with their paddling.

25 Obey River

This year-round run starts at the dam outflow of scenic Dale Hollow Lake and heads past big water scenery to Celina.

County: Clay
Start: Dale Hollow Dam, N36° 32.210', W85° 27.445'
End: Donaldson Park in Celina, N36° 33.353', W85° 29.743'
Length: 6.2 miles
Float time: 2.5 hours
Difficulty rating: Moderate
Rapids: Class I
River type: Dam-controlled coldwater big river
Current: Moderate to swift
River gradient: 4.2 feet per mile
River gauge: Dam Water release schedule (800) 238-2264, press 4, then 35 for Dale Hollow Dam, also available at website listed under contacts/outfitters

Season: Year-round
Land status: Public—Army Corps of Engineers and private
Fees or permits: No fees or permits required
Nearest city/town: Celina
Maps: USGS: Dale Hollow Dam; *DeLorme: Tennessee Atlas and Gazetteer,* Page 66 D1
Boats used: Canoes, kayaks, johnboats, powerboats
Organizations: Cumberland River Compact, P.O. Box 41721, Nashville 37204, (615) 837-1151, www.cumberlandrivercompact.org
Contacts/outfitters: U.S. Army Corps of Engineers Resource Manager's Office, 540 Dale Hollow Dam Rd., Celina 38551, (931) 243-3136, www.orn.usace.army.mil/pao/lakeinfo/dal

Put-in/Takeout Information

To takeout: Coming from Livingston, reach the intersection of TN 53 and TN 52 in Celina, and stay with TN 53 north for 2.0 miles to East Lake Road. Turn left on East Lake Road and follow it 0.9 mile to Jefferson Road. Turn right on Jefferson Road and keep forward at a four-way stop, passing through a residential area. Continue for 0.2 mile to turn right into Donaldson Park, following the main park road for 0.5 mile to dead-end at the boat ramp.

To put-in from takeout: Backtrack to the intersection of East Lake Road and TN 53. Turn left and take TN 53 north for 1.6 miles, bridging the Obey River to turn right onto Dale Hollow Dam Road. Follow it a short distance, passing the Dale Hollow Fish Hatchery. Veer right on Campground Road at the sign for Dam and Powerhouse Recreation Area. The boat ramp is beyond the entrance to the campground.

Paddle Summary

This is a dam-controlled paddle that offers a reliable coldwater float through a tree-lined corridor. It is utilized by anglers fishing for stocked trout as well as by casual

The Donaldson Park boat ramp.

floaters who want predictable flow. The Obey is especially good on a blistering summer day, as the water coming from under Dale Hollow Dam will cool off even the hottest river runner. Also, cool breezes will drift off the Obey while you float. Fall is another good time to make this paddle, when other rivers may be too low. You can enjoy autumn's golden colors as you leave the shadow of Dale Hollow Dam and paddle over clear waters on the last few miles of the Obey before it meets the Cumberland River. Along the way, the Obey turns first around Walker Bend then Peterman Bend, sometimes under impressive bluffs. The final part of the float goes into Celina, where a boat ramp awaits at Donaldson Park. To find out the generation schedule for Dale Hollow Dam, call the above number listed under contacts or go to the web.

River Overview

Most of the main Obey River lies under the waters of Dale Hollow Lake. Its headwaters gather in Fentress County and Overton County, where it flows into two forks. The East Fork gathers to cut an impressive gorge as it heads north, nearing Jamestown. The West Fork gathers in hills and hollows of southeastern Overton, and the two forks meet in a slice of Pickett County. Their confluence is submerged and remains such until the waters are again freed below Dale Hollow Dam to soon meet the Cumberland River. The final flowing miles are encompassed in this float, save for a short distance below the takeout. Whitewater crazies stroke the upper forks of the Obey, while casual paddlers are limited to the river below the Dale Hollow Dam. However, self-propelled kayakers and canoeists can be found exploring Dale Hollow Lake, arguably the most scenic impoundment in the Volunteer State. Paddlers will camp out on the lake banks and islands, extending their trips to several days.

The Paddling

A small dock and a wide boat ramp make putting in easy. An Army Corps of Engineers campground, called Dale Hollow Dam, stands on river right. If you want to include camping in your adventure stay here or at Lillydale Campground, which I think is the best overnighting area on Dale Hollow Lake. See the sidebar below for more information about Lillydale. The Obey extends 140 feet from bank to bank. The shores are lined with autumn olive, ironwood, buckeye, and sycamore. A high bluff stands on river left overlooking the campground. The Obey runs clear, cold, and uniform. Its flow rate is dependent on the generation from the dam, which is a short distance upstream. If you time your paddle with strong generation, you will only have to lift your blade to steer the boat. However, the width of the river makes it subject to winds, especially in the afternoon.

The banks on both sides are U.S. Army Corps of Engineers property. Pass under a major power line shortly after the put-in. An unnamed stream comes in on river left at 0.3 mile. A shoreline trail runs along river right, connecting the dam area to Moody boat ramp, which you reach at 0.7 mile. Grassy and wooded hills rise in the distance.

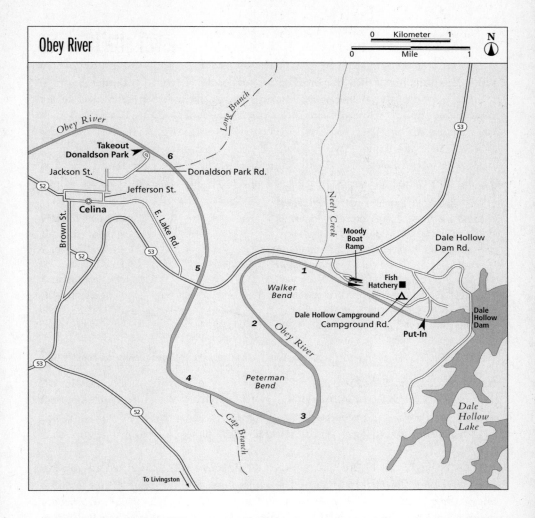

Obey River

At 0.9 mile, Neely Creek flows in through a culvert on your right as the river saddles alongside TN 53. Continue drifting westerly and begin your turn around Walker Bend at 1.2 miles. Many of your fellow boaters will be fishing. This tailwater trout fishery is increasing in popularity but still has a long way to go before it gives the Caney Fork below Center Hill Dam a run for its money.

Beavers are very active along the Obey River. You will see their gnawings along with numerous fallen trees on the banks. When the dam is not generating, the river will flow slower and lower, revealing a few partially submerged trees, covered in moss, along with exposed rocks. Come alongside a stratified bluff at 1.5 miles. You may have noticed by now that the banks are not easy to access, so plan accordingly. Landing isn't impossible, just not easy. When generating, trouble-free access points are submerged.

At 1.9 miles begin a long southeasterly straightaway. The lower Obey is a big river and has both prolonged turns and prolonged straightaways. There is little in the way of hazards in the water, making for clear sailing downstream. Begin curving around Peterman Bend at 2.6 miles, banking up against a high bluff. Wooded hills climb from the banks then apex in sheer rock walls extending 400 feet above the water! These views alone are worth the float. Fields cover the inside of Peterman Bend.

This is one of the cleanest stretches of water in the state. Its banks thus far are undeveloped and all trash upstream is caught by Dale Hollow Dam. Pass Gap Branch on river left at 3.8 miles. Houses begin. The river turns north and passes under the TN 53 bridge at 4.9 miles. You are now 1,500 feet from where you were at 1.7 miles, before the turn of Peterman Bend. More houses appear on river left as you start getting into Celina. Enjoy the relaxed paddling in the ultraclear water. Long Branch comes in on river right at 5.9 miles. Head over to the left-hand bank and began looking for the U.S. Army Corps of Engineers Donaldson Park boat ramp, which you reach on river left at 6.2 miles.

CAMP AT LILLYDALE

Backed against the western edge of the Cumberland Plateau, Dale Hollow Lake is bordered by hills, coves, islands, and fingers forming an interlude of land and water that is very easy on the eyes. The Army Corps of Engineers offers lakeside camping and recreation areas, and Lillydale is the best of the lot.

It offers very large and well-separated campsites. The balance of the campground is located on a hilly peninsula jutting into Dale Hollow Lake, with lake vistas everywhere! A land bridge connects the main campground to a camping island. All the campsites are on the island's edge. Many campers load their boats and boat around to their campsite. The views from the large and spacious sites are great. I highly recommend these campsites. Two modern bathhouses serve the campground. Lillydale Campground has its own recreation facilities. A basketball court and a volleyball court are adjacent to the island camp, as is a swim beach. And the campground has its own boat ramp. However, with so many lakefront campsites, many visitors keep their boats tied up directly in front of their camp. Additionally, the 8-mile Accordion Bluff Trail connects Lillydale Recreation Area with the nearby Willow Grove Recreation Area.

Most campers come here to enjoy water recreation on this pretty lake or float the Obey River below the dam. Fishing, boating, skiing, and swimming are the most common pastimes. Lillydale is primarily a warm weather experience, and the area can be busy on summer weekends. For more information visit www.recreation.gov, then type "Lillydale" in the search box.

26 Roaring River

Tucked away in the hills of Jackson County, this flat travels a designated state scenic river. Paddle it in spring, as it can dry up in summer.

County: Jackson
Start: Intersection of Roaring River Road and New Hope Road, N36° 20.786', W85° 31.400'
End: Fish Weir Dam, N36° 21.172', W85° 35.921'
Length: 7.6 miles
Float time: 3.5 hours
Difficulty rating: Moderate
Rapids: Class I-I+
River type: Small to midsize seasonal plateau river
Current: Moderate to fast
River gradient: 6.7 feet per mile
River gauge: Spring Creek near Dodson Chapel, minimum runnable level 140 cfs

Season: Winter, spring, and following heavy rains
Land status: Mostly private, some public TWRA land
Fees or permits: No fees or permits required
Nearest city/town: Gainesboro
Maps: USGS: Dodson Branch; *DeLorme: Tennessee Atlas and Gazetteer,* Page 56 B1
Boats used: Canoes, kayaks, johnboats
Organizations: Cumberland River Compact, P.O. Box 41721, Nashville 37204, (615) 837-1151, www.cumberlandrivercompact.org
Contacts/outfitters: Tennessee Clean Water Network, 123A S. Gay St., Knoxville 37902, (865) 522-7007, www.tcwn.org

Put-in/Takeout Information

To takeout: From the intersection of TN 56 and TN 53 near downtown Gainesboro, take TN 56/TN 53 north toward Celina. At 1.2 miles, TN 56 heads left, crossing the Cumberland River. You keep forward on TN 53 for another 0.2 mile then veer right on TN 135 toward Cookeville. Follow TN 135 for 4 miles and look left for an unmarked dirt road and turn left to follow it a short distance to reach Fish Weir Dam (if you reach Morrison Road on TN 135, you have passed the left turn onto the dirt road).

To put-in from takeout: From the Fish Weir Dam, return to TN 135 and turn left, resuming toward Cookeville. At 3.9 miles, turn left on Overton Road, passing Overton Cemetery. Bridge Roaring River and at 0.2 mile reach Old Roaring River Road. Turn right on Old Roaring River Road and follow it for 3.1 miles to meet New Hope Road. There is a put-in here, where a stream flows into Roaring River.

Paddle Summary

Not only is the Roaring River a state scenic river, but so are two tributaries, Spring Creek and Blackburn Fork, so expect natural beauty, despite the river being along or near roads the entire paddle. You can use the roads to scout your trip, though the

tough water on the Roaring is upstream of this paddle. This segment flows through a hilly valley just below the Cumberland Plateau. The upper Roaring is oriented toward whitewater paddlers who tackle it at high water. The rapids down here are Class I–I+. This isn't the most scenic section of the Roaring, simply the most doable by the most paddlers in the segment with the longest paddling season. Since the entire watershed is subject to flooding, you will see piles of logs jammed against trees, changing gravel bars, some covered with brush. At higher water flows, when it is most often paddled, the current will take you into brush, so be wary. Spring Creek soon adds to the flow. Downstream the valley widens as Blackburn Fork comes in. Just downstream, on TWRA property is "The Boils," a spring upwelling that flows a short distance into the Roaring. In late summer, the Roaring will be dry in places above The Boils. Tall wooded hills alternate with fields as the Roaring makes its way toward the Cumberland. The hills fall away at Fish Weir Dam a few miles upstream of the confluence with the Cumberland and Cordell Hull Lake. The fast shoals will keep you moving, but there is only one singular drop of note. Important note: The gauge used for this paddle, Spring Creek at Dodson Chapel, is obviously not on the Roaring River, but Spring Creek is a tributary of the Roaring and can help you determine floatability. If Spring Creek is below 140 cfs, then the Roaring River may be too low to float. However, you can also determine floatability while driving along Roaring River Road. Generally speaking, Roaring River is a spring float, and a good one at that.

River Overview

The Roaring River begins in central Overton County where it flows west off Harris Mountain. Its northbound journey heads toward the town of Livingston where Carr Town Creek comes in. Turning west before Livingston, the Roaring River cuts through the Cumberland Plateau, ending its raucous journey around the confluence with Flat Creek. It continues winding west to enter Jackson County and the beginning of this paddle. Here, Spring Creek adds its flow. The Roaring River now travels west and meets Blackburn Fork. Fish Weir Dam slows the water briefly before it continues a short journey to the Cumberland River, which is dammed up as Cordell Hull Lake. An embayment is formed on the lower Roaring River, and it silently meets the Cumberland River near Gainesboro. Casual paddlers can enjoy approximately 20 miles of paddling in the lower Roaring River Valley, whereas whitewater fans have an additional 12 or so paddleable miles to float.

The Paddling

At the put-in the Roaring River averages 35 feet wide. It immediately separates around an island. Sycamores, ironwood, and ash tightly line the banks here. Old

◀ *Dirt Cave can be seen from the Roaring River.*

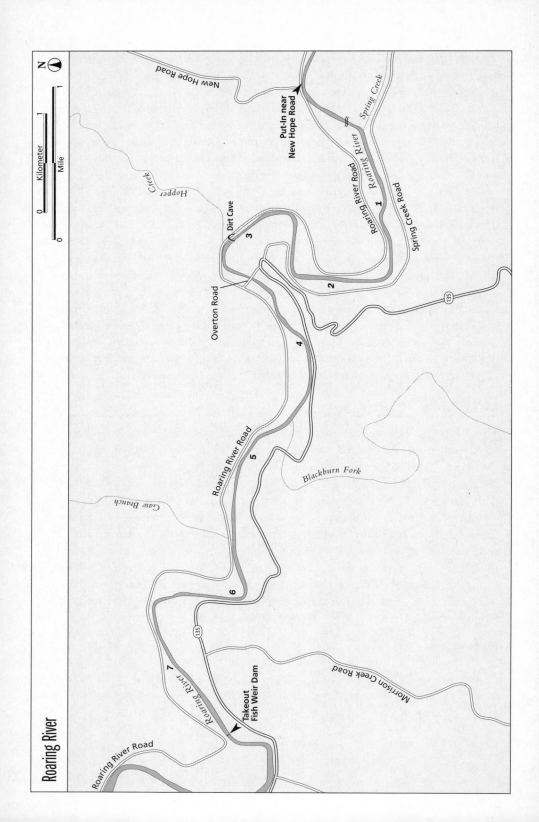

Roaring River

Roaring River Road is within sight. Flats stretch wide away from the river where hills and bluffs aren't present. The wooded flats will be thick with wildflowers in spring. At 0.4 mile, the Roaring River constricts between rock outcrops and forms a simple drop, then meets Spring Creek at 0.5 mile. Spring Creek adds significant flow and may be dingier than the Roaring when the water is up. A slack fishing/swimming hole forms at the confluence.

The Roaring widens as do its gravel bars and overflow areas. Occasional sheer banks rise about 10 feet, then lead to a flat that leads eventually to a hill or bluff in this slender agricultural valley. Roaring River Valley has been farmed for quite a while. Look for old rock walls embedded into the banks of the river, placed by early settlers trying to keep the stream from eroding the rich lands they tilled. You will also see where modern farmers and residents have placed riprap for the same reason. The hand-placed stones are certainly more aesthetically pleasing. At 1.4 miles, the river speeds around a bend as it turns north, then calms down for a gentle float. It seems a hill is always rising in the background, providing a backdrop to the water as it flows over a rock and gravel bottom. Occasional houses are perched well above the floodplain.

At 2.3 miles, the Roaring runs into a cedar bluff, then curves easterly, only to give way to a bluff on river right, as the Roaring River is making a 180-degree turn. Pass Dirt Cave on river right at 3.1 miles. It looks like an old quarry but is a naturally formed opening in a bluff. Dirt Cave is a local landmark mentioned in county court records as far back as the 1870s. Here also is a spring from which locals get mountain water. Unfortunately, the bluff is blighted with graffiti. Hopper Creek comes in at 3.2 miles, in the middle of the bend.

The valley widens. Blackburn Fork comes in on river left at 4.6 miles, calmly flowing after its wild ride off the Cumberland Plateau. A large gravel bar forms here. Another gravel bar builds on river right. The Boils are out of sight and on the other side of this right-hand gravel bar, which is a public Tennessee Wildlife Resources agency access. Pull out and check out the upwelling. The outflow comes in downstream at the lower end of the gravel bar.

The Roaring River spreads wide for about 0.5 mile then gradually narrows. More TWRA land is on river left. Gaw Branch flows through a culvert to meet Roaring River at 5.5 miles. Watch for more hand-placed rock walls along the shore here. A stone-capped citadel stands dead ahead as you float westerly, only to be turned north upon reaching the bluff at 5.9 miles. A large gravel bar at the bend makes for a good stopping spot. The river is slowing as the effects of Fish Weir Dam extend upstream.

The Roaring makes a lazy and wide curve around Roaring River Campground. A high bluff overlooks the flat where the camp lies. The Roaring River has widened considerably. Morrison Creek flows in on river left at 7.1 miles. Drift over to the left-hand bank and begin listening for the Fish Weir Dam flowing over its top. Take out on river left at 7.6 miles, allowing plenty of distance between you and the dam. Anglers will be found fishing below the dam.

THE WILDERNESS TRAIL

The Wilderness Trail is a hiking path located a few miles downstream from Roaring River's confluence with the Cumberland River/Cordell Hull Lake. Located on U.S. Army Corps of Engineers land, it extends 6 miles one way along rugged bluffs of the Cumberland River in Jackson County. Your efforts are well rewarded with vistas, solitude, and a waterfall along the way. Holleman Bend Campground is at the trailhead. It offers ultraprimitive camping, with restrooms only.

Expect far-reaching views from sheer bluffs, cut by deep ravines cloaked in rich woods. Technically a horse trail, the path is also traveled by hikers and only lightly traveled by both groups. It is possible to put a car at the far end. The Cumberland River, dammed but still a ribbon of water, lies to your left. Mile marker signs of various ages and types are nailed into trees alongside the path. A little-used backcountry campsite lies on trail-left before the path crosses a second streambed.

The Wilderness Trail meets Big Branch Road. At this point, a car shuttle would be nice, otherwise you must backtrack. If you choose to set up a car shuttle, back out of Holleman Bend Campground, the main trailhead, and return to TN 53. Turn left, north on TN 53, and follow it to Big Branch Road. Turn left on Big Branch Road to reach the upper end of the embayment of Big Branch, where a large sign on the left, across from the aforementioned house, indicates the Wilderness Trail. To reach Holleman Bend and the beginning of the trail, stay with TN 53 from Gainesboro, heading toward Granville. Turn right on Holleman Bend Road just before Granville and a bridge over Martin Creek embayment and follow it 2.6 miles to a four-way stop at Ragland Lane and Forrester Hollow Lane. Turn into the campground. The Wilderness Trail leaves left from the campground to the right as you face the lake. For more information visit www.lrn.usace.army.mil/op/cor/rec/horseback_trails.

East Tennessee

Steve "Devo" Grayson plying the upper Powell River.

27 Sequatchie River

A paddle down the Sequatchie River is the watery equivalent of sitting on the front porch—it's a relaxing endeavor that we enjoy when we get the chance and would like to do more often.

County: Sequatchie
Start: US 127 bridge near Dunlap, N35° 19.903', W85° 23.518'
End: Frank Tate Bridge, N35° 16.466', W85° 25.793'
Length: 6.2 miles
Float time: 4 hours
Difficulty rating: Easy to moderate
Rapids: Easy Class I
River type: Pastoral valley river
Current: Slow
River gradient: 2.0 feet per mile
River gauge: USGS gauge—Sequatchie at Whitwell, minimum runnable level 70 cfs

Season: Year-round
Land status: Private
Fees or permits: Launching fee at put-in
Nearest city/town: Dunlap
Maps: USGS: Daus; *DeLorme: Tennessee Atlas & Gazetteer,* Page 24 B2
Boats used: Canoes, kayaks, tubes
Organizations: Tennessee Clean Water Network, 123A S. Gay St., Knoxville 37902, (865) 522-7007, www.tcwn.com
Contacts/outfitters: Canoe the Sequatchie, 12800 US 127, Dunlap 37327, (423) 949-4400, www.sequatchie.com/canoe

Put-in/Takeout Information

To takeout: From downtown Dunlap, take US 127 south for 3 miles to the outfitter on the left just before the bridge, passing the put-in. To reach the takeout, continue on US 127 south 1.1 miles farther to TN 283 south. Turn right on TN 283 south and follow it for 4.1 miles to Frank Tate Road. Turn right and immediately come to a bridge over the Sequatchie River. The takeout is on the gravel road before the bridge over the Sequatchie River. A small parking area is on the far side of the bridge.

To put-in from takeout: Backtrack north on TN 283 to reach US 127. Turn left and continue north on US 127, reaching Canoe the Sequatchie outfitter just after the bridge.

Paddle Summary

Trips down here are great for paddlers of all abilities. Even those who are somewhat reluctant to get in the boat may become eager paddling partners after a trip down this beautiful waterway. Put in at the US 127 bridge and begin your trip along an intimate waterway that cuts through what many argue is the most beautiful valley in the state of Tennessee. The generally slow current is broken by easy riffles and shoals that keep your boat moving along but pose no hazards. Tan gravel bars are exposed along the shore in places and make for inviting stops. Hot summer days are made for a trip

Gravel bars on the Sequatchie make for alluring stopping spots.

down the Sequatchie, as the river is mostly shaded, with plenty of deep swimming holes that beckon the paddler. Fallen trees are frequent along the river but generally do not pose an obstacle to a paddler, rather harboring plentiful bass and bream.

River Overview

The Sequatchie River flows through one of the most beautiful valleys in America. Flowing south through the heart of the Cumberlands, it is bordered on the west by the Cumberland Plateau and on the east by Walden Ridge on its course to meet the Tennessee River. It actually starts in Grassy Valley, high in the Cumberlands, then flows underground, springing forth in the northernmost Sequatchie Valley, at the Cumberland-Bledsoe county line. The Sequatchie River meanders through the southwest-trending valley, fed by small tributaries flowing off the wooded ridges. The river becomes paddleable a few miles north of Sequatchie County, beginning nearly 60 miles of canoeing and kayaking pleasure. It passes near Dunlap and Whitwell and finally Jasper before meeting the Tennessee River near the Alabama state line.

The Paddling

Leave the outfitter and immediately pass under the US 127 bridge. The river is 50 to 60 feet wide, flanked by heavily wooded banks. The river's normally clear-green color reflects silver maple, box elder, and ironwood growing thickly on banks 6 to 20 feet high. Higher up the banks, oaks, hickory, and even an occasional pine will overhang the river. Since the Sequatchie is somewhat narrow, trees fallen into the river will narrow the passage opportunities. Rocks and grasses line the immediate shore.

The Sequatchie soon divides around a sycamore-covered island. The left side is generally the better channel. The slow current speeds over shallow gravel riffles, allowing you to see the bottom of the river. Occasionally, fields that occupy the rich agricultural land of the Sequatchie Valley reach the river's edge and dramatically open up the sky overhead. They also allow views of the mountains that border the Sequatchie Valley. Sheer rock outcrops on these mountains add to their scenic value. Faster channels bordered by gravel bars can be as narrow as 15 feet. At 0.6 mile, pass through a rock garden of uptilted strata over which the river speeds. Interestingly, the water-worn rock strata runs almost parallel with the river and you slide through long channels.

At 1.1 miles, the river makes a sharp curve to the right and passes over an old Indian fish trap. At first glance it seems like your average shoal, but a closer look will reveal the land rocks on both sides of the river leading to a central channel through which your boat passes. The Cherokee, who roamed through this area, would station people with woven baskets on the lower side of the river channel, then others would start up the river a ways and start walking down the river, scaring fish downstream into the V-shaped rocks, which would lead the fish into the basket traps. The Tennessee Wildlife Resources Agency would not look kindly if we used this practice nowadays.

At 1.8 miles, the river makes a sharp bend to the right. Here, Kell Branch flows into a large pool. Just downstream of the mouth of Kell Branch, watch for a spring flowing in to form a small but noisy fall that descends over stair-step rock strata.

Gravel bars, rock outcroppings, and small islands with grasses growing upon them characterize the next section. The Sequatchie usually speeds up its lazy flow beside these islands. At 2.9 miles, the river makes a sharp bend to the left and resumes its southerly track. The banks become rocky as a ridge rises to your right. A rocky and easy Class I rapid follows a sharp left turn. The Sequatchie settles into a long slow section where overhanging trees form a canopy over the waterway. At 3.5 miles, the shady solitude is disrupted by a cleared right-of-way and power line passing over the Sequatchie.

At 4.2 miles, pass under the Daus Bridge, on Stone Cave Road. There is a put-in/takeout on the river left before the bridge if you would like to shorten your trip. Stone Creek comes in on the right a little bit before the bridge. By this point, the river has widened some and the straightaway continues. At 4.9 miles, Bryant Branch comes in on your left amid a few grassy shoals that speed the waterway.

The pastoral waterway continues its meanderings toward the Tennessee River. At 5.7 miles, reach the biggest rapid of the trip, which is a 1.5- to 2- foot drop. This is also an old Indian fish trap—look at how the rocks are lined up. Enjoy your last

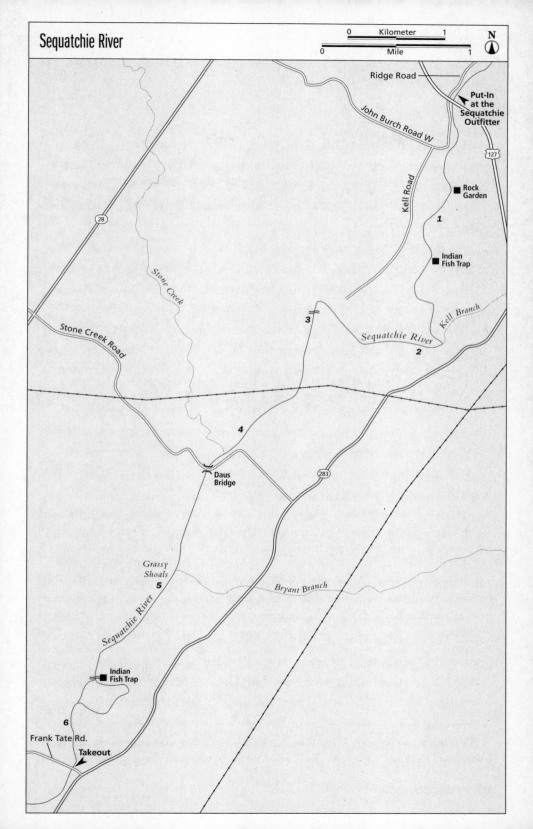

Sequatchie River

Kilometer

Mile

N

Ridge Road

Put-In at the Sequatchie Outfitter

John Burch Road W

127

Kell Road

Rock Garden

1

Indian Fish Trap

3

Stone Creek

Sequatchie River

Kell Branch

2

Stone Creek Road

28

4

Daus Bridge

283

Grassy Shoals

5

Bryant Branch

Sequatchie River

Indian Fish Trap

6

Frank Tate Rd.

Takeout

0.5 mile on the river before reaching the Frank Tate Road Bridge at 6.2 miles. The takeout is on river left under the bridge.

THE CUMBERLAND TRAIL

Atop the eastern mountain rim of the Sequatchie River Valley, known as Walden Ridge, travels part of the Cumberland Trail (CT). The CT is Tennessee's master path, a path in the works that is to extend from Cumberland Gap at the Kentucky state line to Prentice Cooper State Forest down Georgia way. It has been declared the Volunteer State's fifty-third state park.

Cumberland Trail State Park protects the Cumberland Trail. A hardworking, devoted group is building the 300-or-so-mile path. The whole idea of a Cumberland Trail, extending the length of the Cumberland Plateau through Tennessee, dates back to the 1970s. Some trail was built back then, but the builders faded away and the money fizzled out. Fast-forward to 1997, when Rob Weber—a Nashville member of the Tennessee Trails Association—single-handedly revived the idea. Weber formed the Cumberland Trail Conference, which along with the Tennessee Trails Association manages the project, involving land purchasers and trail builders.

The Cumberland Plateau is the final battleground for wilderness preservation in Tennessee. It'll be gone if we don't save a piece of it for future generations. In the course of making this trail, a lot of land is being protected. This trail and the land upon which it travels provide a green corridor for wildlife. The reintroduction of elk on the plateau and bears in the Big South Fork are examples of such successes.

Cumberland Trail Conference volunteers come in all ages, and from all occupations—from college groups on spring break to hiking clubs. Tennesseans and trail locals have been very receptive to the idea of a Cumberland Trail. It preserves the beauty that they have known all their lives. They also see the economic benefits of recreation-based tourism in their counties. Finally, they themselves can enjoy the trail. And the trail mileage keeps increasing.

But the sheer size of the task has been challenging. The act of acquiring miles of trail corridor and adjoining lands takes time. Funding is a challenge, but those who give can be part of something that lasts beyond your lifetime. Sometimes, in the pursuit of money, whether for private or public purposes, we lose sight of life's other rewarding aspects. Not on the Cumberland Trail. The volunteers form bonds through their cooperative efforts in building this long distance path. Tennessee is the Volunteer State. No experience is necessary to volunteer for the Cumberland Trail. If you are interested, visit www.cumberlandtrail.org.

28 Big South Fork National River

A trip down this federally protected waterway is one of the most scenic in the Southeast.

County: Scott
Start: Leatherwood Ford, N36° 28.616', W84° 40.127'
End: Station Camp Crossing, N36° 32.847', W84° 39.873'
Length: 8 miles
Float time: 5 hours
Difficulty rating: Moderate
Rapids: Class I–II (assuming portage of Angel Falls)
River type: Big protected river in deep gorge
Current: Moderate
River gradient: 7.5 feet per mile
River gauge: USGS Big South Fork at Leatherwood Ford, minimum runnable level 120 cfs, maximum 3,000 cfs
Season: Spring, summer, fall

Land status: Public—national park
Fees or permits: Backcountry camping permit needed if going overnight, none needed for day trips
Nearest city/town: Oneida
Maps: Big South Fork National River and Recreation Area; USGS: Barthell SW, Honey Creek; *DeLorme: Tennessee Atlas & Gazetteer,* Page 58 A1, 68 B1
Boats used: Kayaks, canoes, a few rafts
Organizations: Big South Fork National River and Recreation Area, 4564 Leatherwood Rd., Oneida 37841, (423) 286-7275, www.nps .gov/biso
Contacts/outfitters: Sheltowee Trace Outfitters, P.O. Box 1060, Whitley City 42653, (800) 541-RAFT (7238), www.ky-rafting.com

Put-in/Takeout Information

To takeout: From Oneida, take TN 297 west for 5 miles to Station Camp Road. Turn right on Station Camp Road and follow it for 10 miles to dead-end at the takeout. Go to the river and look around to make sure to remember the takeout, which can be recognized by the trail crossing or the wooden steps upstream of the trail crossing.

To put-in from takeout: From Station Camp, backtrack on Station Camp Road to TN 297. Turn right on TN 297 and follow it for 7.5 miles to the Leatherwood Ford access on the right just before crossing the Big South Fork. Use the unloading area at the river access near the gazebo. However, park in the designated parking area.

Paddle Summary

The entire paddle takes place within the confines of the Big South Fork National River and Recreation Area, a National Park Service—run 125,000-acre preserve straddling the Tennessee-Kentucky state line. You will find the area deserving of its national park status as you paddle through a deeply cut gorge with rock bluffs rising forth amid deep green forests above a waterway littered with cabin-sized boulders.

Be apprised this trip has a cost. Two miles into the run, a mandatory portage around Angel Falls awaits. This rapid, originally a waterfall that was dynamited by locals in the 1950s, ostensibly to make it more boatable, is a tough run through constricted boulders, and is recommended only for experts. Don't even try it! The portage is around 120 yards and will add a solid hour to your trip.

The other river rapids are Class I–II. Still other stretches will be calm, where you can admire the scenery. Interestingly, the 8-mile River Trail runs along the east bank of the Big South Fork. You can combine hiking with your paddle or even use the River Trail as a hike or bike shuttle.

River Overview

This brawny and brash watercourse is technically known as the Big South Fork of the Cumberland River. Its short but picturesque journey begins at the confluence of the New River and Clear Fork, within the confines of the Big South Fork National River and Recreation Area. From here it immediately begins cutting into the Cumberland Plateau on an untamed adventure through a gorgeous gorge attracting rafters and kayakers alike. Rapids with names like Jakes Hole and Washing Machine lead paddlers through this upper section to end at Leatherwood Ford. From here, the Big South Fork continues through the recreation area with fewer rapids but still superlative scenery. This section (which includes this paddle) attracts more casual water lovers but also canoe campers who make the 27-mile run from Leatherwood Ford to Blue Heron in Kentucky, easily one of the best overnight runs of its length in the Southeast. The land and waterscapes must be seen to be believed. Massive cabin-sized boulders spill across the river. Lush forests rise to towering rock parapets and sheer stone walls that overlook the river runner. Feeder branches add to the flow as it continues a northward journey to enter the dominion of Kentucky. Hiking, biking, and equestrian trails lace the entire watershed. The gorgeous scenery continues and the river begins to slow down as it flows into Lake Cumberland, finally leaving the recreation area confines, emptying its contents into the Cumberland River.

The Paddling

The put-in is about as nice as it gets. A shady gazebo stands near the loading area. Hiking trails emanate from this gathering spot of the Big South Fork National River and Recreation Area. A concrete ramp leads down to the water and the old Leatherwood Ford Bridge. Put in just below the old bridge at a gravel bar, beside a gentle shoal. The TN 297 bridge is just upstream. The riverbanks are lined with large rocks protruding along the shoreline. Sycamore, river birch, and other moisture-loving species rise from the water. Higher up, hardwoods such as oaks and hickories grow along with pines. As you float, note the streamside gravel bars, where sycamores rise from the rocks. The flood-prone nature of this river is evident as the sycamores all face

Cabin-size boulders and bluffs add national park level scenery on this paddle.

downstream, in reaction to the high waters that push through and continually carve the gorge through which the Big South Fork flows.

A couple of small Class I rapids end in a pool shortly downstream from the put-in. A tan beach extends along the right riverbank and would be a good spot to pull over and regroup, or just hang out. This beach is accessible by the River Trail, also leaving from Leatherwood Ford. Note the access areas with wooden decks along the river. Meanwhile, the John Muir Trail is traveling along the left bank, and does so for the first 2 miles before climbing to the Angel Falls Overlook atop the gorge rim. The vegetation grows extremely thick here along the shores. Small rivulets splash noisily into the river. Cane masses in profusion. Mountain laurel, rhododendron, ferns, and fading hemlock make their presence as well. It won't be long before you see your first bluff downriver. A power line stretches across the board just below the third rapid in the first 0.6 mile. Reach the first huge cabin-size boulders strewn about the river.

At 1.0 mile, Anderson Branch comes in on your right amid an 80-yard Class I shoal. A trail bridge crossing this stream is visible on river right. Ahead, at about 1.5 miles, you can see a large rock outcrop and bluff on river left, Angel Falls Overlook, accessed by the John Muir Trail, which begins at Leatherwood Ford across from the

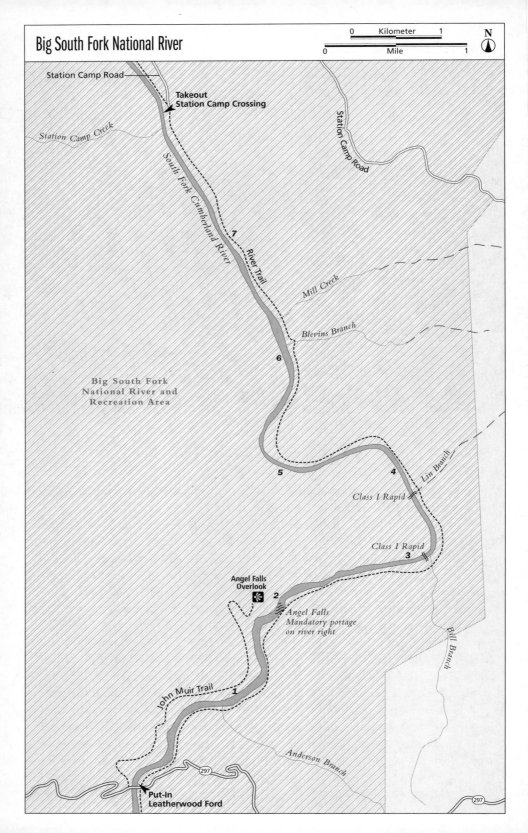

Big South Fork National River

0   Kilometer   1

0   Mile   1

N

Station Camp Road

Takeout
Station Camp Crossing

Station Camp Creek

South Fork Cumberland River

Station Camp Road

River Trail

7

Mill Creek

Blevins Branch

6

Big South Fork
National River and
Recreation Area

5

4

Lin Branch

Class I Rapid

Class I Rapid

3

Angel Falls
Overlook

2

Angel Falls
Mandatory portage
on river right

John Muir Trail

1

Bill Branch

Anderson Branch

297

Put-In
Leatherwood Ford

297

put-in. Begin to watch for the portage trail, on river right, at 1.9 miles. A sign has been posted on river left in the past above the Angel Falls. The portage trail, about 100 to 120 yards in length, climbs from the river to join the River Trail as it passes beneath a bluff, then leaves left down a sandbar, onto a rock slab before reaching a rock-rimmed pool, ideal for swimming on a hot summer day. Factor in a solid hour to your paddle time for this portage and even more time if you are carrying camping gear. Angel Falls is a huge rock jumble that narrows into a whitewater channel of madness. Many a boat has been smashed here. Don't even think about doing it.

Below the falls, the boulder jumble continues to constrict the river, making for an ultrascenic float. Notice also where limbs, brush, and even whole trees will be piled together during floods. At 3.2 miles, the Big South Fork makes a sharp curve to the north as Bill Branch comes in on your right. A rapid occurs here. You will begin to notice that most of the rapids fall where a feeder branch enters the river. At 3.8 miles, another rapid flows at the mouth of Lin Branch. The River Trail continues to run along the right bank.

At 4.3 miles, the river makes a turn to the northwest. Bountiful bluffs are visible near and far. The waters stay quiet. Relax and just absorb the national park–quality scenery. The river widens in excess of 140 feet and settles into a north-northwest course. Bluffs between Blevins Branch and Mill Creek are evident in the straightaway ahead.

Upon entering the long straightaway, the shoreline becomes mainly wooded with fewer exposed rocks. The water remains calm and paddling easy. Feeder streams cut hollows on either bank. As the watercourse appears to narrow and the river makes a slight curve to the right at 7.9 miles, watch on the right-hand bank for wooden steps and the Station Camp takeout. A small shoal and island are just below the Station Camp area. On the left, just before the shoal, Station Camp Creek comes in. It is worth traveling upstream and exploring as you ply your paddle beneath an overhanging tree canopy, forming quite a contrast to the wide-open Big South Fork. However, your takeout is on the opposite side of the river. A second potential takeout is on river right just downstream of the steps. This is the historic Station Camp Crossing ford. For those interested in a hike/bike shuttle to Leatherwood Fork, the River Trail comes in at the upstream side of the Station Camp gravel parking area.

THE SHELTOWEE TRACE

In addition to your paddle, consider adding hiking to your adventure. Hundreds of miles of trails course through the Big South Fork National River and Recreation Area (BSFNRRA), including the Sheltowee Trace, a hiking trail named for Daniel Boone. Sheltowee, meaning Big Turtle, was the name given to Boone when adopted into the Shawnee tribe as the son of the great war chief Blackfish. While being pursued by the Shawnee, Boone hid beneath the waters of a creek, breathing through a reed "straw," thus earning his nickname. Hikers who tread this trail will be "following the turtle," a white painted turtle blazed on trees, extending from the trail's southern terminus in Tennessee's Pickett State Park, north through the BSFNRRA and on through the length of the Daniel Boone National Forest nearly to the Ohio, for a total of 282 miles.

Along the way, hikers will see the best of the Cumberland Plateau, from exquisite arches to bluffs that offer extensive vistas to waterfalls that descend into sandstone cathedrals. The path treads through deep forests in gorges cut by creeks and rivers and atop the plateau, where oak and pine woodlands range long distances. In the BSFNRRA, the Trace nears significant flora and fauna, including threatened and endangered species such as the red-cockaded woodpecker, Virginia big-eared bat, freshwater mussels, and white-haired goldenrod. The black bear has made a comeback in these parts, too.

Starting at nearby Pickett State Park, the Trace explores spectacular natural features amid everywhere-you-look beauty. In its first mile, ST passes a waterfall, an arch, and a rock house while making its way through the Hidden Passage. Rocky vistas extend from Thompson Overlook before reaching the BSFNRRA and Rock Creek. The Trace enters Kentucky to reach Mark Branch Falls, an 80-foot veil of water. Mining history lies ahead along Grassy Fork, as the Trace follows an old mining railroad grade before reaching the big water of the Big South Fork. The river corridor offers sights of its own, such as Yahoo Falls Scenic Area. Yahoo Falls, the highest waterfall in the state of Kentucky at 113 feet, is the centerpiece of this picturesque spot. A set of side trails lead past rock monoliths, Yahoo Arch, overlooks, and other cascades. Beyond here, the trail continues along the river, now backed up as Lake Cumberland, before continuing beyond the recreation area. I had the privilege of writing *Day & Overnight Hikes on Kentucky's Sheltowee Trace* and highly recommend this lesser-used long trail along with spur and loop hikes using connector trails, many in the Big South Fork.

29 Emory River

This river run is the lowermost in the famed whitewater Obed/Emory watershed, part of the Obed Wild and Scenic River system.

County: Morgan
Start: Nemo Bridge, N36° 4.17', W84° 39.67'
End: US 25E at Oakdale, N35° 59.071', W84° 33.462'
Length: 9.9 miles
Float time: 4 hours
Difficulty rating: Moderate to difficult, based on portaging Nemo Rapid
Rapids: Class I–II (III)
River type: Big Cumberland Plateau river
Current: Moderate to swift
River gradient: 7.8 feet per mile
River gauge: USGS gauge—Emory River at Oakdale, minimum runnable level 275 cfs, maximum runnable level 4000 cfs
Season: November through June, then after summer rains

Land status: Public—Obed Wild and Scenic River, Catoosa Wildlife Management Area, Lone Mountain State Forest, also some private
Fees or permits: No fees or permits required
Nearest city/town: Wartburg
Maps: NPS Obed Wild and Scenic River; USGS: Lancing, Camp Austin, Harriman; *DeLorme: Tennessee Atlas & Gazetteer,* Page 58 D1, 42 A2
Boats used: Kayaks, canoes, very occasional raft
Organizations: Obed Wild and Scenic River, P.O. Box 429, Wartburg 37887, (423) 346-6294, www.nps.gov/obed
Contacts/Outfitters: Obed Watershed Community Association, 185 Hood Dr., Crossville 38555, (931) 484-9033

Put-in/Takeout Information

To takeout: From exit 347, Harriman/Rockwood, on I-40 take US 27 north, bridging the Emory River and passing through downtown Harriman to reach TN 328, Georgia Street, at 3.3 miles. Turn left on TN 328 toward Oakdale. Travel for 4.5 miles and turn left on TN 299 south. Follow TN 299 south for 0.2 mile to bridge the Emory River. Turn right just beyond the bridge and circle back under it to reach the takeout under the bridge.

To put-in from takeout: Backtrack on TN 299 to reach TN 328. Turn left and continue north on TN 328, reaching US 27 after 4 miles. Turn left on US 27 north and travel 8 miles to Wartburg. Turn left at the sign for Obed Wild and Scenic River Visitor Center, McNeal Street. Follow it a short distance and T-bone into Main Street. Turn right on Main Street and follow it for 0.6 mile to Maiden Street. Turn left on Maiden Street (the visitor center is reached with a right on Maiden Street) and go just a short distance to turn right on Spring Street at the sign for Nemo River Access. Spring Street becomes Catoosa Road. Follow Catoosa Road for 5.8 miles, then turn right into the Nemo picnic area and boat put-in.

Paddle Summary

The trip down the lower Emory starts off with a bang, as it immediately meets Class III Nemo Rapid, which most paddlers avoid by a short portage or lining their boat along its edges. Then the fun begins, as you travel through a mountain-rimmed valley with protected public lands much of the way. The only intrusion is the Norfolk Southern Railroad, which can be a lifeline if troubles arise. Invigorating and not-too-difficult Class I–II rapids are located at regular intervals throughout the paddle as the Emory travels under the shadow of green ridges and gray bluffs paralleling the watercourse. Impressive boulders add to the scenery.

River Overview

The Obed/Emory watershed, which feeds this paddle, really comprises four drainages that offer paddling of all difficulties. These watercourses—Daddys Creek, Clear Creek, Emory River, and the Obed River—have cut gorges into the Cumberland Plateau, where bluffs overlook rock-choked rivers lying beside thick forests. Upper Daddys Creek is for experts only, but the last 2 miles, from the Devils Breakfast Table, are Class II water. Some sections of Clear Creek are doable by average boaters, but other runs are tough. If you are going to paddle, go with someone who knows the water on your initial trips, and pay attention to water levels. The highest drainages of the Emory start at Frozen Head State Park, another great nearby recreation destination, where streams flow off Bird Mountain. The Emory then gains steam and cuts a canyon with Class II–III water to enter the Obed Wild and Scenic River boundaries. Here it meets the bigger Obed River. The Emory, despite being smaller, retains the name and turns southeast. It continues angling through rugged plateau country, then bisects Walden Ridge and meets the Clinch River under the water of Watts Bar Lake.

The Paddling

Immediately pass under the old Nemo Bridge, which is now part of the Cumberland Trail, then float under the new Nemo Bridge. Be on the watch as Class III Nemo Rapid is around the corner. At higher water levels you can hear its roar. I do not recommend this rapid—I've flipped a few times myself here. Rather portage your boat on the right side of the rapid or just line it through the rapid on the water's edge.

A large pool and rock wall lies below Nemo Rapid. An old trestle stands just below the first rapid beyond Nemo Rapid. The scenery is immediately pleasant and alluring. Boulders line the shore. River grasses grow in the shallows later in the warm season. In slower sections, large pools gather between the strong flows. Sycamore islands, heavy with brush, stand alongside the rapids. Heavy boulders, fallen from the ridgelines above, will be strewn across the river and astride its banks. As you float the

Rapids on the Emory keep the action—and your boat—moving.

alternating pools and shoals, it won't be long before the first train comes down the rail tracks that parallel the river on the left side. This intrusion of civilization is one of the few signs of man to be seen. And though the trains are frequent, they won't degrade from the beautiful scenery that is much like the Obed Wild and Scenic River watershed, minus the hair-raising rapids.

At 1 mile, the river constricts to create a solid Class II shoal with a 3- to 4-foot drop at lower water levels. Sand and gravel beaches will form along the lower end of these larger rapids, exposing themselves at lower river levels. River birches will rise and shade the tan beaches. Sycamore and sweetgum are also prevalent. The Emory runs a long straightaway, allowing you far-reaching looks downstream, where green wooded ramparts stand guard over the river. Look for pine trees silhouetting the sky atop gray bluffs.

Rapids are not continuous but keep the action and water moving. Most are easy Class I shoals, with the occasional more challenging cataract. At 2 miles, where Bear Branch flows in from the left, the river jogs right after a short but solid drop. At 3.2 miles, another short but sweet descent is followed by a slow section. At 4.3 miles,

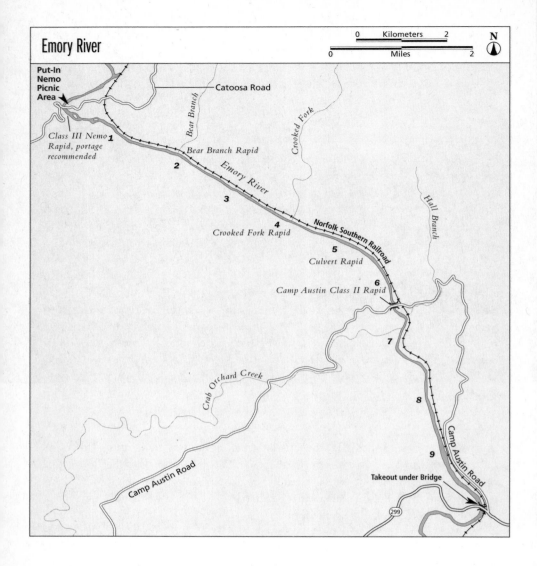

Emory River

0 Kilometers 2

0 Miles 2

N

Put-In
Nemo
Picnic
Area

Catoosa Road

Bear Branch

Crooked Fork

Class III Nemo
Rapid, portage
recommended 1

Bear Branch Rapid

2

Emory River

3

4

Crooked Fork Rapid

5

Culvert Rapid

Norfolk Southern Railroad

Hall Branch

6

Camp Austin Class II Rapid

7

Crab Orchard Creek

8

9

Camp Austin Road

Camp Austin Road

Takeout under Bridge

299

Crooked Fork flows under a rail trestle from your left. A rapid precedes this, and a few more flow near the confluence with Crooked Fork. This is also the beginning of Lone Mountain State Forest on river left.

Steep wooded ridges enclosing the Emory continue to give it a wilderness feel. Stunted sycamores grow out of the rocky islands that border the river in many places. These trees are invariably bent downstream, as the Emory is prone to big floods and wild variations in water levels. Always check the river before coming here. In my ignorant youth, I tried to paddle the river when there was no flow and another time stupidly made this run when the Emory was in the trees. (We flipped three times, but

Camp Austin Bridge and rapid.

lived to tell the tale. I lost a shirt, which I found later hanging from a tree limb after the water receded.)

Cabin-sized boulders often border the river and are also in the flow itself. A keen eye will spot boulders level enough to make ideal picnic spots and river viewing stands. At 5.5 miles, an undersized stream flows through a rail culvert then onto a rock ledge before pouring into the Emory. A rapid lies below here, and the river bends right. The Camp Austin Bridge comes into view—a small rapid occurs before the bridge is reached at 6.3 miles. Get ready for the Class II Camp Austin Rapid below the bridge. It's known for having big train waves in high water. Hall Branch comes in on your left in the rapid. A cliff rises below the rapid, and a recovery beach lies on river right. Just below here, Crab Orchard Creek flows in on river right. The Emory slows below Camp Austin, but the scenery remains impressive with high bluffs, lush woods, and tan gravel beaches, along with the ever present rocks and boulders.

The river separates and comes back together amid a number of islands. Watch for the bridge piling of old TN 299, then pass one last rapid before you reach the high span of current TN 299 and the takeout on river right.

OBED WILD AND SCENIC RIVER: A MULTIPLICITY OF RECREATIONAL OPTIONS

The Obed National Wild and Scenic River, administered by the National Park Service, has come of age. What once was a protected recreation area in name only has now evolved into a multiple outdoor activity destination supported by the community. It all began with die-hard kayakers and canoers plying the whitewater of the Obed-Emory River watershed. Next a few paddle access points were established. Then a segment of the Cumberland Trail was completed. This footpath runs through the heart of the Obed River gorge and starts at Rock Creek Campground, just across from the Nemo access where this paddle begins. The addition of Rock Creek Campground at the Nemo Bridge boat access completes the recreation picture.

When I started coming here over two decades ago, Nemo Bridge was a local party spot. Boy, have things changed. The rough area is now a nice picnic area, put-in, and trailhead. The old Nemo Bridge now is part of the Cumberland Trail. Rock Creek Campground has twelve shaded campsites. The Emory River is just a stone's throw away, and Rock Creek flows alongside camp. The quality design of Rock Creek Campground is immediately evident, with landscaping timbers delineating sites with raised tent pads of coarse sand, offering quick drainage and easy staking of your tent. The picnic tables are of stone embellished with designs, much as you would see in a garden at home. The fire rings and lantern posts are placed to last a long time. Campers should be able to find a site most any weekend if they arrive on Friday. Getting a site is no problem during weekdays and the fall and winter seasons. Summer weekdays are good too. Plan to scramble for a site on spring weekends when the water is right for paddling.

In addition to paddling, what other recreation is here? The rivers are good for fishing. Muskie, bass, bream, and catfish await in the river's deeper holes, most of these accessible by self-propelled boat or foot only. Hikers can take the Cumberland Trail from the campground up the Emory River, climbing away from the water before reaching its confluence with the Obed. At 2.6 miles you will near Alley Ford. Another 2 miles will take you to Breakaway Bluff Overlook. The trail travels on to Rock Garden Overlook and views of rapids before picking up an old railroad bed. It ends after 14 miles at the Devils Breakfast Table on Daddys Creek.

30 Hiwassee River

The Hiwassee makes its way through a mountainous setting, with scenery and views that make it hard to keep your eyes on the frequent attention-demanding rapids.

County: Polk
Start: Below Apalachia Dam powerhouse, N35° 10.863', W84° 26.674'
End: Reliance, N35° 11.296', W84° 30.127'
Length: 5.9 miles
Float time: 2–3 hours
Difficulty rating: Difficult
Rapids: Class I–II+
River type: Dam-controlled whitewater river
Current: Swift
River gradient: 14 feet per mile
River gauge: TVA water release schedule, call (VOL) 632-2264, then follow the prompts to get the release schedule for Apalachia Dam. Or visit www.tva.com.
Season: May–October, dam releases pending

Land status: Public—Cherokee National Forest
Fees or permits: Launching fee at put-in and takeout
Nearest city/town: Etowah
Maps: USGS: McFarland, Oswald Dome; *DeLorme: Tennessee Atlas & Gazetteer*, Page 26 C3
Boats used: Kayaks, rafts, tubes, occasional canoe
Organizations: Cherokee National Forest, 3171 Hwy. 64, Benton 37307, (423) 338-3300, www.fs.fed.us/r8/Cherokee
Contacts/outfitters: Webb Brothers Float Service, Inc./General Store, Hiwassee River, Box 61, Reliance 37369, (423) 338-2373 or (877) WEB-RAFT, www.webbbros.com

Put-in/Takeout Information

To takeout: From Etowah, take US 411 south to bridge the Hiwassee River, then turn left on TN 30 east. Take TN 30 east for 6.2 miles to TN 315 in Reliance. The takeout is at the intersection here at Webb Brothers Country Store.

To put-in from takeout: Take TN 315 across the Hiwassee River and cross the railroad tracks to turn right on Childers Creek Road. Follow Childers Creek Road for 1.3 miles, veering right to stay with Childers Creek Road at an intersection. Then at 1.6 miles, stay right again, now on Powerhouse Road. Travel 3.1 miles up to the Powerhouse boating site.

Paddle Summary

This trip takes place within the bounds of a Tennessee jewel, the Cherokee National Forest. The fun and wild ride is better done with whitewater experience or paddling with those who are experienced. It's an ideal waterway for those wanting to develop/hone their whitewater skills. Having said that, thousands of neophytes go down the river each year in tubes, rafts, and rubber funyaks, using outfitters located here.

Start at the Powerhouse put-in and immediately enjoy the fast-moving water, which leads into some mild shoals before you begin a series of Class II–II+ rapids.

Paddlers put in for the fun ride on the Hiwassee.

Your ears will be filled with the sounds of whitewater throughout the paddle, either from a rapid to come, one you are on, or one you just went down. The roar echoes through the river gorge.

The Hiwassee makes its way around the Big Bend. Continue your trip over The Ledges, Bigneys Rock, and Devils Shoals among other named rapids. Before you know it, the trip will be over and you might be tempted to do it twice in one day. The paddle is just short of 6 miles, but if you want to extend your adventure you can take out at the national forest picnic area 2.5 miles downstream of TN 315 on river left, the Gee Creek boat ramp on river right, or even at the US 411 boat ramp 7 miles downstream on river left. If you choose to use these lower accesses, make sure to look at the access points carefully; it will be different depending on whether the water is being generated. This paddle is dependent on water releases from TVA's Apalachia Dam. Fortunately, TVA makes daily recreational releases for the Hiwassee River from late May through August, with weekend releases earlier in May, and the months of September and October. To find the release schedule, visit the TVA website, www.tva.com, look for reservoir information and then find the release schedule for Apalachia Dam. You can also do it via the phone, (VOL) 632-2264. Releases generally start at

10 or 11 a.m., so be prepared to launch by noon. By the way, you can use your feet to walk back to the put-in via the Benton MacKaye Trail. This particular segment is also known as the John Muir Trail, as the famous naturalist walked the banks of the Hiwassee during his wanderings.

River Overview

The Hiwassee is a Georgia native and is part of the most southeasterly portion of the Tennessee River valley. It begins near Unicoi Gap and the Appalachian Trail, where the stream is small enough to straddle, then heads north where it is impounded as Lake Chatuge. Here, the watercourse enters North Carolina, curving westerly towards the town of Murphy. Here, it flows into Lake Hiwassee. Below this dam the river becomes Hiwassee by name only, minus most of its water—which comes out below Apalachia Dam—and enters the Volunteer State. It is below Apalachia Dam where the river becomes a true river again, and where this paddle begins. The Hiwassee keeps its westerly flow, leaving the mountains and winding westward to meet the Tennessee River, ending its journey.

The Paddling

The large concrete ramp put-in is below the Apalachia Dam powerhouse. Waters rush rapidly as you paddle away. The river is perhaps 250 feet wide, but very swift. Ahead you'll see rock outcrops dotting the mostly forested gorge of the river. Underwater grasses sway in the crystalline, chilly water. Small islands form here and there. The bigger ones are named. A smaller island is immediately downstream of the put-in. In general, keep to the left side of most islands. The banks are heavily forested with river birch, walnut, sycamore, ironwood, and thick brush. A railroad stays along the left bank nearly the entire route. Fog can overhang the river as the cool water mixes with warmer air above it. The wide river can make route finding challenging, but it also has numerous routes on many rapids. Be apprised the Hiwassee is often busy at the put-in immediately after they start generating, but if you have never been on the river, consider following someone to find the best route over the rapids. Just make sure they know what they're doing! If I were to pick someone out of the crowd, I would follow a helmeted kayaker in a hard plastic boat of his or her own, rather than a neophyte renting a rubber funyak.

The first rapid occurs in approximately 0.7 mile, as the river curves left. The main shoals are on the far right-hand side where the Hiwassee flows adjacent to Powerhouse Road. This is a good warm-up for what is to come. More islands follow just below this rapid. At 1.1 miles, the Towee Creek boating access is on river right. Here, paddlers load up, then briefly float Towee Creek before entering the Hiwassee. The second rapid, No. 2 Rapid, is solid drop. Then, the river widens and divides and rounds more islands, the biggest of which is Cane Island. A word about the islands: Once you decide which side of the island you are going on, you will find yourself

Hiwassee River

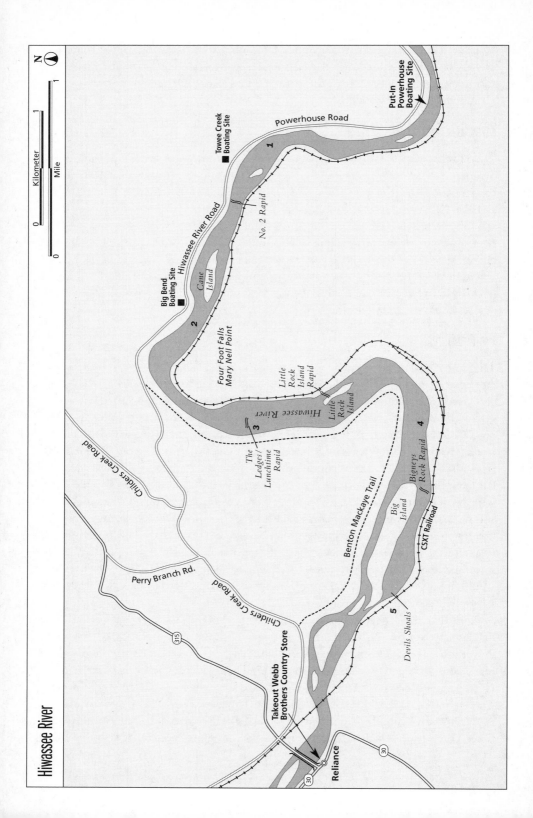

committed to that side for the rest of the rapid. Stay left at Cane Island and work through Thread the Needle Rapid—watch for the rock jumbles on its lower end. Just below Cane Island, at 2 miles, the river comes together and Big Bend boating access is on river right.

Stay on your toes in the Big Bend. First comes Four Foot Falls/Mary Nell Point (rapids on the Hiwassee have many different names, according to whom you ask). Stay left for the biggest drops. Powerhouse Road is no longer beside the river, though the railroad tracks continue on river left.

The river widens. Downstream lies The Ledges/Lunchtime Rapid. This is a series of ledges lasting about 0.25 mile and is very fun. Start on river left then work your way down, ending up on river right, running the calmer water between the ledges to find the next viable chute. An alluring stopping spot is on the right-hand bank at the bottom of the rapid. Look for the rock cliff topped with pine on river left.

Islands resume below The Ledges, the main one being a rocky wooded island topped with white pines rising high. This is Little Rock Island. Aim directly for the nose of the island then go left, spilling over a couple of good Class II drops at 3.4 miles. Now, stay right and look for a small channel cutting through the lower end of Little Rock Island. There's no rapid in the canopied channel, just a fun flow through which to paddle. Open to an area of tiny willow-covered islands.

The river bends to the right and widens. Islands, water, and mountain scenery continue to amaze. Big Island lies ahead. Stay left there and navigate another rapid at 4.3 miles, alternately called Bigneys Rock, Three Chutes, or Funnel Rapid. Multiple chutes allow for your choice of routes. Rhododendron and mountain laurel are regular features of the islands and the riverbanks. The river is wide here, and you can gain great views of Starr Mountain and Chilhowee Mountain, which act as gates through which the Hiwassee flows and exits the highlands a few miles ahead.

Be prepared as the left channel around Big Island builds into some big train waves at the rapid known as Devils Shoals. Open boaters risk swamping here, so be prepared. A final series of easy ledges leads to flowing flatwater with beautiful mountain views. A railroad trestle is in the foreground. Once beyond the trestle stay left and the takeout is on your left just before the bridge.

A TRAIL WITH SOLITUDE

The Benton MacKaye Trail, completed and dedicated in 2005, is 290 miles long. A portion of it travels several miles along the Hiwassee River where this paddle takes place. The idea for the path was spawned in 1979, for two reasons: to honor Benton MacKaye, the man with the original idea for the original long trail—the Appalachian Trail—and to provide an alternative to the overused Appalachian Trail for getting through North Georgia ultimately to the Smoky Mountains.

The Benton MacKaye Trail is what I imagine the Appalachian Trail was like many decades ago—a lesser tamed path, steep in places, rough in spots, and still evolving. The BMT starts at the same place as the AT, Springer Mountain in Georgia. It heads north through the Chattahoochee National Forest, like the AT, and crosses its more famous cousin a few times early before entering Tennessee's Cherokee National Forest. It passes over Big Frog Mountain, crosses the Ocoee River at Thunder Rock, then enters Little Frog Mountain Wilderness to make the Hiwassee River watershed, following Big Lost Creek until it flows into the Hiwassee. Here, it crosses the TN 315 bridge over the Hiwassee, then heads upstream along it, the part you can use for a shuttle, then leaves the river north through the Cherokee in the Citico Wilderness to ultimately reach the Great Smoky Mountains National Park. It then courses through the Smokies to terminate at Davenport Gap, on the Smokies' east end.

The BMT is more remote than the AT and certainly less traveled. The BMT isn't as easy to hike, either. Often, the trail goes straight up and down ridgelines, rather than gently switchbacking its way while changing elevations, which range from 1,500 feet to over 4,200 feet. There aren't conveniently located shelters, or supply points or hostels. Campsites are less frequent and not always obvious. The route can be overgrown. However, these may be the very qualities you are looking for: a challenging trail that takes effort to follow, a path where you must carry many supplies, and very few overcamped spots—in other words, a trail with solitude. For more information, visit www.bmta.org.

31 Little River

This segment of the Little River makes for a fun float. It offers cool clear aqua emanating from the Smokies in a mix of swift and slow segments.

County: Blount
Start: Mill Dam near Melrose, N35° 44.942', W83° 50.219'
End: Wildwood, N35° 47.933', W83° 52.949'
Length: 7.7 miles
Float time: 4 hours
Difficulty rating: Easy to moderate
Rapids: Class I–I+
River type: Pastoral river exiting mountains
Current: Moderate
River gradient: 4.4 feet per mile
River gauge: USGS gauge—Little River above Townsend, minimum runnable level 100 cfs

Season: May through October
Land Status: Private
Fees or permits: Parking fee at takeout
Nearest city/town: Maryville
Maps: USGS: Kinzel Springs, Wildwood, Maryville; *DeLorme: Tennessee Atlas & Gazetteer,* Page 44 B1, 43 B7
Boats used: Canoes, kayaks, a few johnboats
Organizations: Little River Watershed Association, www.littleriverwatershed.org
Contacts/outfitters: River John's Outfitters, 4134 Cave Mill Rd., Maryville 37804, (865) 982-0793, www.blountweb.com/riverjohns/

Put-in/Takeout Information

To takeout: From downtown Maryville, take TN 33, East Broadway Avenue, toward Knoxville to turn right on Wildwood Road. Follow Wildwood Road for 3.8 miles, bridging the Little River, then turn right at 3.9 miles onto Cave Mill Road. Follow Cave Mill Road for 0.5 mile and turn right into the River John's Outfitters.

To put-in from takeout: Leave the outfitter, turn right on Cave Mill Road, and follow it for 0.6 mile to reach Wildwood Road. Turn right on Wildwood Road and follow it for 1.1 miles to reach US 411. Turn right on US 411 and drive for 0.3 mile to reach River Ford Road. Turn left on River Ford Road and follow it for 1.5 miles, then turn right on Ellejoy Road. Follow Ellejoy Road for 0.6 mile then turn left on Old Walland Highway. Follow Old Walland Highway for 1.9 miles, then turn right on Melrose Station Road, crossing the Little River. Follow Melrose Station Road for 0.2 mile to reach US 321. Turn right on US 321 south and follow it for 0.2 mile, then turn right into the TWRA river access.

Paddle Summary

Leave a historic mill dam to immediately experience the shoal and pool pattern that will keep you moving, with a gradient of over 4 feet per mile. Throughout the run, islands divide the river into channels, though the main flow is almost always easy to discern. These islands harbor wildlife such as deer and also mitigate the possibility of having to land on private shores or backyards of riverside residents. Occasional gray bluffs provide backdrop for deep holes frequented by anglers and swimmers on warm weekends.

Rapids pose little problems and you only have one significant 2-foot drop at 4.9 miles. The rest of the shoals are Class I riffles flowing over gravel, with an occasional rocky chute that keeps the paddling interesting. The paddle ends at River John's, which makes for a safe place to leave your vehicle.

River Overview

The Little River and its tributaries drain the highest mountains of the Volunteer State, tumbling down the north slope of Clingmans Dome, at 6,642 feet the single loftiest point in Tennessee. Held fast within the confines of the Great Smoky Mountains National Park, trout-filled Grouse Creek, Fish Camp Prong, and Goshen Prong gather among dense rhododendron thickets shaded by magnificent forests to meet and form the Little River, which flows many protected miles through the Smokies before exiting the park at Townsend. From here, the Little exhibits both mountain and valley characteristics while heading through Blount County. Entering the expanding suburbs of Maryville, the river slows down before becoming entirely slackened by the Tennessee River near Knoxville. Whitewater crazies enjoy the challenging 15 miles starting at Elkmont through the Smokies where Class III–IV rapids and a gradient of over 70 feet per mile keep your average paddler off the water until it leaves the park. That being said, tubers float sections of the river there. Excellent swimming holes, such as The Sinks, draw in others. (I broke my foot at The Sinks, jumping into the water from an outcrop. Unfortunately I didn't jump far enough out.) Leaving the park, more casual paddlers have over 30 miles of river to ply. The rapids are mostly Class I with a few Class II ones closer to the park. As you head away from the Smokies, pools increase in size and shoals ease. Roads parallel the river nearly its entire distance, which makes scouting the river easy and adds to your paddling possibilities on this watercourse draining the highest lands in Tennessee.

The Paddling

The trip begins just below the old Melrose Mill dam, spilling loudly as you load your boat. (We used this area as a swimming hole during my days at the University of Tennessee.) Put in and immediately float down the left side of an island. The Little River flows translucent green over gravel. It extends 50 to 60 feet in width and is heavily wooded on both sides with box elder, sycamore, and river birch. Together they overhang the river, at times nearly canopying the shallow waterway. This makes for a shady venue along one bank or another. However, civilization is present just beyond the banks in the form of occasional first homes, resort houses, and camps standing 5 to 20 feet above the waterway. River grasses grow on the shoreline in summer, and on the island edges.

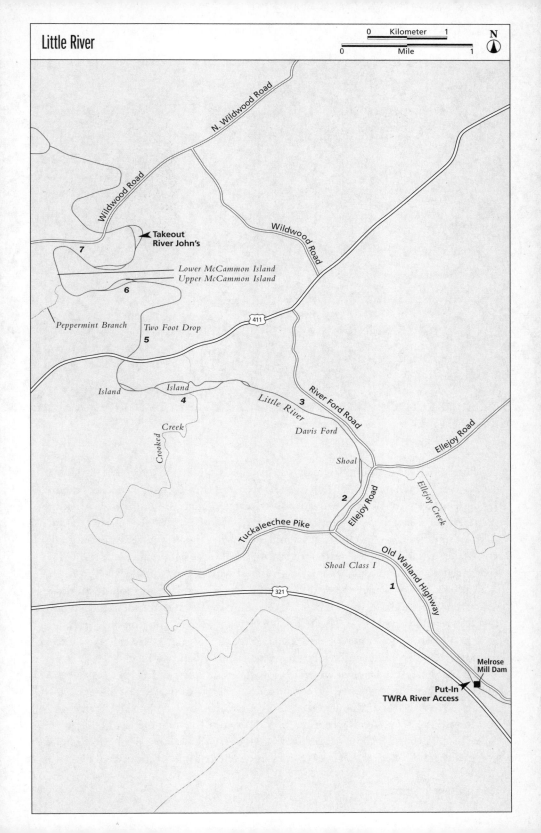

Little River

Kilometer
Mile

N

Melrose Dam stands just above the put-in.

The initial shoal through which you paddle is typical of the river—a gradual, steady descent where the current speeds over shallows to end in a deeper pool. Underlying rock strata show beneath still waters and contrast with the gravel of the shoals. At 1.1 miles, the river curves left and widens to 80 to 100 feet. Reach the first shoal of significance at 1.3 miles. It is similar to earlier shoals, yet has a steeper gradient. Make sure and look upstream for views of Chilhowee Mountain behind you. The river narrows again and passes around an island with speedy riffles that lead to the Tuckaleechee Pike Bridge at 1.7 miles. This is an alternate put-in should you desire to shorten this paddle. A small rock bluff rises on river left and overlooks a deep pool that forms below the bridge. This is a popular swimming/fishing hole for locals. The long pool narrows to a chute where Ellejoy Creek meets Little River. Ellejoy Creek can sometimes be muddy and cloud the waters over which you float.

The Little temporarily widens just below the confluence of Ellejoy Creek. At 2.7 miles, pass the Old Davis Ford. You can still see the ford on river right—it is now used as a river access. In this area lazy pools are broken by babbling shoals that push you toward the Tennessee River. Finer homes are located along the river here. At 3.5 miles, reach a large sycamore-covered island, which follows a big pool. At 4.0 miles, potentially muddy Crooked Creek comes in on the left side of this island. The river speeds up—enjoy a 150-yard shoal. Pass under the US 411 bridge at 4.8 miles. Enjoy a speedy little rapid just below the bridge before you reach the biggest rapid of the float—a 2-foot drop.

The final portion of the paddle works around some sharp bends with bluffs among many islands, collectively known as Upper McCammon Island, which you work around at 6.0 miles. Be careful picking your channel, as the lower flow channels may be obstructed by trees or have too little water. Peppermint Branch flows in on river left at 6.6 miles. Lower McCammon Island and a shoal wait as you make your final turn to enter a slow area. Unnamed isles lie downstream in this slow section. The river comes together before reaching River Johns, itself located on an island. Take out at the head of the island, reached at 7.7 miles.

TROUT FISHING THE UPPER LITTLE RIVER

I couldn't help but notice the onset of spring while headed up the Little River Trail. Spring flowers sparkled under a growing canopy of trees, whose leaves were that bright shade of green only seen in the season of rebirth. Insects flew industriously in the afternoon sun. Birds lighted from one branch to the next. The Smoky Mountains had sprung back to life after the winter dormancy. My backpacking partner Wes Shepherd and I hoped the trout were now feeding with renewed vigor, for we were engaging in one of the finest outings available in Tennessee: backpack fishing in the Smokies.

If you like to hike, camp, and fish, you can do it all in one fell swoop on the Little River in the Smokies. After a 3-mile hike to Rough Creek backcountry campsite, we hurriedly set up camp, taking time to hang our food from bears, who were probably famished after emerging from their winter dens. With my felt-soled boots on to handle the slippery rocks of the Little, I set out upstream from the campsite, spinning rod in hand. In the Smokies, the fishing rules are simple. You must have a valid Tennessee or North Carolina license. Only single hook artificial lures may be used. A total of five fish, at least 7 inches in length, per person, may be kept.

My 5-foot ultralight rod was tipped with a gold spinner while I crept along a pool gathering beneath a 4-foot fall. I tossed the lure at the foot of the fall, let it sink briefly, and retrieved it at a pace slightly faster than the current. A fish struck! With a stiff tug, I set the hook. The rainbow trout leapt in an effort to free itself, but to no avail. I reeled the 10-incher in and put it on my stringer.

I forged up the beautiful mountain valley and met with more success. Back at camp, Wes had a warming fire going while preparing our mountain feast. Potatoes were baking in the coals and a can of beans was heating at the fire's edge. Wes breaded our fish in corn meal, then fried them in oil. Under the glow of candlelight, by the gurgling Little River, we ate our delicious meal. Later, by the campfire, Wes recounted his fishing venture. Just about dark, he had hooked a real fighter but had somehow lost it as the fish swam downstream, slackening the line. He wasn't concerned with his loss, for he knew there would be other days of fishing in these clear highland streams. We retired under the stars, sleeping away the cool night.

The next morning, after coffee, we once again fished the Little, releasing all the fish we caught, broke camp, then returned downstream to the Goshen Prong Trail, toward our destination, Camp Rock backcountry campsite. The Goshen Prong Trail paralleled Fish Camp Prong. We would see if the waters of Fish Camp Prong lived up to their name. They didn't disappoint. Later that afternoon we were cleaning our fresh trout, under trees whose leaves seemed to be greening and growing before our very eyes. Our fish camp on Fish Camp Prong was made complete as we dined on rainbow trout that evening.

Wes and I were sad to see our trip end the next day while hiking back to the trailhead, a warm breeze blowing down the valley. Spring had arrived in the Smoky Mountains, and we knew we'd be back for more.

32 French Broad River Blueway: Seven Islands

You will be surprised at the beautiful nature of this paddle so close to Knoxville. Paddling potential is enhanced by the establishment of the French Broad River Blueway, a series of put-ins and takeouts along the river in Tennessee.

County: Sevier, Knox
Start: Kelly Lane boat ramp, N35° 57.10', W83° 41.00'
End: KUB boat ramp, N35° 56.49', W83° 49.25'
Length: 15 miles
Float time: 8 hours
Difficulty rating: Moderate to difficult
Rapids: Class I
River type: Wide river broken by islands with occasional shoals
Current: Moderate to swift
River gradient: 1.6 feet per mile
River gauge: TVA—French Broad at Newport, also TVA Douglas Dam release schedule (865) 632-2264, no minimum runnable level

Season: Spring, summer, fall
Land status: Mostly private, Seven Islands Refuge—public
Fees/permits: No fees or permits required
Nearest city/town: Knoxville
Maps: USGS: Boyds Creek, Shooks Gap; *DeLorme: Tennessee Atlas & Gazetteer,* Page 44
Boats used: Canoes, kayaks, johnboats
Organizations: French Broad River Conservation Corridor, 2447 Sutherland Ave., Knoxville 37919, (865) 215-6600, www.knoxcounty .org/frenchbroad
Contacts/outfitters: River Sports Outfitters, 2918 Sutherland Ave., Knoxville 37919, (865) 523-0066, www.riversportsoutfitters.com

Put-in/Takeout Information

To takeout: From exit 398 on I-40 east of Knoxville, take Strawberry Plains Pike south for 3.4 miles to TN 168, John Sevier Highway. Turn left and take TN 168 west for 1.7 miles to Asbury Road. Turn right and follow Asbury Road for 0.4 mile to National Drive. Turn left on National Drive and follow it for 0.3 mile to Water Plant Drive. Turn left on Water Plant Drive and follow it 0.6 mile to dead-end at the river. The paved road will split at the river. Look for a clear path to the water at the split. This is the takeout. However, go physically look at the takeout from the river so you can recognize it before you proceed to the put-in.

To put-in from takeout: Return to the light at TN 168 and Asbury, then proceed through the light, crossing TN 168 on Asbury Road. Shortly merge into Thorn Grove Pike. Stay with Thorn Grove Pike for 3.5 miles, then veer right onto Kodak Road. Stay with Kodak Road for 5.5 miles and look for the right turn onto small Kelly Lane. Turn right on Kelly Lane and follow it for 0.4 mile then turn left for the canoe/kayak launch for Seven Islands Refuge. Follow the paddle access for 0.6 mile to dead-end at the launch.

The French Broad at Seven Islands Refuge.

Paddle Summary

This route travels the lowermost part of the French Broad River, passing through the Seven Islands Refuge, where the wide waterway breaks apart and flows in chattering shoals. The river continues its westerly course in sweeping bends below green hills. Islands occasionally appear, and the gentle river speeds. Tan bluffs rise from the water here and there, including Paint Rock Bluff, just before the bridge at John Sevier Highway. The final part of the trip becomes less bucolic near the takeout at the old Knoxville Utilities Board property at Forks of the River Industrial Park. Also, consider exploring the hiking trails at Seven Islands Refuge, which also begin at the Kelly Lane boat ramp. The refuge encompasses 360 acres and is managed by Knox County Parks and Recreation. Also, before embarking check the Tennessee Valley Authority Douglas Dam release schedule. Releases usually coincide with peak power use, which generally occurs in the later afternoon, though there may be some light generation during the earlier part of the day. Call (865) 632-2264, then follow the prompts for scheduled water releases. The releases will affect current speed but not the overall paddle.

River Overview

Purportedly the third oldest river in the world (only the New River of West Virginia and the Nile River of Egypt are older), the French Broad River is a large waterway by the time it gets down to Knoxville, where it joins the Holston River to form the Tennessee. Born in the high mountains of western North Carolina near the town of Rosman, it passes 116 miles in a wide arc through Asheville and the Tar Heel State to push through the crest of the Appalachians into Tennessee, where it is one of the original rivers included in the 1968 Tennessee Scenic Rivers Act. An already big waterway by the time it reaches the town of Newport, Tennessee, the French Broad continues dropping in shoals and pools before being slowed as it enters Douglas Lake. It once again begins flowing below Douglas Dam and travels a little less than 40 miles to its end, for a total of 102 miles in the Volunteer State.

The Paddling

Leave the Kelly Lane ramp and paddle into the wide waterway, extending 250 or more feet across. Houses are scattered on the far bank. The Seven Islands Refuge lands stand off to the right, heading downstream. A walking trail, which starts at the put-in, travels along the refuge shore. Wooded banks are thick with sycamore, ash, locust, silver maple, and willow. For the first 2 miles, the French Broad forms the Knox-Sevier county line. Curve northwesterly after a big bend. Just before reaching the Seven Islands, Bays Mountain leaves left, away from the river. Note the planted cypress at the head of the upper stream island, which is known as Newman's Island. The best route is to stay left here, passing the Kimberlin Heights boat ramp. Class I riffles and shoals extend along the Seven Islands and even a bit beyond them. Wildlife is abundant— you may spot deer. Birders should enjoy this paddle—I have seen a bald eagle here. Pelicans and geese are more commonly seen birds. Also look for beaver or muskrat.

The French Broad begins a long southeasterly sweep, passing Kodak Road and the old Huffaker Ferry landing at 5.5 miles, now a boat ramp. Hills continue rising in the distance and add to the scenery. Huffaker Shoals form a riffle below the landing. Reach Johnson Island at 7 miles. Stay right in the narrow channel, then continue northwest, passing Cement Shoals. You may notice a pattern to the rocks here. In the early 1900s the Army Corps of Engineers tried to "improve" the river for transportation, and this is the remnant. Steamboats plied the river from the 1870s to the 1920s, falling off when a railroad connected Knoxville to Sevierville. Pass a smaller unnamed island at 9.5 miles, just as the river curves left. Hills and farms continue, with occasional houses in an overall rural landscape. The French Broad pushes for Knoxville, passing Hines Creek on the left at 12 miles.

At 13.5 miles, Paint Rock Bluff rises on the right bank. The black and tan rock promontory is unmistakable. Just ahead, the river passes under the Johnson Sevier Highway Bridge, TN 168. The scenery abruptly changes from rural to industrial on river right, as you have reached the Forks of the River. The backup of Fort Loudon

French Broad River Blueway: Seven Islands

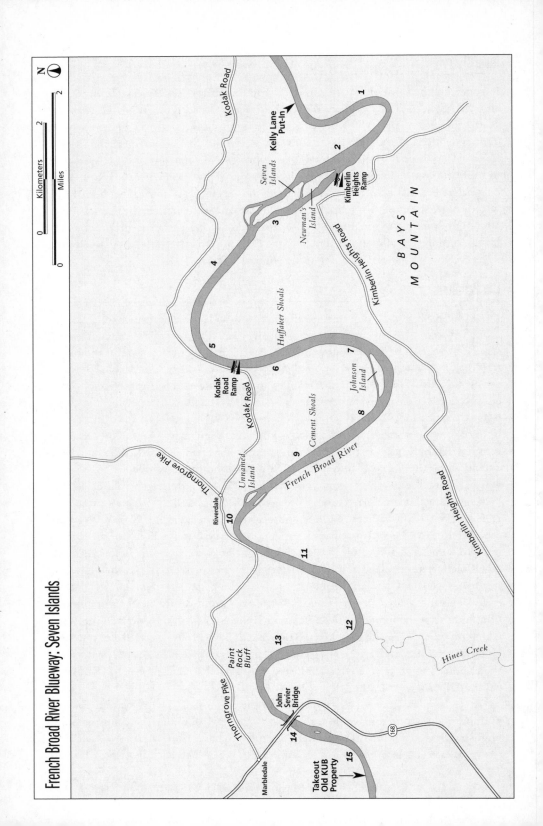

Lake now slows the French Broad. Begin hugging the right bank, and keep an eye peeled for the KUB parking area, which is up the bank to your right at 15 miles. By the way, make sure and look out on the river to mark the spot when you leave a shuttle vehicle, as there is no ramp.

FRENCH BROAD: AN UNUSUAL NAME

Before you ever see this scenic waterway, you will undoubtedly take note of its name. Early European explorers came upon the river and dubbed it the French Broad, as it was flowing toward the French-claimed Mississippi River basin and secondly for the wide nature of the river.

Before that, it was historically Cherokee country, as were most of the Southern Appalachian Mountains. After gathering below North Carolina's highest peaks, it heads through the heart of Asheville. Shortly before crossing the Tennessee state line it passes through an area visited by not only the Cherokee but even tourists of today—to seek relief in the warm waters near the town of Hot Springs. The Appalachian Trail bridges the river here. Beyond Hot Springs the river enters a gorge where whitewater thrills await those in kayaks, rafts, and the occasional canoe.

Bigger boats plied the river in days gone by. Steamboats were working their way up the Tennessee River watershed and made their way to the French Broad. To enhance steamboat traffic the Army Corps of Engineers got in on the act. In the early 1900s, the French Broad was still being altered for the purpose of steamboat navigation, since it was part of the Tennessee River watershed. At one time it was officially opened for steamboat navigation for 46.5 miles upstream from its mouth to the town of Dandridge, Tennessee. The Army Corps of Engineers cited the nearly 130,000 tons of freight moved along the river in 1917 as a testimony to its work. Having a 2-foot draft on the entire river was the definition of navigable for steamboats. At higher waters, the river was opened for 20 miles farther upstream to the community of Leadvale. Today, the flowing Volunteer State portion of the river sees only smaller craft as it flows broadly toward the Mississippi, once occupied by the French, via the Tennessee and Ohio Rivers.

33 Powell River

Floating this part of the Tennessee countryside will take you back to a quieter, more relaxed time.

County: Hancock, Claiborne
Start: TWRA boat ramp at TN 63, N36° 33.359', W83° 22.769'
End: Brooks Bridge at TN 63, N36° 32.095', W83° 26.810'
Length: 8.9 miles
Float time: 4.5 hours
Difficulty rating: Easy to moderate
Rapids: Class I
River type: Moderate moving mountain river
Current: Slow to moderate
River gradient: 2.4 feet per mile
River gauge: USGS gauge on web—Powell River at Arthur, minimum runnable level 350

cfs, also TVA, call (865) 632-2264, then press 3, then listen for Powell River at Arthur
Season: Spring, summer, fall
Land status: Private
Fees or permits: No fees or permits required
Nearest city/town: Harrogate
Maps: USGS: Coleman Gap; *DeLorme: Tennessee Atlas & Gazetteer,* Page 68 D4, 69 D5
Boats Used: Canoes, johnboats
Organizations: Upper Tennessee Roundtable, 366 West Main St., Suite 400, Abingdon, VA 24210, (276) 628-1600, www.uppertnriver.org
Contacts/outfitters: Heavys Barbecue Canoe & Camp, 233 Benfield Lane, Harrogate 37752, (423) 869-9024

Put-in/Takeout Information

To takeout: From Harrogate, take TN 63 east for 12 miles to the Brooks Bridge, crossing the Powell River. Park on the southeast side of the bridge.

To put-in from takeout: From Brooks Bridge, continue on TN 63 for 0.4 mile to TN 345, Alanthus Hill Road. Turn left on TN 345/TN 63, Alanthus Hill Road, and follow it for 5.4 miles to the Tennessee Wildlife Resources Agency boat ramp, on your left, just before reaching Mulberry Gap Road.

Paddle Summary

Every time I paddle the Powell I wonder why more people aren't on it. At the put-in, the Powell has recently entered the Volunteer State and is making a meandering southwesterly course through hilly terrain. Wallen Ridge forms a rampart to the southwest. Mulberry Creek contributes to the river flow just below the put-in. Here, the normally clear-green Powell flows gently over gravel bars past partly wooded bluffs that rise across from sloped meadows where cattle lazily graze. Occasional riffles in the shallows speed the current, but it is mostly a relaxed float amid the mountain scenery. You will likely have this river to yourself. The Powell is floated by a few area anglers in johnboats, and next to no "outsiders." That being said, the locals have been nothing but helpful to me during my adventures here.

Mountain views are common on the Powell River.

River Overview

Springing forth from the ridges of Wise County and Lee County of southwest Virginia, the Powell becomes truly riverine with the addition of the South Fork Powell River, after passing through the town of Big Stone Gap. Paddling in the Old Dominion is more of a spring affair. The upper watershed above Big Stone Gap is more for heavy whitewater paddlers, but it does settle down into Class I–II water below Big Stone Gap. Entering the mountains of East Tennessee after 80 miles in Virginia, the Powell River courses through superlative scenery, where pastoral meadows lie tucked away between steep wooded ridges. Houses are infrequent. I have paddled the river from the state line to Norris Lake in one shot and pronounce it a great adventure. Despite being enveloped in steep terrain, the Powell in Tennessee is an easy float with no challenging rapids from the Virginia state line 70 miles to where the river is stilled at Norris Lake. The Powell is absorbed into the Clinch at Norris Lake.

The Paddling

Leave the put-in just below the TN 63 bridge. Maynard Creek comes in on the left, but the Powell remains about 60 to 80 feet wide. Sycamore, box elder, and ironwood

Powell River

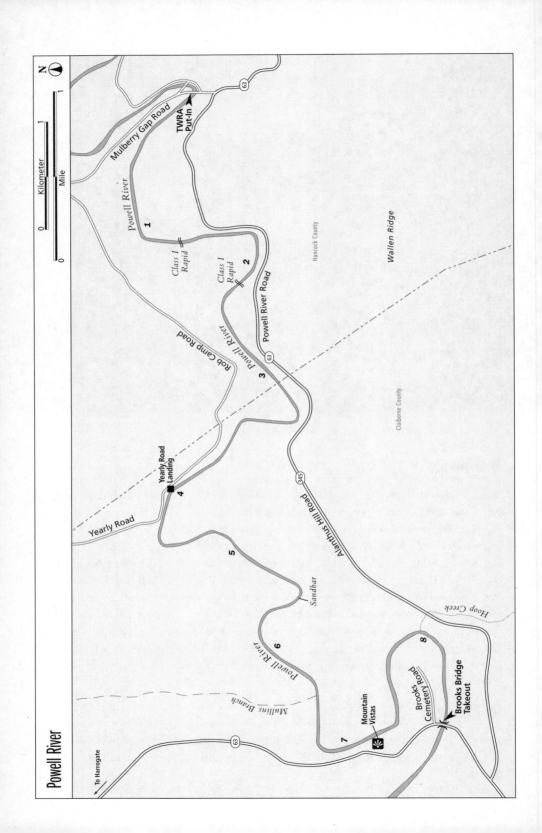

N

To Harrogate

Mulberry Gap Road

Powell River

TWRA Put-In

1
Class I Rapid
Class I Rapid
2

Powell River Road

Rob Camp Road

Powell River

3

Hancock County

Wallen Ridge

Claiborne County

Yearly Road

Yearly Road Landing

4

5

345

Alanthus Hill Road

Sandbar

6

Powell River

Hoop Creek

Mullins Branch

7

Mountain Vistas

8

Brooks Road

Cemetery Road

Brooks Bridge Takeout

63

Kilometer
0   1

Mile
0   1

grow to the water's edge, along with the occasional basswood. Sycamore and grasses round out the vegetation. At times pastureland runs almost to the river. The river is clear-green in its normal state. Copious mussel shells will be reflecting off the rocky river bottom. The Powell River and the Clinch are the two most intact rivers in the upper Tennessee River drainage and house some of the richest mussel habitats on the planet. Most of the bivalves have long scientific names, but just know the clean moving water of the Powell is ideal habitat for these life forms.

The river alternates between shallow Class I riffles and deeper pools from which cedar-topped bluffs rise. Other bluffs rise more covertly through a screen of trees. Along the water, mud banks will be bordered by thick vegetation and overhanging or fallen trees. At 1.3 miles, flow through a long Class I riffle with a river birch–covered island off to the right. Shortly come along TN 63, as the Powell makes a long bend. Encounter a second Class I shoal at 2.2 miles. By 2.8 miles, bluffs recede from both sides of the river. A line of trees screens pasturelands beyond. But flatlands are infrequent in this valley, and bluffs rise again by 3.3 miles. Cane crowds the bluffs, especially ones back from the river, as opposed to promontories rising directly from the water's edge. This thick brush can sometimes prohibit your landing. Consider small gravel bars for ingresses, though they will be partly covered with grasses as the warm season progresses.

In its convolutions, the Powell will sometimes lend long looks toward mountains rising afar, a view that complements the closer ridges rising directly from the valley. At 4.2 miles, reach a gravel landing on river right. This is just off Yeary Road. The current speeds, and a shallow clear stream comes in on the right. This riffle continues for some distance as the river curves back to the south.

Reach a willow-shaded sandbar at 5.6 miles, on a sharp bend to the right. A sheer prominence rises across the water. The spot is an alluring stop, but you may be sharing it with cows coming down for a drink. At 6.6 miles, Mullins Branch comes in on the right across from rising gray bluffs on your left. Long, drooping weak-leaf yucca plants grow amid the gray rock. In spring, delicate blooms of old man's beard infrequently whiten the gray rock. The bluffs are often a series of multiple ledges leading down the river, broken by grasses and flowers, with cedars aplenty on the south- or west-facing areas. On the low side of the river, sloped pastureland rises beyond riverside trees. At 7 miles, the Powell makes a long southbound straightaway where mountain vistas impress. The straightaway ends at 7.4 miles, as the Powell curves to the left, creating a large gravel bar suitable for stopping. Beyond the gravel bar the river widens in excess of 100 feet. At 8.1 miles, on a long 180-degree bend, Hoop Creek comes in on the left. The Powell speeds at a shoal here. Just beyond Hoop Creek one last beautiful bluff ascends from the river and the TN 63 bridge shortly comes into view. The takeout is on river left before the bridge. A privately owned ramp is on river right, but you must get permission from the landowner in the house nearest the northeast side of the bridge to use it. Consider offering to pay to park/disembark at the private ramp.

COAL TO TREES?

The headwaters of the Powell River flow through the heart of Virginia's coal country. It drains 353,000 acres of land in Wise and Lee Counties. Prior to the 1970s unregulated mining tampered not only with the Powell River but also groundwater supplies and just about anywhere else water flowed within its watershed, making it a problem for residents and river critters alike. Virginia's coal production peaked in 1990. Though still a force in the region, coal production is down. Over time, we have learned what to do with the areas after coal production has ceased. Places such as the Powell River Project and Research Center and researchers at Virginia Tech have developed various methods of reclaiming lands to benefit not only the Powell River watershed but also the lands through which they flow and residents living in those lands.

One such idea is to use post-mining land for commercial forestry. Whether we want it or not, most mining land will become forested either through planting or through the works of nature over time in a process known as succession. This is where land slowly grows from pioneer plants such as grasses eventually to trees. Some lands may be developed for human use or pasturage, but most will end up as woodland. Commercial foresters can plant valuable species such as white pine rather than low value nonmarketable trees that might spring up on their own. A road system that can handle trucks needed for timber harvesting is usually already in place from the mining activity.

Successful land reclamation such as commercial forestry, environmentally-minded yet sensible mining regulations, along with cleaning up past abuses such as acid mine drainage will continue to improve the health of the Powell River from its headwaters in Virginia to its tailwaters in Tennessee.

34 Clinch River

This long run offers great scenery as the river cuts its way through rugged scenic terrain that threatens to take your eye off the many angled shoals.

County: Hancock, Claiborne, Grainger
Start: Old Manning Ferry, N36° 26.903', W83° 20.935'
End: US 25E near Norris Lake, N36° 24.056', W83° 27.577'
Length: 16 miles
Float time: 8 hours
Difficulty rating: Moderate
Rapids: Class I–II
River type: Large river bordered by mountains with ledge rapids aplenty
Current: Moderate
River gradient: 6.2 feet per mile
River gauge: USGS gauge—Clinch River above Tazewell, minimum runnable level 300 cfs

Season: Spring through fall
Land status: Private
Fees or permits: No fees or permits required
Nearest city/town: Tazewell
Maps: USGS: Swan Island, Howard Quarter; *DeLorme: Tennessee Atlas & Gazetteer,* Page 61 A5, 62 A4
Boats used: Canoes, johnboats, occasional kayak
Organizations: Upper Tennessee Roundtable, 366 West Main St., Suite 400, Abingdon, VA 24210, (276) 628-1600, www.uppertnriver.org
Contacts/outfitters: River Place on the Clinch, 2788 Hwy. 70, Kyles Ford 37765, (423) 733-4400, www.clinchriverecotourism.com

Put-in/Takeout Information

To takeout: From Tazewell, take US 25E south for 9 miles to Clinch River Road, which is just before the bridge over the Clinch. Turn right on Clinch River Road and follow it a short distance. The boat ramp is just below the old bridge over the Clinch River.

To put-in from takeout: Backtrack to US 25E and turn left back toward Tazewell. Follow 25E north for 0.9 mile and turn right on Upper Caney Valley Road. Go for 7.8 miles to reach Porter Johns Road. Turn right on Porter Johns Road and follow it for 0.7 mile to drive over a small culverted creek. Immediately make a left turn on an unnamed dirt road and follow it for about 80 yards. You can drive almost to the river, but be careful, as the dirt road can get muddy. Even consider parking out on Porter Johns Road and carrying your stuff in if you feel uncomfortable about the condition of the dirt road. You've gone too far on Porter Johns Road if you start climbing a very steep hill to a dead end at a homestead.

Paddle Summary

This is a fun trip. After I did it for the first time, I wondered how come it took me so long to get here. Actually, one of the reasons is the lack of public access. You'll note that this river trip is 16 miles, a long day trip. Reason: a lack of public river accesses. So start early then expect to have a great time on the Clinch. Put in at the site of forgotten Manning Ferry. Here, the Clinch begins cutting into a series of knobs and ridges, creating sheer bluffs on one side or the other of the river. Simultaneously, numerous rock ledges cross the river and make for fun rapids to run. The shoals are primarily Class I–I+ with a few Class II shoals thrown in, especially when the ledges run irregularly, necessitating good route finding. Just remember to start early and don't tarry too long at any one spot with 16 miles to travel.

River Overview

The Clinch River is born near Tazewell, Virginia, where the South Fork and North Fork converge a little south of the Old Dominion's border with West Virginia. The Clinch then begins its southwesterly journey, absorbing tributaries as it flows some 70 miles to the Volunteer State. It is quite a paddler's river in Old Virginny and its bluffs, banks, and bottoms harbor rare flora (see sidebar for more). Generally considered float-able by the time it reaches Richlands, Virginia, the Clinch avails some Class II+ waters before settling down to more pedestrian rapids. The river enters Tennessee in the midst of a long straightaway, hemmed in by Copper Ridge and Big Ridge. It finally leaves the mountainous straitjacket above Kyles Ford, curving a bit, then resumes its nearly linear track until about 5 miles below Sneedville. From here on, the Clinch winds and works its way through rising mountains for about 25 gorgeous miles before being slowed at Norris Lake. Under the still lake, the Powell, a major tributary also detailed in this book in chapter 33 (page 188), feeds the Clinch. The now-bigger Clinch is released below Norris Dam as a tailwater trout fishery of regional fame. From here it flows through the town of Clinton before being dammed again near the city of Oak Ridge as Melton Hill Lake. Below Melton Hill Dam the river is briefly freed one last time before meeting the Tennessee River under the waters of Watts Bar Lake.

The Paddling

A small gravel bar serves as the put-in. A tributary comes in just above that. The Clinch is about 100 feet wide at this point and bordered by a mix of field and forest with hills rising in the distance. Box elder, willow, and sycamore are the predominant riverside tree species. Walnuts and sumac have a presence as well. Cane often mixes in the waterside growth. The banks are rock and mud ranging about 5 feet high. The river makes the first of many bends as it cuts deeper into the War Ridge and Comby Ridge and their adjacent hills. Immediately turn into a shoal. Rapids here are gener-ally Class I–I+ rock riffles and ledges of irregular rock that extend across the river. A bluff rises on river right in the middle of the rapid. This is just a precursor for what is to come. The river immediately curves back right and a bluff rises on river left. Shoals wait around the bend, continuing fast-moving water since the paddle's beginning. A few ledges add spice to the flow.

Occasional farmhouses and such are visible in the riverside flats. At 2.4 miles, Big War Creek comes in on your left. Despite the added flow, the river narrows, curves right, and flows over angled ledges, working its way around Craneneck Bend. A large bluff rises on river left. The river briefly slows, where a white church on Paw Paw Road stands within sight. As the Clinch curves north, rapids resume, flowing over another angled ledge, and rapids continue with just a few breaks. This is known as Macks Shoals.

It's interesting—the river ledges run southwest to northeast no matter which way the Clinch curves, making each rapid dissimilar. A good example stands at 5.2 miles. Here the ledges run almost parallel with the river. Cedar bluffs continually rise from the shoreline.

Taking a break among the many ledge shoals of the Clinch River.

Begin curving around Lee Bend at 5.6 miles. Calm stretches divide Bulls Shoals and Johnson Shoals, each with big bluffs rising above them. Johnson Shoals is a long series of moderate rapids. At 7.5 miles, you'll see a concrete structure resembling a mini tower on your right. It's an old USGS water monitoring station. This marks the entrance into the bend circling around The Narrows. Grissom Island Baptist Church stands on river right. Locals, with permission of the church, put in here, then float 10 miles to the US 25E bridge. Grissom Island, actually a series of islands, begins below the church. The river continues one of the sharpest bends along the route and passes a high bluff. Look for the exposed rock spire flanked by cedars. The water speeds below the spire.

At 10.5 miles, drop over a ledge crossing perpendicular to the river flow, a classic rapid, and begin making the big curve of Posey Bend. A bluff rises on river right. Here, the Clinch widens to around 150 feet and begins a series of sweeping loops, penned in by River Ridge to the south and Caney Ridge to the north. Pass Sycamore Island amid a long shoal at 11.5 miles. The river is cutting its way ever deeper toward Norris Lake. Steep hills lead down to the river's edge, broken by occasional flats on

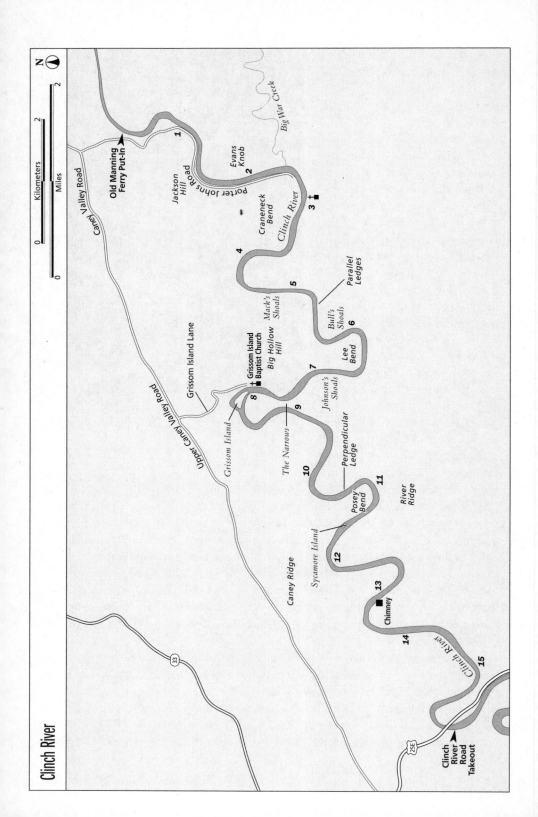

Clinch River

Old Manning
Ferry Put-In

Caney Valley Road

Jackson Hill

Porter Johns Road

Evans Knob

Big War Creek

Clinch River

Craneneck Bend

Mack's Shoals

Parallel Ledges

Bull's Shoals

Lee Bend

Johnson's Shoals

Grissom Island Lane

Upper Caney Valley Road

Grissom Island
Baptist Church

Big Hollow Hill

Grissom Island

The Narrows

Perpendicular Ledge

Posey Bend

River Ridge

Caney Ridge

Sycamore Island

Chimney

Clinch River

Clinch River
Road Takeout

N

Kilometers

Miles

one side or the other. Watch for an old chimney at the base of a rapid, marking a forgotten homestead on river left at 13.2 miles.

A large gravel bar appears on river left below the chimney. Wide shoals continue. The Clinch makes one final turn, running parallel with 25E. There's a long gravel bar used by locals here. Pass under the new 25E bridge, then the old one and the ramp is on the right just beyond the old bridge at 16 miles. Should you want to continue this already long day trip, you can paddle for 1.3 miles downriver to a TWRA boat ramp on river right. The still waters of Norris Lake usually start near the bridge; however, they can rise as far as 0.5-mile upstream at higher water levels and as far as a mile down at lower water levels.

MUSSEL CENTRAL

I bet you didn't know that the Clinch River is the number one spot in the United States for rare and imperiled mussel species. The Clinch River, along with its tributary the Powell, harbors an impressive concentration of freshwater mussels, over forty in all. The names might not mean much, but they do sound like they were coined by mountaineers who settled this country: birdwing pearly mussel, rough rabbitsfoot, shiny pigtoe.

Today, more and more people are settling in the Clinch River Valley. And who can blame them for wanting to live in such a beautiful place? Unfortunately, some residents old and new allow pollution to enter the river, which is tough on the mussels. See, mussels are sedentary feeders, basically filtering the river to obtain nutrients. Thus when toxins enter the river the mussels absorb them. Mussels are the proverbial "canary in a coal mine" for rivers. Today, we have an ever-increasing awareness of how our practices affect rivers. Now you will see more protection of the land along the rivers, as in keeping banks vegetated and feeder streams shaded, and simply awareness that dumping something in the river does have consequences. On the Clinch, groups such as The Nature Conservancy have purchased land and islands along the river to preserve mussel habitat. The group has helped set aside over 1,000 acres in the greater Cleveland, Virginia, area to preserve not only the mussel habitats but also dolomite barrens on bluffs overlooking the river. They also have an 850-acre tract near Kyles Ford, Tennessee, among others in their greater Clinch Valley Program, designed to help preserve this great Appalachian River.

35 Nolichucky River

This trip takes you on waters typical of the lower Nolichucky River. Quieter sections lead past agricultural land, but repeatedly the river will gather to descend in shoals that keep the paddling exciting.

County: Washington, Greene
Start: Bailey Bridge, N36° 9.376', W82° 35.429'
End: Davy Crockett Birthplace State Park, N36° 12.320', W82° 39.598'
Length: 9.2 miles
Float time: 5 hours
Difficulty rating: Moderate
Rapids: Class I–II
River type: Large valley river with solid drops
Current: Slow to fast around rapids
River gradient: 5.8 feet per mile
River gauge: USGS gauge—Nolichucky River at Embreeville; also call TVA (865) 632-2264,

then press 3, minimum runnable level 500 cfs
Season: Spring, summer, fall
Land status: Private
Fees or permits: No fees or permits required
Nearest city/town: Johnson City
Maps: USGS: Telford, Chuckey; *DeLorme: Tennessee Atlas & Gazetteer,* Page 62 C4
Boats used: Canoes, kayaks, a few johnboats
Organizations: Middle Nolichucky Watershed Alliance, P.O. Box 145, Greeneville 37744, www.middlenolichuckywatershedalliance.org
Contacts/outfitters: Cherokee Adventures, 2000 Jonesborough Rd., Erwin 37650, (800) 445-7238, www.cherokeeadventures.com

Put-in/Takeout Information

To takeout: From Johnson City, take US 11E south for 17 miles to the signed turn for Davy Crockett Birthplace State Park on South Heritage Road. Follow South Heritage Road for 1.2 miles, crossing Limestone Creek. Turn right on Davy Crockett Road and follow it for 1.2 miles and turn right on Keebler Road. Reach the state park at 0.9 mile and stay left. Continue on beyond the Davy Crockett birthplace site to the boat ramp at the far end of the park.

To put-in from takeout: From the state park, backtrack on Keebler Road for 0.9 mile, then stay right, still on Keebler Road for 0.9 mile farther, then turn right onto Corby Bridge Road. Follow Corby Bridge Road closely as it twists and turns. Along the way you'll cross the Nolichucky River. Travel 5.9 miles, then reach a stop sign at TN 353. Turn left on TN 353 and follow it for 0.1 mile, then turn left on Bill Mauk Road. The put-in is just a short distance down the road on your right, across from a house and downstream of Bailey Bridge.

Paddle Summary

Paddlers will enjoy this Nolichucky experience all the way to its end at Davy Crockett Birthplace State Park, where you can learn a little history about one of Tennessee's most colorful characters. First you will go through a surprisingly solid rapid,

Author navigates a rapid and scouts ahead at another.

then past some impressive bluffs. More bluffs appear periodically, and the wide river allows views of the state line crest through which it flows. Islands form near Mitchell Bluff, giving you route options. The paddle is 9+ miles, which makes it a full day trip, especially when you include stops. Gravel bars are ample for stopping at normal water levels.

River Overview

I have paddled this river every bit of its 100 miles through Tennessee. The entire waterway is a great paddling resource for residents of the Volunteer State. However, before you put in anywhere realize some hairy rapids fall in its uppermost sections. The waters of the Nolichucky come from the absolute highest point in the East, Mount Mitchell in the Black Mountains of North Carolina. Mount Mitchell is drained by the Toe River, which meets the Cane River just east of the Tennessee state line in the shadow of Cane Mountain near the humble hamlet of Huntdale, North Carolina. Here, the Nolichucky River is born and immediately begins a raucous journey (along with a companion rail line) through the Nolichucky Gorge of white-water fame, entering the Volunteer State. It then slices a second chasm between Buffalo Mountain and Rich Mountain. Beyond the second gulf at Embreeville, the river turns into the southwest-trending ridge and valley province (along with most other rivers) of East Tennessee. It then opens into rolling agricultural lands of Washington and Greene Counties, before it is briefly stilled near Greenville as Davy Crockett Lake, once a TVA power generator. From there, the Nolichucky continues southwesterly as a wide river broken with frequent shoals, with the small Enka Dam in the way, before meeting the French Broad River at the upper end of Douglas Lake.

The Paddling

The most challenging rapid of the entire float is immediately below the put-in—Woods Rock Shoals. It is a solid Class II rapid. At high water it has a tendency to fill your boat and at low water it can be rocky, banging you around into a potential flip, especially since there's no "practice rapid" before you begin floating. There's a large catch basin at the bottom bordered by a gray rock bluff. Paddlers most often take the right-hand channel, and it will be the only channel available at lower water. However, the left channel is a good sneak route to avoid swamping. Carry around it if you feel uncomfortable.

The river valley in Washington and Greene Counties offers a rural flavor the entire paddle. Box elder, sycamore, river birch, and ironwood line the banks. In other places homes and fish camps occupy the shores. The Nolichucky averages 120 to 140 feet in width. It is normally green but can become muddy after rains, since much of it borders agricultural and pastureland. Watch for rock outcrops that occur throughout this section of river. At 1.1 miles, float through Blackburn Shoals, a long Class I rapid. The water is especially deep at the base of the shoals, where an outcrop rises on river left. More shoals soon follow. Make sure and look upstream for some inspiring mountain views. Reach Winter Jacob Bales Shoals, another long Class I shoal, ending at a bluff and deep hole on river right. Here, the Nolichucky curves to the north at the base of Yarbrough Cliff—a sheer bluff on river left that overlooks a large sandbar on the inside right bank from which pastureland rises. Note the craggy cedars atop the cliff.

The Nolichucky divides around an island just before reaching Snapp Bridge at 3.3 miles. Small, sometimes shallow shoals keep your boat moving in this cattle and agriculture country where the riverbanks are wide. Rock bluffs resume as the river curves northwest. Fun-to-float rapids resume and the river narrows here as well. Small islands form, dividing the Nolichucky. Little Limestone Creek comes in from the north. The river reconvenes below cedar-clad Mitchell Bluff at 4.9 miles. A small beach is on river left.

The river continues its big curve, passing sycamore-covered Broyles Island on the right. The floating is fun here while navigating long but easy Wilson Shoals that speeds your boat along. Mountain views open up and Big Butt—over which the Appalachian Trail travels—stands proudly in the distance. The water slows and bluffs soon rise on river left. Pass Corby Bridge Road, part of your shuttle run, at 7.2 miles. Ahead you can see the hand-cut pillars of abandoned Smith Bridge, also known as Glaze Bridge. Notice the historic brick farmhouse near the bridge on this wide and slow section. The "Noli" speeds at Blaine Shoals, a Class I+ rapid with a

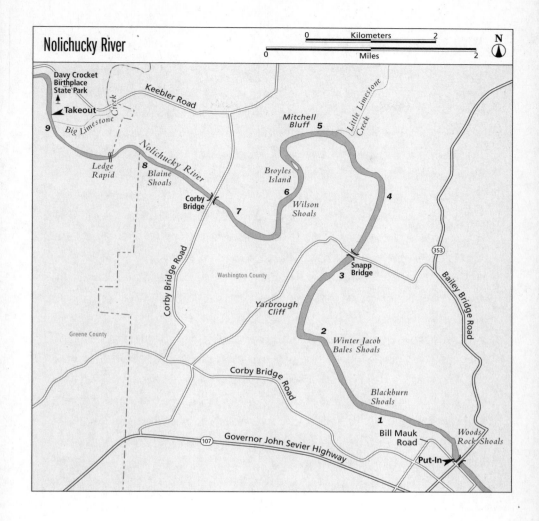

Nolichucky River

Davy Crockett Birthplace State Park

Keebler Road

← Takeout

Mitchell Bluff 5

Little Limestone Creek

9 Big Limestone Creek

Nolichucky River

Ledge Rapid

8 Blaine Shoals

Broyles Island

6

Corby Bridge

7

Wilson Shoals

4

353

Washington County

Snapp Bridge

3

Bailey Bridge Road

Corby Bridge Road

Greene County

Yarbrough Cliff

2

Winter Jacob Bales Shoals

Corby Bridge Road

Blackburn Shoals

1

Governor John Sevier Highway

107

Bill Mauk Road

Woods Rock Shoals

Put-In →

N

0   Kilometers   2
0   Miles   2

straightforward drop of a few feet at the base of which the flow gathers and can fill your boat at higher water levels.

Enter Greene County at 8.0 miles. The river bends left then comes to an unusual rapid. Here, an angled ledge extends across the left-hand side of the river. The main flow of the river travels alongside the ledge. Below the rapid sycamore trees rise from a sand and rock beach that begs a stop. Pass one little rapid as you go beneath a power line. Big Limestone Creek comes in on your right just before reaching the state park boat ramp on river right at 9.2 miles. Don't miss the boat ramp, because there's a doozy of a drop a couple hundred yards below the ramp. A shaded picnic area is adjacent to the boat ramp and adds to the possibilities when exploring the birthplace of Davy Crockett, a true Tennessee hero. If you wish to camp out overnight along the way, make sure and register your car at the state park office.

AN OLD TIME CANOE TALE

Davy Crockett Birthplace State Park marks the beginning of the life of one of Tennessee's most notable residents. During his time, he was always known as David Crockett. It was only after the 1950s television series trilogy put forth by Disney, in which he was dubbed "Davy Crockett," that this erroneous name came to rise. The state of Tennessee ought to know better than to name the state park as they did. Perhaps they were trying to cash in on the Davy Crockett craze that followed the shows. Ironically, the state correctly named David Crockett State Park near Lawrenceburg, where he later settled during his lifetime ramblings.

Name aside, Crockett was born here at the mouth of Limestone Creek in August of 1786, after his dirt-poor father, John, had moved here from North Carolina. The elder Crockett had fought in the Revolutionary War's Battle of Kings Mountain as part of the Overmountain Men and perhaps heard about the wonders of what was to become East Tennessee. It was on the banks of the Nolichucky at the state park takeout where young David relates a story in his worth-reading autobiography, *A Narrative of the Life of David Crockett*. It seems an older boy named Campbell was playing with David's four older brothers when they decided to get in John Crockett's canoe. Campbell, inexperienced with a paddle, led the five of them backwards toward a fall in the river (you can see it today) just below the current landing. David stood helpless on the shore. A farmer named Kendall was hoeing a field across the water and dashed toward the kids, stripping as he ran, then half swam/half floundered to grab the canoe just before it went over the falls. Even so, the force of the current pulled mightily, and by force of will Kendall dragged the boys to shore and out of danger. So while you are here at the state park make sure to walk down to the falls, along with the very bank where Crockett walked remembering this little tale.

36 Holston River

This easy water paddle heads down the upper mountain-bordered valley of the Holston River, below the town of Kingsport.

County: Hawkins
Start: A. S. Derick Park, N36° 31.468', W82° 40.947'
End: Christian Bend boat ramp, N36° 28.423', W82° 46.195'
Length: 10.4 miles
Float time: 5 hours
Difficulty rating: Moderate
Rapids: Class I–II
River type: Wide slow valley river bordered by mountains
Current: Slow to moderate
River gradient: 2.9 feet per mile
River gauge: USGS gauge—South Fork Holston near Damascus, VA; no minimum runnable level

Season: Year-round
Land status: Private
Fees/permits: No fees or permits required
Nearest city/town: Church Hill
Maps: USGS: Church Hill, Lovelace, Plum Grove, Stony Point; *DeLorme: Tennessee Atlas & Gazetteer,* Page 70 B3, 62 A3
Boats used: Canoes, johnboats, occasional kayak
Organization: Holston River Watershed Alliance, (423) 246-2017, www.kingsport tomorrow.org
Contacts/outfitters: Tennessee Clean Water Network, 123A S. Gay St., Knoxville 37902, (865) 522-7007, www.tcwn.org

Put-in/Takeout Information

To takeout: From exit 1, West Stone Drive, on I-26 take 11W south for 8.6 miles to Goshen Valley Road and a traffic light. Turn left on Goshen Valley Road and follow it for 1.3 miles to Christian Bend Road. Turn right on Christian Bend Road and follow it for 3.3 miles to the boat ramp on your right (stay right at 2.1 miles, as Christian Bend Road turns right at an intersection).

To put-in from takeout: Backtrack to 11W and follow it north for 2.1 miles to Silver Lake Road and a traffic light with a McDonald's on the corner. Turn right on Silver Lake Road and follow it downhill just a short distance to turn left on Ordnance Drive. Follow Ordnance Drive just a short distance to turn right on Bucky Cooper Road. Follow Bucky Cooper Road into A. S. Derick Park and dead-end at the boat ramp on the Holston River.

Paddle Summary

Leave the Church Hill area on a wide river dotted with islands large and small. Occasional shoals speed the generally slow-flowing Holston, which widens in excess of

Wooded ridges border the wide Holston.

350 feet in places, making it a potential fairway for winds. However, the wide river reveals impressive scenery, as wooded ridges rise near and far. Adjacent riverside flats stretch out in fields and houses.

Underwater grasses sometimes slow the pace on this full day paddle. The mountain scenery and the river islands are the highlights of this trip. The river islands divide the river into channels, which completely changes the atmosphere from large river to intimate canopied stream, only to open again. Furthermore, these islands are good habitat for wildlife. You will undoubtedly see deer, and a keen eye will also spot otters, muskrat, and beaver. I've even seen a raccoon on the riverbanks.

River Overview

The Holston is primarily known as being one of the two rivers, along with the French Broad, that together form the Tennessee River. The Holston begins as three forks flowing out of the southwest Virginia mountains. The North Fork Holston River and South Fork Holston River meet shortly above this paddle in Kingsport, Tennessee, to form the main Holston River. From there, the Holston widens as it winds southwesterly with mountains near and far. After 40 or so miles, the river is slowed as it reaches the dam of the John Sevier Steam Plant. Just beyond the spillway it enters Cherokee Lake.

Beyond Cherokee Lake the river is unleashed. A popular coldwater trout fishery and paddling lie below Cherokee Dam. The river warms and makes its way toward Knoxville, eventually meeting the French Broad just east of downtown to become the Tennessee River.

The Paddling

A. S. Derick Park offers picnic tables, a walking track, and a shelter. A concrete boat ramp makes the put-in an easy affair. The Holston River is a couple of hundred feet wide at this point and is flowing sluggishly. From here you cannot go upstream very far because the Holston Army Munitions Plant doesn't allow river passage through their property. Downstream, pass the private VFW put-in. Holston River Mountain and surrounding ridges appear in the distance, and it isn't long before you reach the first of many river islands. This one is known as Negro Island. The water speeds up at a shoal around the island. The shoreline is forested with occasional grassy areas at this point. Box elder, silver maple, and sycamore crowd the shoreline. Grasses sway under the water and on the surface and can be troublesome to paddlers and anglers alike. These grasses have proliferated in the past decade. Mussel shells reflect the sun in the shallows. Small creeks form gravel out-washes that will be submerged at high water.

Reach large mile-long Hawkins Island at 0.8 mile. The smaller channel stays left with the main river on the right. The smaller channels of these islands are the preferred route for paddlers. Occasional shale bluffs, pocked with brush and cedars, rise from the river. U.S. Army property continues on river left. The Army property is a de facto game preserve, and you may see deer in this area.

Return to the main river and Canebrake Mountain rises directly before you. Laurel Run comes in on river left, just below a bluff. A shoal forms here. At 2.8 miles, at the lower end of Laurel Run Park, pass the park boat ramp. Stop and look upriver for some spectacular mountain views. Curve away from the mountains at this point, though ridges are always in view.

The shoreline is primarily forest here with fields behind it, though fields do occasionally creep to the river's edge. At 3.8 miles, you'll pass a smaller isle before reaching large Smith Island. Goshen Valley Bridge comes into view from the lower end of Smith Island. A large field is on your right. The river widens back out to 350 feet or more. The current quickens to pass under the Goshen Valley Bridge at 5.5 miles. Notice the pilings of the old bridge here. The Holston begins a bend to the south, McPheeter Bend, after passing fairly close to US 11W. Below Goshen Valley Bridge, the river narrows, deepens, and slows down, splitting around Hord Island at 6.3 miles. The smaller channel, 60 to 80 feet wide, heads left. Beyond Hord Island, the river speeds to a long Class I shoal and shortly divides around a small unnamed island. The smaller channel, to the left, is but 20 feet wide.

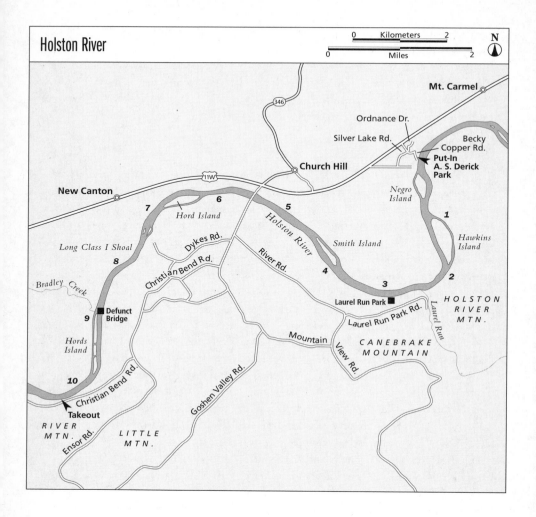

0   Kilometers   2

N

0   Miles   2

Mt. Carmel

Ordnance Dr.

Silver Lake Rd.

Becky Copper Rd.

Church Hill

Put-In
A. S. Derick Park

New Canton

Negro Island

7

6

5

1

Hord Island

Holston River

Hawkins Island

Long Class I Shoal

Smith Island

8

Dykes Rd.

River Rd.

Christian Bend Rd.

Bradley Creek

4

Defunct Bridge

9

3

Laurel Run Park

HOLSTON RIVER MTN.

Laurel Run Park Rd.

Laurel Run

Hords Island

2

Mountain

CANEBRAKE MOUNTAIN

View Rd.

10

Christian Bend Rd.

Goshen Valley Rd.

Takeout

RIVER MTN.

Ensor Rd.

LITTLE MTN.

Ahead, an old defunct bridge spans the Holston and ridges rise in the distance. Pass under the old span at 8.8 miles. Note Bradley Creek coming in on the right. Reach Hords Islands, a collection of isles. Smaller channels to the right will be of more interest to paddlers. River Mountain looms larger. The current speeds here, as it is prone to do whenever islands divide the Holston. The far right channel is nearly canopied and diversifies the atmosphere. You are on a dead on course for River Mountain, which forces the river to bend to the right. Move to the left bank below the islands and reach the takeout at Christian Bend Road.

THE HOLSTON/TENNESSEE NAME DEBATE

Today, the beginning of the main Holston River is not in doubt. It officially starts just below the town of Kingsport, where the South Fork Holston River and the North Fork Holston River meet, just above historic Long Island, which was a haunt of the Cherokee, and later a meeting place for pioneers, settlers, and soldiers. Long Island was the starting point for Daniel Boone's famed Wilderness Road, which led through Cumberland Gap and into Kentucky. Some say that the state of Tennessee got its name from the Indian word "Tana-see" which referred to Long Island, but the general belief is the name came from a Cherokee village named "Tanasi" on the banks of the Little Tennessee River in what is now Monroe County, near where the "Little T" meets the Tennessee River. The Little Tennessee River brings us to the next part of the story. See, the Holston didn't always end where it does today, at the confluence with the French Broad near Knoxville. For most of American history the Holston ended at its confluence with the Little Tennessee River, some 50 miles downstream of where it "ends" today. When the Tennessee Valley Authority (TVA) was created, the U.S. Congress mandated its headquarters to be on the Tennessee River. Well, TVA had decided to put its headquarters in Knoxville, which at the time was on the Holston. In grand government fashion it decided to "move" the official Tennessee River upstream to the confluence of the French Broad and Holston, which is conveniently just upstream of Knoxville. So, TVA got its headquarters on the Tennessee and the Holston lost 50 miles of river.

37 South Holston River

This tailwater paddle is a long one, but the current is good and the streamside scenery better. Mostly easy shoals keep you moving on this nationally recognized trout fishing destination.

County: Sullivan
Start: South Holston Weir Dam, N36° 31.365', W82° 6.428'
End: Bluff City Recreational Park, N36° 28.358', W82° 15.497'
Length: 14 miles
Float time: 6 hours
Difficulty rating: Moderate, has one Class II rapid
Rapids: I–II
River type: Dam-controlled coldwater river
Current: Moderate to fast
River gradient: 6.4 feet per mile
River gauge: TVA South Holston release schedule, www.tva.com/river/lakeinfo/index—South Holston, check release schedule or call (865)

632-2264, runnable during dam generation
Season: March–October when South Holston Dam is generating
Land status: Private
Fees or permits: No fees or permits required
Nearest city/town: Bristol
Maps: USGS: Holston Valley, Bristol, Keensburg, Bluff City; *DeLorme: Tennessee Atlas and Gazetteer,* Page 70 D1, 71 B7, 63 A7
Boats used: Canoes, kayaks, dories, rafts
Organizations: Holston River Watershed Alliance, (423) 246-2017, www.kingsport tomorrow.org
Contacts/outfitters: Tennessee Clean Water Network, 123A S. Gay St., Knoxville 37902, (865) 522-7007, www.tcwn.org

Put-in/Takeout Information

To takeout: From exit 36 on I-26 near Johnson City, take TN 381 1.6 miles north to Bristol Highway, US 11E. Take US 11E north for 11.7 miles to TN 394. Take TN 394 east for 0.2 mile to TN 390 south. Turn right on TN 390 south toward Bluff City and cross the bridge over the South Fork Holston River at 2.1 miles, then turn right into Bluff City Recreational Park. There is a boat ramp here.

To put-in from takeout: Backtrack from Bluff City on TN 390 north to TN 394. Turn right and take TN 394 east for 7.5 miles to reach a stoplight and US 421 south. Turn right on US 421 south and follow it for 2.9 miles, then turn right on Emmett Road (look for a sign indicating South Holston Dam). At 0.5 mile, stay right on Emmett Road, then at 1.0 mile keep straight, now on Holston Dam View Road to cross the South Fork Holston at 0.3 mile. Just beyond the bridge look left for a sign stating SOUTH HOLSTON DAM and CANOE LAUNCH. Turn left into the parking area and the put-in is just below the weir dam.

Fog rises from the cool, trout-filled waters of the South Holston.

Paddle Summary

The South Fork Holston flows cold and clear below the dam that backs its waters near the Tennessee-Virginia line. Here it travels over a weir dam, which oxygenates the water and makes it one of the best trout habitats in the state. It is at this weir dam where paddlers begin a scenic and lively trip through a river valley backed by mountains. Paddlers will be surprised at the speed of the current and the fun but doable shoals that are almost all Class I–I+. It is every bit of 14 miles from the dam to Bluff City, where the South Holston slows as it becomes Boone Lake. However, don't let the distance scare you off—the current is swift and the mileage can be easily surmounted with even a moderate amount of paddling. The current gives way just before reaching Bluff City. If you choose to paddle this when the TVA isn't generating, then plan to sleep in your boat. Stopping points are limited when the dam is generating, due to private land and inundated islands, though there are some roadside accesses that will allow you to take a break.

Occasional bluffs are interspersed with pastureland. Houses are more common along the river toward Bluff City. The South Fork Holston has been discovered both as a trout fishing venue and as a place to live. That being said it is still underutilized as a paddling destination, especially with anglers, who prefer to wade the river when TVA is not generating.

South Holston River

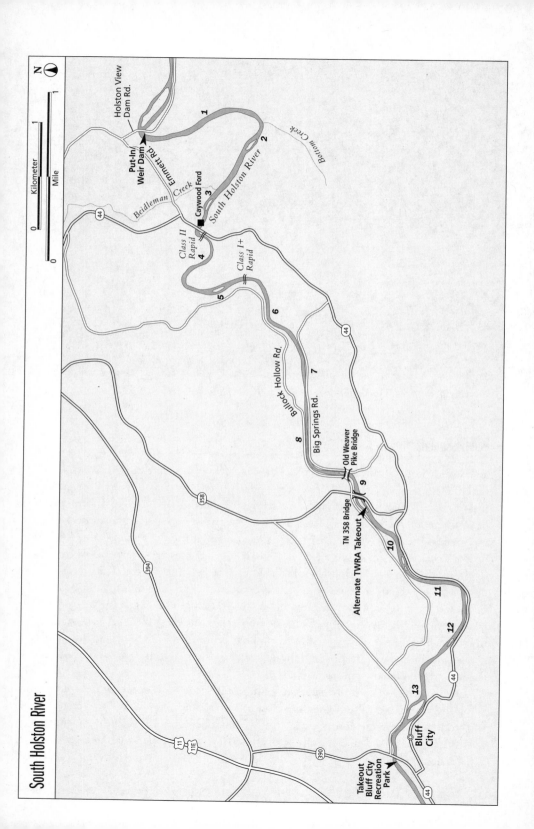

River Overview

The South Fork Holston River is born in the Old Dominion, near the town of Marion in Smyth County. Here, the South Fork drains much of Mount Rogers National Recreation Area, containing Virginia's highest point—Mount Rogers—then flows into Washington County, Virginia, where it meets the Middle Fork Holston River. The river is slowed as South Holston Lake and enters the Volunteer State. This paddle begins southeast of Bristol, where the river is once again freed below South Holston Dam, heading southwesterly through ridge and valley country until it is slowed as Boone Lake near Bluff City. It barely has a chance to flow again before it is dammed as Fort Patrick Henry Lake. Once again loose, it passes historic Long Island in Kingsport, then meets the North Fork Holston at the Hawkins/Sullivan County line and becomes the Holston proper, which flows southwesterly to Knoxville and becomes part of the Tennessee River. At higher water levels, paddlers can enjoy the free-flowing river in Virginia above South Holston Lake. Otherwise they are limited to stillwater paddling on lakes.

The Paddling

Leave the canoe launch and immediately pass under the access road bridge. When generating, the South Fork Holston will have quite a current as it speeds left around a corner. The icy cold water will sometimes make a fog in summer. No matter whether TVA is operating one generator or two, the waters will be swift. Holston Mountain comes into view as you slide down your first fun shoal, which is characteristic of the river—a lot of water and very few rocks, which make navigating them a simple read and run process. The South Fork extends 120 feet wide and is generally shallow, especially in fast-moving sections. The bottom is easily visible through the crystalline water. Smaller gravel and stones alternate with a hard rock bottom underneath the flow. Sycamore, tulip trees, white pine, fading hemlocks, and grasses line the shore, which is occasionally punctuated with low rock bluffs.

Pleasant Class I riffles with playful waves continue to push you downstream. The water stays swift between shoals. Bird lovers will enjoy herons, kingfishers, swallows, and even osprey as they cruise the river. At 1.7 miles, the South Fork makes a westerly curve as Bottom Creek enters on river left. The river then breaks around small islands, which will occur the rest of the float. At 2.6 miles, the mountains have receded somewhat and the pasture borders the shoreline. At 2.9 miles Beidlman Creek enters on river right. A large island divides the river just downstream, creating a shoal at the old Caywood Ford site. The ford is now replaced by the TN 44 bridge, which you pass under at 3.4 miles. The South Fork curves left and reaches the Class II rapid. It is a straightforward drop but does have some rocks to avoid. The white noise will put you on alert.

Pass around an island shoal at 5.0 miles. These islands, despite their tree cover, are brushy around their edges and not conducive for stopping when the dam is generating. Navigate a Class I+ ledge drop at 5.4 miles. The water continues pushing westerly toward Bluff City. Pass through a long Class I riffle at 7.8 miles. Watch in this area for gravel accesses on the river left off Big Springs Road that you can use for stopping. Pass under the Old Weaver Pike Bridge at 8.9 miles, then the TN 358 bridge at 9.2 miles. There is a gravel public access on river right under the TN 358 bridge, if you want a shorter paddle. The South Fork has now widened to 140 feet or more and is often broken by islands. Pass through a long island shoal at 10.3 miles. More swift but simple shoals lie ahead, including a single shoal that extends for 0.5 mile starting at 12.1 miles. It is these shoals that keep the water moving and make the 14-mile day trip very doable. At 12.8 miles, pass a water treatment facility on river right. The current begins to moderate as you near the backwaters of Boone Lake. You may see motorboaters in this slower stretch plying the waters of Boone Lake. Pass under a swinging pedestrian bridge, then the Norfolk Southern railroad bridge. Come along the Bluff City boardwalk, situated along the South Fork. The takeout is on river left just beyond the TN 390 bridge.

THE SULLIVAN COUNTY GRAND SLAM

South Holston Lake, which chills the waters of this paddle, is a fine destination itself. The mountainous Cherokee National Forest nearly surrounds the lake and makes this impoundment one of the most beautiful in the state. Paddlers can explore the area from a base camp known as Little Oak, on South Holston Lake within sight of South Holston Dam. I have paddled the South Fork and camped here and highly recommend the experience. Little Oak is laid out atop the remnants of Little Oak Mountain after the Holston River Valley was flooded to create South Holston Lake. Little Oak has many spacious lakeside sites. Short paths slope from each lakeside site to the water's edge.

After setting up camp, we launched the canoe into the lake, paddling around some islands as the sun set over South Holston Lake. Next morning we took a vigorous hike on the Little Oak Trail that loops the campground. For a different perspective, take the Little Oak Mountain Trail. It begins near the pay station and ascends a mountainside before making a loop.

In East Tennessee, the high country is never far away. Little Oak is near the Flint Mill Scenic Area, offering a broad representation of Southern Appalachian flora and fauna and elevations exceeding 4,000 feet. Turn right from the campground onto Forest Service Road 87 and drive 1.4 miles. The Josiah Trail (Forest Trail #50) starts on your left and ascends for 2.2 miles to a saddle on Holston Mountain and Forest Trail #44. To your left at 4.3 miles are the Appalachian Trail and the Double Springs Gap backcountry shelter. To your right after 3.4 miles is the Holston Mountain Fire Tower and views aplenty. Flint Mill Trail (FT #49) climbs 1 steep mile to Flint Rock and some fantastic views of South Holston Lake and Little Oak Campground. The trail is 2.2 miles on the left beyond the Josiah Trail. For more information, please visit www.fs.fed.us/r8/Cherokee.

38 Watauga River

This float below Wilbur Dam offers mountain scenery and fast cold water. End in Elizabethton after some fun rapids.

County: Carter
Start: Wilbur Dam, N36° 20.311', W82° 7.417'
End: Riverside Park near Riverside Stadium, N36° 21.185', W82° 13.552'
Length: 8.5 miles
Float time: 3.5 hours
Difficulty rating: Moderate, has one Class II–III Rapid
Rapids: Class I–II (III)
River type: Dam-controlled coldwater river
Current: Moderate to fast
River gradient: 11.7 feet per mile
River gauge: TVA Wilbur Dam release schedule, www.tva.com/river/recreation/schedules.htm, (865) 632-2264, runnable following dam generation

Season: Follows TVA recreational generation schedule—late May through early September, plus Saturdays in September and October
Land status: Private except for near Wilbur Dam
Fees or permits: No fees or permits required
Nearest city/town: Elizabethton
Maps: USGS: Elizabethton; *DeLorme: Tennessee Atlas and Gazetteer,* Page 63 A7
Boats used: Rafts, canoes, kayaks, dories
Organizations: Tennessee Clean Water Network, 123A S. Gay St., Knoxville 37902, (865) 522-7007, www.tcwn.org
Contacts/outfitters: Mountain Adventure Guides, 2 Jones Branch Rd., Erwin 37650, (866) 813-5210, www.mtnadventureguides.com

Put-in/Takeout Information

To takeout: From exit 24 on I–26 near Johnson City, follow the signs for Elizabethton, joining US 321 north/TN 67 east. Travel for 7.2 miles to reach Elizabethton and a traffic light in a commercial area (US 321/TN 67 becomes West Elk Avenue in Elizabethton). The road leading right at the light will be McArthur Street, but you take the road leading left—West Mill Street. Turn left on West Mill Street and follow it for 0.2 mile, then turn left on Ash Street, a residential road. Follow Ash Street for 0.2 mile to meet Riverside Drive. Turn left on Riverside Drive and travel just a short distance to reach a parking area near a picnic pavilion and the Watauga River.

To put-in from takeout: Backtrack to US 321/TN 67/West Elk Avenue. Turn left and resume US 321 north/TN 67 east to travel for 1.4 miles to reach a major intersection. Turn right here, now joining US 19E south, Veterans Memorial Parkway, toward Roan Mountain, Mountain City, and Boone, North Carolina. Follow US 19E south for 0.4 mile to a traffic light. Turn left on Siam Road and follow its windings, watching for signs for TVA Watauga Dam. At 3.5 miles, turn left, joining Wilbur Dam Road. Follow Wilbur Dam Road for 0.5 mile to reach a T intersection. The Watauga

River is dead ahead. Turn right here, still on Wilbur Dam Road, and trace it for 1.7 miles to reach a left downhill turn to the put-in below Wilbur Dam.

Paddle Summary

The Watauga River is a local·favorite of mine. Flowing cold and clear out of one of Tennessee's most scenic impoundments—Watauga Lake—the dam-controlled waterway offers paddlers a lively mountain float in pristine waters. TVA manages the Watauga as one of its recreational rivers and thus has a dependable warm weather recreation release schedule for rafters, canoers, and kayakers. At the appointed hour, paddlers assemble at the put-in and the dam begins releasing. Watauga enthusiasts enter the frigid, trout-filled aqua, immediately joining the swift stream to flow over some fun shoals before reaching Bee Cliff Rapid, a Class III white flow also known as Anaconda. Fortunately, there is a cheat route and you can avoid the worst of the rapid if you so desire. Beyond Bee Cliff Rapid, the river continues to speed, passing pastoral lands in a backdrop of fine scenery dominated by Holston Mountain. Streamside houses become common heading toward Elizabethton, but your eyes will be on the swift but easy Class I–II rapids, divided by occasional islands. The cold water sometimes generates a cool fog blanket that lies upon the river. Stay off the river if TVA is not generating, as the current is otherwise negligible and you may have to pull your boat. However, when TVA is generating stopping points are limited, not only by private property but simply by high water inundating the shore. The fast waters will have you at Riverside Park in Elizabethton before you know it.

River Overview

The Watauga River is born on the slopes above Grandfather Mountain just off the Blue Ridge Parkway in western North Carolina. Tributaries flowing from the highlands of Watauga County widen the westerly-turning Watauga. It cuts a gorge while entering the state of Tennessee in Carter County. Here, it is soon dammed as Watauga Lake, where the Elk River adds to the flow. It is but a short distance between Watauga Dam and Wilbur Dam. This paddle begins below Wilbur Dam. The Watauga then flows icy cold as it heads westerly to and through Elizabethton, passing historic Sycamore Shoals, where the Overmountain Men mustered during the Revolution to fight the British at the Battle of Kings Mountain in South Carolina. Beyond Sycamore Shoals, the Watauga speeds more before being stilled as Boone Lake, where it meets the South Holston River and ends. A small creek flowing behind my home in Johnson City lies within the watershed of the Watauga River. Whitewater paddlers can ply the seasonally high section of the Watauga River upstream of Watauga Lake in Tennessee and North Carolina, but it is for advanced paddlers only. Watauga Lake makes for scenic stillwater paddling for sea kayakers and canoe campers. The best and most reliable run is described below.

Paddlers need to keep an eye on the fast-moving Watauga River, despite the mountain scenery.

The Paddling

The put-in is within earshot of Wilbur Dam. Enter still water before paddling into the fast flow just below the dam. The clear-green water is frigid to the touch. Make sure and have your life jacket on for the first mile at least—Bee Cliff Rapid comes quick. Sycamore, tulip trees, and other lush vegetation line the banks. Anglers may be vying for the trout that inhabit the river. A protruding cliff lies just around the corner from the put-in. Commercial rafting operations often stop here so clients can jump off the 15 or so foot rock into the water. Tie your boat in well if stopping here.

The first rapid comes at 0.2 mile and is a welcome warm-up. Like most other rapids on this paddle, it is a simple read and run drop with few if any exposed rocks. Ahead, an old swinging bridge spans the 100-foot-wide river. Keep generally on river left. At 0.7 mile, the river begins to curve left and passes over some mild shoals. Move river left and you will soon hear the white noise of Bee Cliff Rapid, aka Anaconda. You may see the vertical tan wall on river right that gives the rapid its name. Keep within 5 feet of the left shore and you can successfully run an even gradient, avoiding the froth of white in the middle of the Watauga.

Watauga River

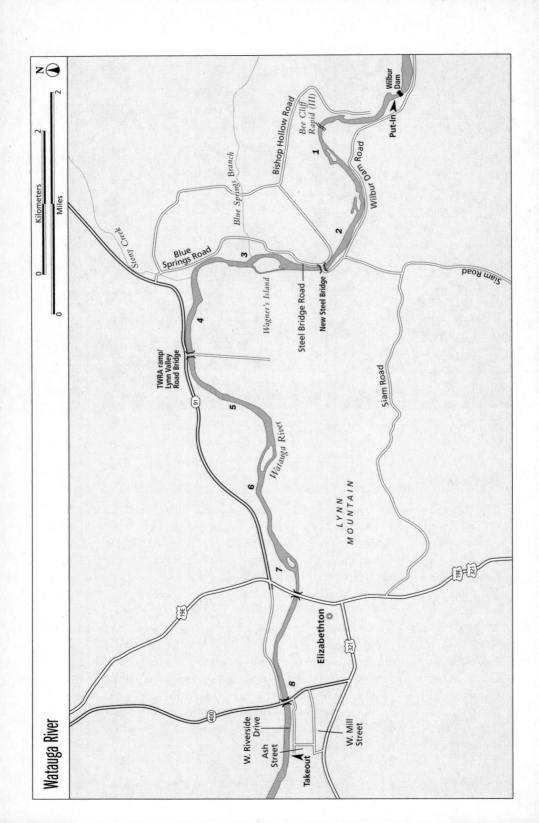

From here on out you've got it made. Enjoy the splashy shoals and mountain scenery. Another fun shoal lies a short distance downstream. The current continues moving at a hasty pace as you pass by old bridge abutments at 1.9 miles. Holston Mountain dominates the skyline, while Lynn Mountain rises in the foreground. Pass under the New Steel Bridge at 2.3 miles. Islands occasionally divide the river. Streamside houses become more common. At 2.6 miles, Blue Springs Branch comes in on river right while you curve around the right side of Wagner's Island in a relatively slow section. At 3.6 miles, the river passes under a power line, then curves left in a speedy extended shoal. Stony Creek flows in on river right here.

At 4.4 miles, Lynn Valley Road Bridge spans the Watauga. There is a Tennessee Wildlife Resources Agency boat launch on river left, just before the bridge, that makes for a dry and legal stopping spot. Take advantage. A Class II shoal flows just below the bridge. The Watauga begins to widen where the frequent rapids are not present. Islands continue to divide the river, but the main channel is evident. Paddlers beware taking the narrower channels as the strong current is sometimes forced into trees or other obstacles. The rapids of the main channels are clear-cut with splashy water the only potential troubles.

Noteworthy shoals occur at 6.0 and 6.4 miles. Pass under the US 19E bridge at 7.0 miles. Enjoy a fast-moving riffle just below the bridge. At 7.3 miles, you will pass by an abandoned bridge abutment followed by another fun shoal created by the confluence with the Doe River coming in on river left. The Doe drains the highlands of Roan Mountain to the south, then passes through the heart of Elizabethton. More rapids make a fast trip even faster. Pass under the TN 400 bridge at 8.0 miles. Below this bridge Riverside Park comes into view on your left. Shift over to the left shoreline. The takeout is at the lower end of the park near the shaded picnic pavilion. Riverside Stadium is in view beyond the park. Be careful, as there is no official landing and the river is flowing swiftly when generating where you will be taking out.

WATAUGA CAMPING

In addition to your paddle you may want to visit—or even camp—on Watauga Lake. Upstream of the paddle put-in lies a TVA campground and picnic area. But even better are the Cherokee National Forest recreation areas on the east shore of the lake near the community of Hampton, with the highlight being Cardens Bluff Campground.

If Cardens Bluff were private land it would go for big, big bucks. The scenery is that outstanding. Luckily, we can overnight here for cheap. Tall mountains rise from the clear blue/green water of Watauga Lake. The camping area stands on a peninsula jutting into the dammed Watauga River. The U.S. Forest Service offers traditional drive-up campsites, walk-in tent sites, and a bathhouse with showers. A dense forest screens the sites from one another and provides good shade for summer days. Attractive rockwork and site leveling enhances the hillside camps. Nice summer weekends will fill. Get here early if you can. You can find a site most any weekday, save for summer holidays.

The Rat Branch boat ramp is just down the way, where you can launch your boat and have a ball, whether you are fishing or just boating. Also down the lake is the Shooks Branch Recreation Area, which has a swim beach. Maybe they put the swim beach here for the Appalachian Trail through-hikers, since the AT runs right by the beach. If you leave south from Shook Branch on the AT, enter the Pond Mountain Wilderness and climb to Pond Flats 4 miles distant. If you head north, the AT skirts around the lake to reach Watauga Dam in 3 miles. The northbound hiking is easier. The Cardens Bluff Trail is also easy. It leaves near campsite #12 and circles around the shoreline. The Watauga Point Recreation Area is only a mile down TN 67. This spot also has a swim beach, picnic area, and a gravel path looping through the woods. This whole area is known as the Watauga Recreation Corridor, all part of the Cherokee National Forest and as you can read, there is plenty going on here. For more information, please visit www.fs.fed.us/r8/Cherokee.

Paddling Index

Other Books by Johnny Molloy

50 Hikes in Alabama
50 Hikes in the North Georgia Mountains
50 Hikes in the Ozarks
50 Hikes in South Carolina
50 Hikes on Tennessee's Cumberland Plateau
60 Hikes Within 60 Miles: San Antonio & Austin (with Tom Taylor)
60 Hikes Within 60 Miles: Nashville
A Canoeing & Kayaking Guide to the Streams of Florida
A Canoeing & Kayaking Guide to the Streams of Kentucky (with Bob Sehlinger)
A Falcon Guide to Mammoth Cave National Park
A Paddler's Guide to Everglades National Park
Backcountry Fishing: A Guide for Hikers, Backpackers and Paddlers
Beach & Coastal Camping in Florida
Beach & Coastal Camping in the Southeast
Best Easy Day Hikes: Cincinnati
Best East Day Hikes: Greensboro / Winston-Salem
Best East Day Hikes: Jacksonville
Best East Day Hikes: Richmond
Best Easy Day Hikes: Springfield, Illinois
Best Easy Day Hikes: Tallahassee
Best Easy Day Hikes: Tampa Bay
Best Hikes Near: Cincinnati
Best Hkes Near: Columbus
The Best in Tent Camping: The Carolinas
The Best in Tent Camping: Colorado
The Best in Tent Camping: Florida
The Best in Tent Camping: Georgia
The Best in Tent Camping: Kentucky
The Best in Tent Camping: Southern Appalachian & Smoky Mountains
The Best in Tent Camping: Tennessee
The Best in Tent Camping: West Virginia
The Best in Tent Camping: Wisconsin
Day & Overnight Hikes in Great Smoky Mountains National Park
Day & Overnight Hikes on Kentucky's Sheltowee Trace
Day & Overnight Hikes in Shenandoah National Park
Day & Overnight Hikes in West Virginia's Monongahela National Forest
From the Swamp to the Keys: A Paddle through Florida History
Hiking the Florida Trail: 1,100 Miles, 78 Days and Two Pairs of Boots
Hiking Mississippi

Mount Rogers National Recreation Area Guidebook
The Hiking Trails of Florida's National Forests, Parks, and Preserves
Land Between the Lakes Outdoor Recreation Handbook
Long Trails of the Southeast
Paddling Georgia
Trial By Trail: Backpacking in the Smoky Mountains

Visit the author's website: www.johnnymolloy.com.

About the Author

Johnny Molloy is a writer and adventurer with an economics degree from the University of Tennessee. He has become skilled in a variety of outdoor environments and written over three dozen books, including hiking, camping, paddling, and comprehensive regional guidebooks as well as true outdoor adventure books. Molloy has also written numerous articles for magazines, websites, and blogs. He resides in Johnson City, Tennessee, but spends his winters in Florida. For the latest on Molloy's pursuits and work, please visit www.johnnymolloy.com.